Rational Behavior Therapy

Rational Behavior Therapy

Maxie C. Maultsby, Jr., M. D.
University of Kentucky—College of Medicine

Prentice-Hall, Inc., Englewood Cliffs, New Jersey 07632

Library of Congress Cataloging in Publication Data

Maultsby, Maxie C.
  Rational behavior therapy.

  Bibliography: p.
  Includes index.
  1. Rational-emotive psychotherapy. I. Title. [DNLM:
1. Behavior therapy.   WM 425 M449r]
RC489.R3M384   1984   616.89'14   83-9519
ISBN 0-13-752915-5
ISBN 0-13-752907-4 (pbk.)

Editorial/production supervision and
  interior design: Maureen Connelly
Cover design: 20/20 Services, Inc./Mark Berghash
Manufacturing buyer: Ron Chapman

Printed in the United States of America

10 9 8 7 6 5 4 3

ISBN 0-13-752907-4 {P}
ISBN 0-13-752915-5 {C}

Prentice-Hall International, Inc., *London*
Prentice-Hall of Australia Pty. Limited, *Sydney*
Editora Prentice-Hall do Brasil, Ltda., *Rio de Janeiro*
Prentice-Hall Canada Inc., *Toronto*
Prentice-Hall of India Private Limited, *New Delhi*
Prentice-Hall of Japan, Inc., *Tokyo*
Prentice-Hall of Southeast Asia Pte. Ltd., *Singapore*
Whitehall Books Limited, *Wellington, New Zealand*

Contents

Part V
THE APPENDICES   *211*

Foreword

This book represents an important milestone in psychotherapy. To my knowledge, it is the first treatment manual which attempts to integrate a system of psychotherapy with what is currently known about brain function. Attitudes, thought processes, and behavior are not simply independent epiphenomena but are rooted in the biology of man, capable of serving adaptive and maladaptive purposes. Dr. Maxie C. Maultsby, Jr., from his unique perspective and experience, provides the reader with a "rational" world view within which man's strivings and sufferings can be better understood.

Rational Behavior Therapy, a derivative of rational emotive therapy, represents a practical and effective approach for treating a wide range of emotional and behavioral problems. It is relatively "culture free" in its application and can be used by the entire spectrum of therapists, regardless of professional discipline. It also can be adapted easily for use by lay groups.

In my estimation, one of Dr. Maultsby's great virtues as a clinician has been his willingness to test his theories through research and to incorporate the latest scientific thought into his conceptual system. In this volume, he not only draws attention to a wide range of scientific findings but also makes reference to holography and other recent developments to illuminate his views.

Dr. Maultsby has a special interest in short-term therapy and self-help techniques. He is a pioneer and innovator in his field. Within this volume, he has managed successfully to include a wealth of clinical insights and intriguing speculations about the nature and process of therapy. The reader should find particularly fascinating the author's observations about right and left hemisphere functioning and how that relates to certain attitudes and perceptions of the world.

This book is "must" reading for any student and practitioner of psychotherapy. Writing in a simple and straightforward instructional style, the author offers penetrating and practical applications of his system of therapy. This is not just a book on theory. It also represents a manual for practice. If the reader is willing to assume the role of student, he will be rewarded with many helpful suggestions and guidelines for his clinical practice.

Arnold M. Ludwig, M. D.
Evalyn A. Edwards Professor of Psychiatry
College of Medicine
University of Kentucky

Acknowledgments

Many thanks go to Eleanor Royalty and Barbara Johnson for cheerfully typing the drafts of this book. I gratefully acknowledge the helpful contributions of Barbara Benson, Walter Gaffield, and Arnold Ludwig, who read the original draft and made valuable critical comments. Special appreciation goes to Barbara Benson for her critical and editorial intelligence, and her commitment to this work. Full responsibility for the contents of the book, however, remains with the author.

Rational Behavior Therapy

PART ONE

Introduction

Part One consists of two subdivisions:

Introduction

RBT (Rational Behavior Therapy) (Chapter 1)

The introduction describes what to expect from the book. It also suggests how best to read the book to get the maximum recall with the least effort.

Chapter 1 describes how and why Rational Behavior Therapy is a comprehensive, short-term, cross-cultural, drug-free, cognitive-behavioral psychotherapy that produces long-term results.

Introduction

Introduction

IMPORTANT FACTS ABOUT THIS BOOK

This book will give you two immediate, pleasant surprises. Your first pleasant surprise will be learning that a scientific book, written for professionals, doesn't have to be boring to read and difficult to understand. In fact, prepublication readers say this book is both easily understandable and enjoyable reading.

And here's your second pleasant surprise. The behavioral concepts and techniques in RBT apply to healthy, or desirable, behaviors as well as they apply to unhealthy, or undesirable behaviors. Therefore, as soon as you understand an RBT concept or technique, you can immediately try it out on yourself. It is strongly recommended that you do because such self-application will give you the most immediate, in-depth, and personally meaningful learning experience possible.

Remember, you don't have to have personal problems to apply RBT to yourself; that's one of its main advantages. Both RBT theory and its techniques accurately apply to the behavior of anyone who has a healthy, undrugged brain. So whether you want to improve some aspect of your self-control, or whether you just want objective insight into your own unique personality traits, RBT theory and its techniques will let you achieve either.

BOOK CONTENTS

This book introduces you to basic RBT theory and therapeutic technology. As much as possible, the book covers the same material that is covered at the RBT Center in our intensive training courses for psychotherapists and counselors.[1] In short, this book represents the essence of many years of research and experience in giving health professionals rapid, intensive training in Rational Behavior Therapy.

EXPECTED READERS

This book was written for practitioners and students of the helping professions who have these three personal goals:

1. They want to help emotionally distressed people faster and safer, without using drugs, than they can help them by using drugs.
2. They want the people they help to be better able to cope successfully with future problems in living than they were ever able to cope with them before.
3. They want to use a psychotherapy or counseling technique that also helps people prevent future problems in daily living.

FORMAT AND AIDS TO RAPID, SELF-REINFORCING LEARNING

Each chapter begins with a preview, followed by the Special Vocabulary used in that chapter. The Special Vocabulary gives you the operational definitions of concepts and terms unique to RBT.[2]

RBT therapists emphasize *saying what you mean* and *meaning what you say*. That emphasis is not simply to improve interpersonal communications; it also has important clinical applications. As this book repeatedly shows, one of the most common causes of emotional distress is that people both think what they don't mean and mean what they don't think, all the while believing every word of it. The following excerpts from a favorite teaching tape clearly demonstrate that fact.

I call this tape the "Mouse Lady" tape. It's the recording of the intake interview of a young, attractive, and intelligent woman, the day after she had tried to commit suicide. When I asked her, "Why did you think that suicide was the only solution to your problem? What could be that terrible about your life?" she said, "I'm such a mouse." I said, "A mouse?" And she said, "Yeah, I'm just a gutless mouse; that's why I did it." And I said, "Well, if I were to take a picture of you and show it to my staff, would they say, 'Oh, what a cute little mouse'?"

The Mouse Lady thought for a moment; then said, "No, I haven't felt very attractive lately, but I don't think I look like a mouse." And I said, "Well then, why do you call yourself something you don't look like?" And she said, "Well,

---

[1] For information about these training courses, write to Training Coordinator, RBT Center, College of Medicine, University of Kentucky, Lexington, KY 40536.

[2] Expect some of the operational definitions used in RBT to differ from Webster's definitions. Remember, Webster is concerned with generally accepted word usage. But RBT is concerned with the most generally healthy use of words by emotionally distressed people.

you see I feel like a mouse.'' Then I asked, ''When was the last time you asked a mouse how it felt?''

Now, you probably think that by this point, this attractive, intelligent woman was willing to give up the self-image of herself being a mouse, especially after she had just admitted she didn't look like one. But oh, no; instead, she explained, ''Well you see, if you get after a mouse, it'll run; well, that's what I do.'' Then I pointed out, ''But if you get after an elephant, he'll run too. Are you an elephant? If you get after a lion, he'll run, too. Are you a lion?''

''No'', she explained, ''what I mean is, I'm so afraid of rejection, I don't stand up for myself; I just let people take advantage of me.'' Then, because RBT is excellent, short-term, yet comprehensive therapy for fear of rejection, the interview immediately began to move in a rapidly therapeutic direction.

But let's take a few seconds to see why those excerpts accurately demonstrate the hazard of people thinking what they don't mean, and meaning what they don't think, and believing every word of it. The Mouse Lady's last comment, ''I'm so afraid of rejection,'' showed she hadn't meant what she said when she called herself a mouse; nor had that self-label said what she meant. But by feeling as if she were a mouse, this lady showed that she believed, at least at that moment, that ''mouse'' was the most appropriate label for her. That common cognitive habit has this emotional hazard: It can cause people to be suicidally depressed about beliefs that could never be facts.

Remember, one of the oldest, and still most useful insights into human self-control is ''Every way of people is right in their own eyes'' (Proverbs 21:2). Or, as we say in RBT, ''Normally, people voluntarily maintain and act out *only* the ideas and emotional reactions they believe are right for them at the moment they act.'' That's the most clinically useful explanation of why the Mouse Lady stubbornly defended her incorrect label; she sincerely believed her self-label was right for her at that moment, even though she didn't mean it.

Sincerely clinging to obviously incorrect self-labels is a common self-defeating habit of emotionally distressed people. But, as you saw with the Mouse Lady, getting patient-clients (P-Cs) to answer simple, yet obviously reality-oriented questions is an ideal way to help them quickly give up that self-defeating habit.[3]

Now let's go back to the format of this book. After each chapter's Special Vocabulary, you will find Focus Items. Focus Items are questions that, first, highlight important points to remember and, second, increase your self-instructive concentration. I have also included occasional mnemonic illustrations. These illustrations help you vividly conceptualize unfamiliar concepts, parts of the brain, and explanations of events that, if described with words alone, might be vague and nonspecific.

To increase your short- and long-term memory, I have put a list of Memory Aids for each chapter in Appendix A. Each aid is a leading question—rather than a

---

[3]Out of respect for the semantic preferences of non-physician and physician psychotherapists and counselors, I refer to people receiving psychotherapy or counseling as patient-clients or P-Cs.

simple statement—about an important fact to remember. Therefore, these questions don't attempt to test you; they merely help you convert your short-term and initial recognition memories to long-term memory.

Most readers read the Memory Aids immediately after each chapter. Other readers wait until they have read the whole book. In either case, expect the answers to the questions to be easy and obvious to you. As I said, the leading questions are merely statements of important facts in question form. Questions elicit more active reader participation than simple statements of facts. And active reader participation is what increases long-term memory.

Several weeks or months after reading any book, even the best memories begin to fade. That will be a good time for you to review the Memory Aids; you'll be amazed at how your memory will instantly reapproach maximum recall without having to reread the actual chapters.

If you are like most people, you tend to read every book as if it were a novel; that is, once through, from front to back as quickly as possible. But since this is not a novel, *resist* that tendency with this book.

Novels are *not* meant to instruct you; they are meant only to entertain you. Therefore, the faster you read novels, the more you will enjoy yourself per unit of time and effort. You neither expect nor want to remember many of the details in novels. You just want a few enjoyable hours.

But this is a self-instructional book; it's designed to change the way you do psychotherapy and maybe even change your life. Therefore, it deserves a special reading routine.

HOW BEST TO READ THIS BOOK

First skim the book, reading only the chapter previews, Focus Items, Special Vocabularies, chapter headings, subtitles, mnemonic illustrations, and Memory Aids. But don't try to answer the Memory Aids on your skim-through.

After you skim the book, immediately start reading it at your usual reading rate. Even then, it's best to skim each chapter first. Then go back and read the chapter, word for word, at your usual rate.

You may now be thinking, "That sounds like work." You are right. But remember, this is a self-instructional book; it's especially designed to make your short-term reading experience give you long-term professional results. It's usually best to read such books rapidly at first; then again more slowly; and, ideally, again even more slowly and thoughtfully a third, and maybe even a fourth time. It also helps if you remember this fact: *Trouble is the only thing you can usually get fast and easy, on the very first try.*

THE CASE HISTORIES

Wherever possible, case histories have been included to illustrate the clinical use of RBT theory and technique. Naturally, though, identifying data were changed to protect the privacy of my former P-Cs.

ABOUT REFERENCES

This book is well referenced. But the references are concentrated on the behavioral scientists who have had the greatest personal influence on me or whose research and theories form the scientific basis of Rational Behavior Therapy or both. That choice made it inevitable that some authentic pioneers in behavior therapy and cognitive behavior therapy would be omitted. I now apologize for that.

Understandably, I make a few claims to relative originality for myself. I say relative originality, because I sincerely believe, ''The thing which has been is that which shall be; and that which is done is that which shall be done; and there is no new thing under the sun'' (Ecclesiastes 1:9).

WHAT ELSE TO EXPECT FROM THIS BOOK

Expect to learn an ideal form of cognitive behavior therapy. But also expect to learn many neuropsychophysiological facts that will be clinically useful in any type of psychotherapy. That's why, in order to add RBT to your present technique of psychotherapy or counseling, you do *not* have to give up what you already do well therapeutically.

The theory and techniques in RBT are based on research-supported learning theories of normal human behavior; therefore, they fit into any other research-supported psychotherapy or counseling approach. So you can immediately use any RBT concept or technique you thoroughly understand. But remember! No one RBT concept, insight, or technique alone can reproduce the excellent clinical results described in this book. Understandably, therefore, for consistent results like these, you must use all of RBT, the way it is described here. Otherwise, you will not be giving Rational Behavior Therapy an adequate clinical trial.

Another thing: Expect this book to challenge a few of the ''sacred cows'' of traditional psychotherapy, especially those about what should and shouldn't be done. And expect some of those challenges to feel wrong when you first read them. New facts always feel wrong when they conflict with old beliefs. For example, when the first people said that the world is round, that idea felt so wrong that most other people just laughed and ignored it. But their laughter did not change the round shape of the world.

So don't worry when new ideas in this book feel wrong; instead, just do these two things: Remember that the world was round a long time before it felt right to believe it. Then, as you read, be your most objective self. Temporarily ignore any conflicting ''gut feelings.'' But keep an open mind. Look closely at the clinical advantages RBT will give you and your P-Cs. Then ask yourself, ''Do the contrary traditional ways give me or my P-Cs or both as many clinical advantages as RBT will give?'' When in doubt, list the pros and cons of RBT versus traditional methods. Then let the facts speak for themselves.

The Memory Aids for the Introduction are on page 213.

What is RBT? What makes RBT an ideal cognitive-behavioral psychotherapy? Where did RBT come from? What's rational in RBT? This chapter gives you the answers to all four questions.

SPECIAL VOCABULARY

Apperception: any personally meaningful cognitive unit consisting of a perception plus a personally meaningful label or an evaluative thought about the perception, or both. The distinction between apperception and perception rarely is important clinically. Therefore, except when the distinction has important theoretical implications, the word *perception* will be used in this book as if it were synonymous with apperception.

Camera Check of Perceptions: self-help maneuver in RBT that helps ensure that what seems real to people objectively fits the obvious facts of the situation.

Cognitive behaviors: the symbolic activities of the brain that collectively form the most widely accepted concept of the human mind. In RBT, the two most important cognitive activities for psychotherapeutic focus and change are (1) people's habitual perceptions, that is, what they usually pay attention to about themselves and the external world, and (2) people's sincere habitual thoughts and attitudes about their perceptions.

Emotive behaviors: the subjectively positive, negative, or neutral emotional feelings, plus the interactions of people's vital organ systems that are usually associated with their emotional feelings.

Mental image: in RBT, the mental reproduction of any concept, object, or event. Although visual reproductions are probably the most common mental images in sighted people, any sensory stimulus, or combination of sensory stimuli, can both make up and trigger a mental image. *Synonyms:* mental picture, mental picture-map, and mental impression.

Obvious facts: objectively real events, and descriptions of such events that accurately reflect the way video cameras or other mechanical recording devices would have recorded them. *Antonym:* fiction. *Synonym:* correct statement.

Perception: any stimulus registered in the brain.

Psychotherapy: verbal attempts by trained helping professionals to help people improve their emotional and other behavioral control without using drugs, psychosurgery, or physical or electrical stimulations. In short, RBT therapists agree with Pavlov: "Psychotherapy is essentially word therapy, directly affecting the second signal system (that is, people's language) . . . and the internal milieu" (Pavlov as quoted in Volgyesi 1954, slightly paraphrased).

Rational Self-Counseling: the emotional self-help method routinely included in RBT (Maultsby 1976).

FOCUS ITEMS

1. What do RBT therapists mean by the word *rational*?
2. How is that concept relevant to optimal emotional health?
3. What is the logic behind the Camera Check of Perceptions?
4. What is "From Missouri-itis"?
5. Why is the Camera Check clinically useful?
6. What is some obvious evidence indicating that rational behavior really means emotionally healthy behavior?

CHAPTER 1

RBT (Rational Behavior Therapy)

RBT is an ideal cognitive behavior therapy because it has each of the six characteristics that identify all ideal psychotherapies. RBT is: (1) comprehensive, (2) short-term, (3) cross-cultural, (4) drug-free, (5) it produces long-term results, and (6) the behavioral concepts and emotional self-help techniques used in RBT (Maultsby and Hendricks 1974; Maultsby 1976, 1978, 1982) enable public school and community groups to offer to interested people effective, yet economical and preventive mass mental-health programs.

RBT is comprehensive because it deals directly with all three groups of human behaviors: cognitive, emotive, and physical.

RBT is short-term psychotherapy because it includes teaching emotionally distressed people the research-tested, drug-free technique of Rational Self-Counseling. This emphasis on scientific emotional self-help enables people to help themselves at will, between therapy sessions. That greatly speeds up the therapeutic process while making it as comprehensive as possible.

RBT is cross-cultural psychotherapy because it is acceptable to and effective for people whose ages, races, cultural values, and lifestyle preferences are widely different from those of their psychotherapists (Brandsma et al. 1979; Fowler 1980; Maultsby 1975, 1980; Maultsby et al. 1975, 1976; Patton 1976; Ross 1978; Ruhnow 1977; Schwager 1975; Werito 1980). Hence, RBT is an excellent method for treating not only traditionally ideal psychotherapy candidates, but also for treating people who are often neglected as psychotherapy candidates: adolescents, the elderly, the poor, and members of racial and ethnic minorities.

Medical science has not yet been able to improve on nature at its best. That is why RBT therapists believe that healthy, undrugged brains are psychotherapists' safest and most reliable therapeutic aids. That's also why RBT is drug-free psychotherapy for people with physically healthy brains.

RBT produces long-term results because adequately treated people learn proven, effective emotional self-help skills. Such people are better able than ever before to cope successfully with future problems in daily living (Maultsby 1982).

Our research in teaching Rational Self-Counseling as a regular classroom course (Maultsby, Costello, and Carpenter 1976) indicates that it is an ideal way to help normal people help themselves to happiness. And local chapters of I'ACT (The International Association for Clear Thinking; see Quinn 1980) are excellent examples of how community groups, by teaching classes in Rational Self-Counseling, can give their communities effective, economical programs in mass mental-health improvement.

WHERE RBT CAME FROM

After completing medical education as a physician, I spent fifteen years conducting an in-depth study of nine scientific approaches to understanding and helping people help themselves emotionally.

The first approach was simply the art and science of practicing family medicine.

The second approach consisted of completing specialty training in adult and child psychiatry.

The third approach consisted of the neuropsychological theories of Hebb (1949, 1966) and Luria (1960, 1966, 1966a, 1968, 1973, 1976).

The fourth, fifth, and sixth approaches were the classical conditioning theory of Pavlov (as described in Beritoff 1965); the operant learning theory of Holland and Skinner (1961), and Skinner (1953, 1957); and the learning theories of Mowrer (1960, 1966) and Rotter (1954, 1966).

The seventh approach included the conditioning and learning research and writing of Hudgins (1933), Jones (1924, 1924a), Lacey and Smith (1954), Osgood and Suci (1955), Razran (1935, 1949, 1961), Staats and Staats (1957, 1958), Watson and Rayner (1920), Wolpe and Lazarus (1966), and Wolpe (1973).[1]

The eighth approach was the psychosomatic research of Grace and Graham (1951) and Graham et al. (1958, 1962).

The ninth approach was Albert Ellis's theory and technique of Rational Emotive Therapy (1963).

In the eight years after those in-depth studies, I combined these nine learning experiences into one ideal system of psychotherapy and counseling, called Rational Behavior Therapy, or RBT.

[1]One of my fondest memories of Dr. Wolpe is that during my brief study with him, in 1968, he kindly critiqued my first published paper.

THE RATIONAL IN RBT

The "rational" meaning of the word *rational* is quite different from what most people assume rational means. Most people use *rational* to describe their sincere ideas and actions. And they assume that *irrational* describes the contrary ideas and actions of other people.

Check that claim objectively right now: When you tell people that their ideas or actions are irrational (or they tell you), are you and they usually in agreement or disagreement? A good bet is that you and they are in disagreement almost every time this happens. This also applies to most other people who have healthy, undrugged brains.

People with healthy, undrugged brains almost never knowingly hold personal beliefs that they consider wrong or irrational. But if such people's pretherapy beliefs and disbeliefs were the only things they needed to solve their emotional problems satisfactorily, they wouldn't need psychotherapy. To be healthy and therapeutic, therefore, *rational* has to have a meaning that goes beyond personal beliefs and disbeliefs.

In RBT, the word *rational* equals optimal health. That's why, when RBT therapists say "rational behavior," they mean cognitive, emotive, and physical behaviors that simultaneously obey at least three of:

THE FIVE RULES FOR OPTIMAL HEALTH

1. Healthy behavior is based on obvious fact.
2. Healthy behavior best helps you protect your life and health.
3. Healthy behavior best helps you achieve your short-term and long-term goals.
4. Healthy behavior best helps you avoid your most undesirable conflicts with other people.
5. Healthy behavior best helps you feel the emotions you want to feel.

If you change the word healthy to *rational* in these five rules, you'll have the five rules in RBT that describe *rational* thoughts, beliefs, attitudes, emotional feelings, and physical actions. These rules also define the "rational" meaning of *rational*.

Remember, though, that it's not enough for cognitive, emotive, and physical behaviors to obey one or two of those rules. To be rational, behaviors must obey at least three of the five rules at the same time.

IRRATIONAL BEHAVIORS

The Five Rules for Rational Behavior make it easy to recognize irrational behaviors. In RBT, irrational behaviors mean cognitive, emotive, and physical behaviors that simultaneously disobey three or more of these five rules.

At this point, you may wonder, "What about a behavior that obeys one or two of the rational rules, disobeys one or two and is irrelevant to the others?" That behavior cannot be rational. At best, it will be nonrational. But nonrational behavior is not good enough to produce optimal emotional health. So RBT therapists reject it as readily as they reject clearly irrational behavior.

THE ORIGIN OF THE RBT CONCEPT OF *RATIONAL*

Shortly after my training with Dr. Ellis, I was treating Dan, a college student, for his preexam anxiety. In the third session Dan said, "Okay, so you are saying it's the irrational things I think about exams that make me anxious. But that's the way I've always felt about exams; I don't know what else to think about them. So, suppose you tell me what I should think, and I'll try that."

That was when I made the surprising discovery that I had no trouble intuitively pointing out to my P-Cs their rational and irrational thinking in their therapy sessions; but I couldn't describe clear-cut objective criteria that would help my P-Cs recognize and practice rational thinking between their therapy sessions. Such criteria, however, would have been greatly helpful to Dan.

What did I do? I went back to theoretical basics. The basic theoretical assumption underlying rational psychotherapy is this insight from stoic philosophy: Human beings are disturbed not by things, but by the views they take of them (Ellis, 1963, p. 54).[2]

Me: Think about the facts, because facts don't cause panic. For example, you now tell yourself that you can't stand to flunk a test. But is that a fact? No! You've flunked at least two tests and you didn't die either time; that proves you can stand it. Granted, you stood it miserably both times; but you still stood it. Yet you continue forcing yourself to react emotionally as if your incorrect belief were an obvious fact. But the obvious fact is, you not only survived twice, but, with a little extra work, you made up for both flunked exams well enough to maintain an overall B average, right?

P-C: Right.

Me: Well then, for starters, tell yourself the obvious facts, because facts don't upset people.

Author's Note

At that moment, my session timer indicated the session was over.

Me: Well, I see our time is up; we'll have to stop here. But I want you to remember that one insight; and when I see you next week, we will pick up at that point. Okay?

[2]The following excerpts were taken, with Dr. Ellis's permission, from my article "The Evolution of Rational Behavior Therapy" (1975).

A THERAPEUTIC CHALLENGE

At that point, I had seven days to come up with useful, scientifically valid criteria for rational thinking. I read many different definitions of rational; but none made consistently useful sense to me. Then I made an obvious insight and a logical deduction.

The insight: Psychotherapists try to help people improve their emotional health.

The logical deduction: To be therapeutically useful, the criteria for rational thinking must reveal, as well as lead to, optimal emotional health.

I read numerous definitions of emotional health, but none seemed comprehensive, yet practical enough for everyday use. But by combining the two most practical-sounding definitions, I got a pleasant surprise. This combination stated that emotionally healthy people are reality oriented and are committed to living productive lives with maximum personal and social approval and minimal undesirable emotional conflict.

Those ideas made useful sense. So I restated them as the following four rules for rational thoughts, emotional feelings, and physical behaviors (Maultsby, 1970).

THE FIRST RULES FOR RATIONAL BEHAVIOR

1. What's rational is based on as nearly accurate a description of objective reality as is currently possible.
2. Regardless of the circumstances, what is rational is most likely to preserve your life.
3. What's rational enables you to most efficiently achieve your personal goals.
4. What's rational is least likely to result in your having either significant emotional conflict or significant environmental conflict.

Those four rules worked out well for about six months. Then Connie, an obsessive-compulsive P-C, asked:

1. "What if my behavior is irrelevant for one of the four rules for rational, but obeys the other three? Will my behavior be rational or not?"
2. "How much conflict is significant?"
3. "What if I am not having significant conflict, but I am causing significant conflict for other people? Am I then being irrational or not?"

Again, my session timer rescued me and I said, "I see our time is up. But we shall discuss each of your questions in detail in your next session."

When I later rethought the event, I clearly saw the therapeutic value of Dr. Ellis's repeated advice: "You've got to remember that human beings are fallible.

And because they are fallible, they all have an incurable tendency to mess up.[3] That makes it irrational for people to try to be perfect.''

That memory led me to these useful insights: About the only thing a fallible human being can do perfectly well all the time is die. But with the new life-supporting machines and vital organ transplants, even dying perfectly well is becoming difficult, if not impossible to do. So it's almost certain that no one will ever live in a perfectly rational way all the time.

To be maximally accurate, therefore, a therapeutic concept of rational behavior had to be formulated in relative, rather than absolute terms. It then became obvious that rational behavior could be any behavior that's more rational than irrational. So, even if behavior obeyed only three of the four rational rules, it would still be more rational than irrational. Therefore, it would meet the criteria of relative rationality.

Having solved that problem to my satisfaction, I turned my attention to the question "How much conflict is significant?" I saw immediately that I didn't know how much conflict would be significant for anyone except me. The only thing to do was to let these obvious facts speak for themselves.

People react differently to the same stimuli. Therefore, what is significant enough for one person to get upset about may not be all that significant for another person. Therefore, to be maximally useful, significant conflict had to be the amount of conflict that each person dislikes enough to work to avoid.

That definition opened my eyes to these two obvious, yet often ignored clinical facts: (1) What's rational for one person may not be rational for another. If therapists ignore that fact, psychotherapy can become an expensive waste of time. When P-Cs ignore that fact, they often end up in significant interpersonal conflict. (2) What's rational for people at one time, or in one situation, may not be rational for them at other times, or in other situations. When P-Cs ignore that fact, they usually cause themselves significant personal conflict.

Rational Behavior Therapists recognize and accept those two facts. That's why RBT therapists don't try to impose their beliefs or value systems on their P-Cs. And by structuring psychotherapy around those facts, RBT therapists free themselves to do efficiently effective, drug-free, cross-cultural psychotherapy, regardless of the age, sex, race, social status, or lifestyle preferences of their P-Cs.

Next I attacked Connie's third question, "What if a person's behavior is a stimulus for significant emotional conflict in other people?" I decided that this question was irrelevant. The American Revolution and the civil rights protests of the 1950s and 60s were two obvious demonstrations that people can rationally be stimuli for significant conflict in and with others, without causing significant conflict for themselves.

To emphasize that fact, I separated the old fourth rational rule into two rules.

[3]Dr. Ellis used a more colorful four-letter word—perhaps that's why I remembered the advice so well.

Then I saw that "significant conflict" could be replaced with "your most undesirable conflict" without any loss of meaning. Making that switch eliminated the need for P-Cs to learn the definition of significant. That was an improvement because *the less that emotionally distressed people need to learn to help themselves, the faster they usually progress.*

Finally, I rewrote the five rules for rational behavior using the simplest wording I could think of. Clinical experience had taught me that the simpler self-help language is, the more rapidly people learn to help themselves by using it. Now:

THE FIVE RULES FOR RATIONAL BEHAVIOR

1. Rational behavior is based on obvious fact.
2. Rational behavior best helps you protect your life and health.
3. Rational behavior best helps you achieve your short-term and long-term goals.
4. Rational behavior best helps you avoid your most undesirable conflicts with other people.
5. Rational behavior best helps you feel the emotions you want to feel.

These five rules for rational behavior enable emotionally distressed people to assess accurately how emotionally healthy or unhealthy their behaviors are. Helping P-Cs begin to make that behavioral assessment automatically is an important as well as unique feature of Rational Behavior Therapy.

WHY REALITY MAY NOT BE OBJECTIVELY REAL

Most people are confident of their ability to recognize obvious facts. Still, the first rule for rational thinking (that is, thinking based on obvious facts) is the rule that emotionally distressed people usually misuse the most. Why? Because emotionally distressed people usually have varying degrees of "From Missouri-itis."

From Missouri-itis means having the incorrect idea that what you see is really right before your eyes. In fact *what people see is never right before their eyes; it's always a mental picture or image formed in the back of their brain.*

This fact indicates that human brains work like cameras (Pribram 1971). But the brain is much more flexible than a real camera. When a real camera forms images, it can only use input from the outside world. The human brain doesn't have that limitation. Human brains can and sometimes do ignore the outside world, forming images based solely on people's imaginations, memories, and emotional feelings. That's why it's important for psychotherapists to make sure their P-Cs know and remember the next three facts. First, Eccles's work (1958) clearly shows that healthy human brains do not automatically separate mental pictures or images that are based on people's imaginations, memories, and emotional feelings from mental pictures or images that are based on obvious facts.

Second, the origin of the brain's mental pictures doesn't matter; the brain still uses those mental pictures, whatever their origins, to control people's cognitive, emotional, and physical reactions.

Third, obvious facts do not adjust themselves to people's arbitrary mental pictures or apperceptions. Therefore, when obvious facts are in significant conflict with people's apperceptions of them, the people often end up in undesirable conflicts with those obvious facts.

Bower's work (1974) with newborn infants indicates that the human brain seems to be genetically programmed to trigger consistently similar mental reproductions of similar events in the external world, plus consistently similar emotional and physical responses to those reproductions. Bower's earlier work (1971) also indicates that when humans discover that external reality is significantly different from their brain's reproductions of it, they seem to have an innate tendency to get emotionally upset about that fact.

For example, Bower (1971) induced naive infants to reach for optical illusions; they naturally grabbed hands full of air. The youngest infants responded with intense crying reactions; in addition to crying, older infants also banged their hands against their chairs. To help P-Cs avoid or quickly eliminate similar emotional upsets, RBT therapists teach them to do the Camera Check of their Perceptions. As you recall, I started that teaching process in my first interview with the Mouse Lady (see pp. 4–5). Her self-perception could not pass the Camera Check. (See Figure 1-1.)

1-1   The Camera Check of Perceptions

The Camera Check of Perceptions helps people make sure their brain is working at least as accurately as a simple camera would work. For example, I asked the Mouse Lady if a photo of her would look like a mouse. That question got her to do a Camera Check of her self-perception, even though she had never heard of that valuable emotional self-help maneuver. But because she was not psychotic, the Mouse

Lady said that a photo of herself would not look like a mouse. Then I pointed out, "Since a camera's picture or image of you wouldn't look like a mouse, it's neither objectively accurate, nor fair to yourself, to call yourself a mouse. And your label is doubly irrational because you make yourself feel like a mouse; or more accurately, you feel the way you believe a mouse should and would feel if a gutless mouse could feel."

At this point a few bright but inexperienced graduate students often ask, "Are you saying that everything I can take pictures of is reality?"

My answer is, "No, no, no; the Camera Check of Perceptions only makes people aware of mental images that do *not* describe obvious facts. The logic is that if a camera could not have recorded an event the way people described it, then their description is probably more arbitrary opinion than obvious fact."

Yes, people have a right to their opinions. But people's sincere but irrational opinions often cause them unhealthy emotional or physical conflict, or both, with the outside world. When that's the case, what's the most emotionally healthy thing for them to do? RBT therapists believe the answer is, "Rationally change those opinions." That belief makes obvious the main therapeutic strategy in RBT: Getting P-Cs to recognize and replace their sincere, but irrational, opinions with rational ones.

Unfortunately, people generally resist changing the opinions they believe are facts. It seems we all have a touch of From Missouri-itis; that is, people normally believe that their mental pictures are obvious facts. That's why people tend to cling to the inaccurate mental images that their unnoticed but incorrect opinions trigger. In addition, people often act out their incorrect mental pictures and images to self-defeating ends. Consequently, getting emotionally distressed people into the habit of doing the Camera Check of Perceptions has both a strongly self-protective as well as therapeutic effect.

Here's another question graduate students often ask: "What is the evidence that the Five Rules for Rational Thinking reliably define emotionally healthy behavior?" There are three classes of readily observable evidence.

First, if you look objectively at each rule separately, what immediately becomes obvious? You immediately see that consistent, significant deviation from the established healthy norm for any one of those rules is almost always a sign of major psychiatric disorder.

Second, if you do behavioral assessments of emotionally healthy people, you will rarely find anyone whose general day-to-day thinking or other behavior consistently *disobeys* three or more of those rules at the same time. Instead, almost all of those people's behavior will consistently *obey* three or more of those rules at the same time.

Third, if you do behavioral assessments of emotionally distressed people who need psychotherapy or counseling, here's what you'll find: Almost without exception, in their situations of distress these people's thinking and other behaviors will consistently *disobey* three or more of the Five Rules for Rational (and therefore emotionally healthy) Behaviors.

These are the three main reasons why the Five Rules for Rational Behavior guide every aspect of RBT.

The Memory Aids for this chapter are on page 214.

PART TWO

The Neuropsychophysiologic Basis of RBT

Thinking is the single most important thing people do. It triggers and directs their emotional feelings and physical actions. Because thinking occurs only in people's brains, the next fact seems odd, to say the least: Rarely do books on psychotherapy or counseling even mention that people have brains.

That oddity may be due largely to this fact: People almost never consult psychotherapists or counselors because they're concerned about the way they've been thinking lately; it's almost always because of concern about the way they've been feeling lately.

But would you take your car to mechanics who had learned their trade by studying books that didn't mention that cars have engines? Think about your answer if you think it's odd for this book on psychotherapy to discuss

The Human Brain in Self-Control (Chapter 2)
One Head, But Two Brains (Chapter 3)
Rational Cognitive-Behavioral Learning Theory (Chapter 4)

These chapters give you the neuropsychophysiological basis of RBT theory. They also give you useful clinical examples of the applications of the theory. Therefore, these chapters give you basic facts about the brain and show you the direct tie-in between the brain, principles of normal human behavior, and RBT technique.

CHAPTER **2**
The Human Brain in
Self-Control

People's brains are their single most important organs of survival, comfort, and self-control. And it's people's naive misuses of their healthy brains that create their needs for psychotherapy. Fortunately, though, people's brains also control all their behaviors that psychotherapy can influence. That's the main reason why Rational Behavior Therapy focuses on teaching P-Cs the healthiest possible use of their brains.

For some reason books about psychotherapy rarely mention that people have brains, much less discuss the healthiest way for them to use their brains. That seems odd—it's like writing books about auto-mechanics but not mentioning automobiles have engines or how the engines work.

This chapter illustrates and describes the main parts of the brain that control the behaviors that psychotherapy can influence. This chapter also briefly summarizes the three functional brain units and the essential mental functions they have in behavioral control. (For a more detailed discussion of these important topics, see Luria 1973, pp. 43–102.)

SPECIAL VOCABULARY

Holography: a special type of photography that uses split laser beams as its source of light. Holography seems to provide the best current model for how the brain produces and reproduces a person's experiential reality.

Sagittal View: a look at the inner surface of an organ that has been split into right and left halves from top to bottom, length-wise. Example: a watermelon split into length-wise halves.

FOCUS ITEMS

1. What are the three major parts of the brain that control the behaviors that psychotherapy can influence?
2. Who described the three functional brain units?
3. What essential mental activities for survival, comfort, and self-control does each of the functional brain units control?

4. Why is the third functional brain unit the most important one in making possible independent, truly adult living?
5. What important mental capacity does the holographic theory of the mind help explain?

CHAPTER **2**

The Human Brain in Self-Control

It is useful to think of human brains as being ultrasophisticated organs that produce symbolic information. The raw data for the human brain's symbolic outputs are people's multivaried internal and external stimuli. Human brains usually process those stimuli sequentially. This is done in the brain's three major neuropsychological divisions which are called the first, second, and third functional brain units. These three functional units are connected by numerous intercommunicating channels of nerve-impulse transmission. A stimulus in any one of the units, therefore, simultaneously influences the mental activities in all three units.

In the first functional brain unit two major components are the ascending and descending reticular formations. The main body of these formations is in the brain stem, shown below.

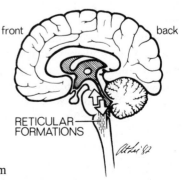

2-1 Sagittal View of the Brain and Brain Stem

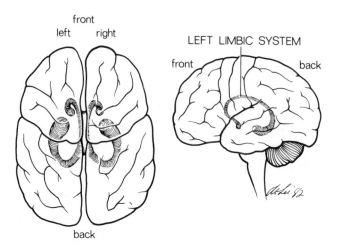

2-2   The Limbic Systems

This loose network of ascending and descending nerve cells has reciprocal connections with the other major components of the first functional brain unit: the right and left limbic systems, shown above in a view of the brain. You can see the right and left limbic systems in their usual position embedded in the inner walls of their corresponding hemispheres. The limbic systems control the body's autonomic nervous systems and, through them, coordinate the body's vital organ systems.

The actions and interactions of the body's vital organ systems create the physiologic basis of emotional sensations. The limbic systems, therefore, are primarily responsible both for the positive, negative, and neutral emotive or feeling parts of human emotions and their secondary motivational urges.[1]

Most P-Cs come to therapy believing the incorrect idea that their emotive feelings are their total emotions. But early in RBT, P-Cs learn that their emotive feelings are only a part of their total emotions. Equally important, P-Cs learn that, for rational self-understanding, their emotive feelings are the least important parts of their emotions. The clinical importance of that fact will become clear in Chapter 4, in the description of the A, B, C model of emotions (Ellis 1963) used in Rational Behavior Therapy.

Because of the direct tie-in between the reticular activating systems and the limbic systems, every sensory stimulus triggers either a positive, negative or neutral state of arousal. The brain then stores that information in its emotive memory bank for future use in behavioral motivation. The main functions of the first functional brain unit, therefore, are clear. It creates and maintains the levels of alertness and motivation for reinforceable behaviors that are essential for survival and drug-free emotional comfort.

---

[1]In *Help Yourself to Happiness through Rational Self-Counseling* (Maultsby 1976), I called the limbic systems the feeling parts of the brain. But as this chapter shows, that label is somewhat inaccurate. Still, it's a clinically useful fiction for giving most P-Cs quick, helpful insights into healthy brain control.

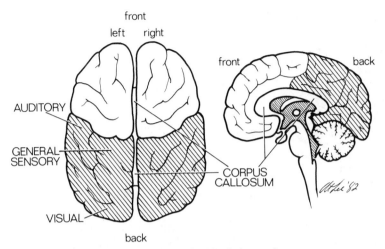

2-3   Second Functional Brain Unit (shaded areas)

The second functional brain unit shown above consists largely of the middle and posterior regions of each hemisphere on the convex surfaces; those surfaces include the visual, auditory, and general sensory areas. The main functions of this brain unit are receiving, analyzing, and storing information as past experiences. Without that experiential memory, future goal-directed behavior would be impossible.

The corpus callosum is the huge mass of nervous tissue shown above connecting the brain's left and right hemispheres.

The corpus callosum normally functions like the control box of a master intercom that usually has most of its channels open; consequently, the right and left hemispheres normally stay well informed about each other's current activities. In this way the two hemispheres maintain their usual, dynamic, functional balance of individual influences on their owner's emotive and physical behaviors. When internal or external circumstances demand it, however, one or the other of the hemispheres can and will flood the corpus callosum with one-way communications; then that hemisphere will temporarily exercise primary control over the person's behavioral responses (Galin 1974; Galin and Ornstein 1972).

The third functional brain unit consists largely of the frontal areas of the brain shown on pg. 28, anterior to the precentral gyrus.[2] (See Figure 2-4.)

This brain unit is concerned primarily with creating goal-directed intentions, plans for action, and with gathering feedback essential for distinguishing successes from failures. The third functional brain unit does not become fully active until after the age of language. Then, for the following two reasons, this unit rapidly becomes the most important brain unit for independent adult survival, drug-free emotional comfort, and self-control.

[2]This area of the brain I usually call the "thinking parts of the brain" (Maultsby 1976), or the neocortex. Again, as with the concept of the "feeling parts of the brain," the concept of the "thinking parts of the brain" is merely a useful fiction for communicating easily with P-Cs.

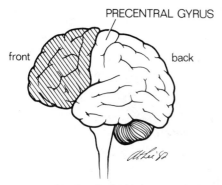

PRECENTRAL GYRUS

front   back

(LEFT HEMISPHERE)   2-4   Third Functional Brain Unit (shaded areas)

First, the third functional brain unit has the neurocellular design that makes it ideal for coordinating the activities of the first and second brain units (Luria 1973, pp. 79–99). Understandably, therefore, this unit ultimately gains direct or indirect control of people's voluntary and involuntary reactions.

Second, as human infants mature, their uniquely human mental activity of language quickly takes over ultimate control of the psychophysiological reactions essential for behavioral self-control (Lamendella 1977; Luria 1960, 1966, 1966a, 1973; Mowrer 1966). Then, the main function of the brain's third unit seems to be converting a person's "world-of-words" (Lee 1941, p. 16)—that is, a person's personal self-talk or thoughts—into the logical behavioral plans, intentions, and mental picture-maps that are needed to change symbolic information into corresponding emotional and physical reactions (Luria 1973, pp. 229–340).

HUMAN BRAINS AT WORK

In processing stimuli, human brains work like cameras first and then second work like preprogrammed computers. That's why people never perceive reality directly; they perceive only their mental images and semipermanent, computer-program-like, neuroelectrical maps of reality. When those images and maps are well-learned, they trigger and direct habitual reactions correctly, with minimal-to-no conscious thoughts.

Before healthy human infants learn to talk, their brains (like ordinary cameras) record reality most accurately. Granted their brains can also blur reality as well as record it out of focus. But, except when other humans arbitrarily create illusions for human infants (as in Bower 1971), their brains *don't* seem able to make mental images of things that don't exist in the world outside their minds. Language, however, enables infants' brains to overcome that limitation on their ability to form mental images.

In addition to forming images of the objective, factual, "world-of-not-words" (Lee 1941, p. 16), when people learn to talk, their brains can and do ignore objective reality and form realistic mental images based on verbal memories and on imagination. Regardless of their origins, however, people's mental images of reality, together with their programmed reactions to these images, control people's emotional and physical behaviors. That neuropsychophysiologic fact makes people's verbal thoughts the single most important factors in their emotional and physical control.

People are a part of, live in, and interact with the world of objective reality outside their minds. To live and control themselves in emotionally healthy ways, however, people must consistently make sure their brains do these two things:

1. create mental images that accurately describe the outside factual world-of-not-words illustrated later in this chapter and
2. create intentions, goals, plans, and mental programs of actions that accurately reflect the objective cause-and-effect principle that seems to govern the world-of-not-words outside human minds.

Those facts make it clear why the first rule for both rational, as well as emotionally healthy, living is that *the behavior must be based on obvious fact.* That's also why one of the first things that people receiving RBT learn is how to do the Camera Check of their problem-related perceptions before they act on them.

Granted, the analogy of the human brain with a camera is only superficially accurate. Even holography (Russell 1979), the most sophisticated theory and technology of photography, can't begin to simulate even ten seconds of human fantasy. Yet, impressive research data (cited in Pribram 1969; 1971) indicate that the holographic theory of human brain and mind functions is the best current working model for the photographic and mnemonic activities of the human brain. This is why comprehensive neuropsychological theories of human behavior include concepts from holography.

SUMMARY OF HOLOGRAPHY

To take a holographic image or picture, the camera sends laser beams through a laser-beam splitter. Half of the beams go directly to the special holographic plate; the other half of the laser beams are diverted to the object being photographed; from that object the beams are reflected to the holographic plate where they reunite with the undiverted beams. But the holographic plate does not record the direct image or outline of the object being photographed. Instead, the holographic plate records only the patterns of interference of the laser beams. Those patterns have no obvious resemblance to the object photographed. (See Figure 2-5, p. 30.)

To see the image of a holographically photographed object, you must reilluminate the holographic plate with its original laser beams. Then, you will see the first of the three most remarkable features of holography: The image of the photographed object appears to the human eye as a three-dimensional reproduction of the object suspended in space. (See Figure 2-6, p. 30.)

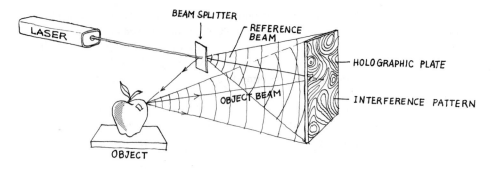

2-5 Holographic Photography

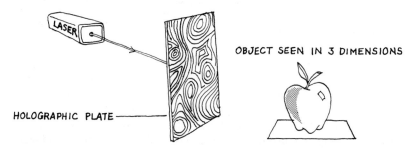

2-6 Holographic Reproduction

Second, however small a piece of holographic plate you may break off, if you reilluminate it with the original laser beams, that small piece of holographic plate will reproduce the complete image of the photographed object. Only the detail and clarity of the whole image decrease, as the fragment of the original holographic plate decreases in size. (See Figure 2-7.)

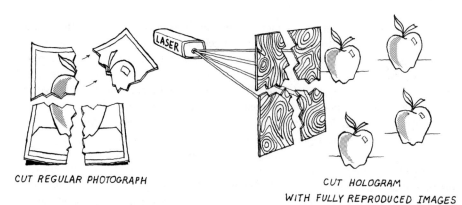

CUT REGULAR PHOTOGRAPH   CUT HOLOGRAM
                                                      WITH FULLY REPRODUCED IMAGES

2-7 Holographic Vs. Photographic Reproduction

Third, if an exposed holographic plate is merely rotated a degree or two, a second image can be recorded on the same holographic plate without disturbing the first image. Consequently, just one cubic centimeter of holographic plate can record and store 10 billion bits of information. (For a more detailed, documented description of this process, see Russell 1979, p. 151.)

Now let's look at the two main facts that make the holographic theory of the mind so attractive. First, more than 10 billion bits of information can be recorded and stored on one cubic centimeter of holographic plate. The human brain contains about 1,500 cubic centimenters. In addition, the proteins used to form brain images are much smaller than the molecular particles on holographic plates. Mathematicians say, therefore, that if people were to use only ten percent of their brains' capacity for holographic data processing, they could still record and store a hundred new bits of information per second, every second of their lives. That's far more mental activity than the average person usually engages in.

Pribram's work (1969; 1971) indicates that the holographic recording activities of the brain include neuroelectrical input from all the sensory organs. I interpret that to mean that the combined sensory inputs of people's neuropsychophysiological reproductions of reality are the analogues of the laser beams in holography. In addition, any sensory area of the brain is the analogue of a part of a holographic plate. But unlike the laser beam of holography, the neuroelectrical activity triggered in the brain by any sensory organ can function like the whole laser beam, thereby reproducing the complete holographic gestalt, merely by activating its own sensory and memory areas of the brain. This view is consistent with the data indicating multidimensionality of memory (Gazzaniga and Le Doux, 1978, p. 132). This view also gives you a plausible explanation for why only a chord or a few notes from a specific symphony can trigger a holographic, mental reproduction of an evening at the concert, or why the fragrance of a certain perfume can trigger the holographic, mental reproduction of a long past romantic interlude, and why people are able to recognize other people and pets after seeing only a small part of their faces or bodies, or after merely hearing their voices.

At best, though, the holographic camera is still an inadequate analogue for the human brain. Probably the biggest defect in any camera analogy with the brain is this: No camera can generate its own stimuli for making images, independent of the outside, objective world-of-not words.[3] Human brains don't have that limitation. Linguistic ability gives people the complete second world of subjective mental experiences that Lee called the world-of-words. And as Pavlov pointed out, "For people, the word is an entirely real stimulus; it signals and substitutes for every other stimulus and induces every kind of reaction other stimuli induce" (Pavlov as quoted in Volgyesi 1954, slightly paraphrased).

The diagrams on page 32 show that the external realities in the world-of-not-words have no intrinsic, nor direct, nor invariable relevance to the arbitrary word-sounds that trigger the mental images of them. Yet those word-sounds trigger peo-

---

[3]In blind people that world-of-not-words may consist largely of the neuroelectrical equivalent of the nonvisual images produced by their functioning organs of smell, hearing, and the other senses.

THE WORLD OF WORDS   THE WORLD OF NOT WORDS

2-8   The World of Words and the World of Not-Words

ple's mental images of reality and their voluntary and involuntary reactions to it. That's why in human emotional and physical self-control, people's sincere words (that is, their beliefs and attitudes) are often more important than obvious facts.

In Chapters 3 and 4, you will read about how the right and left hemispheres of the brain seem to work together. If you then recall the holographic model of the mind and the ways words trigger mental images, you will make this insight: There is ample neuropsychological justification for RBT's unique therapeutic emphasis on objective precision in how words are used for one's beliefs and thoughts. In addition, you will see clearly why it's clinically useful to get P-Cs (such as the Mouse Lady) to say what they mean and mean what they say.

The Memory Aids for this chapter are on page 214.

PREVIEW

People have only one head, but they have two complete brains. That insight is quite old. Hippocrates, the father of medicine, realized it over 2,000 years ago. But A. L. Wigan, a nineteenth-century English physician, seems to have been the first physician to publish clinical data clearly supporting that insight. In the words of Dr. Wigan: "I believe myself able to prove 1. That each cerebrum [that is, *hemisphere*][1] is a distinct and perfect whole as an organ of thought. 2. That a separate and distinct process of thinking or ratiocination may be carried on in each cerebrum simultaneously" (Wigan as quoted in Bogen 1969a, p. 151).

Since Dr. Wigan's discovery, much neuropsychological research has made the concept "one head, but two nonduplicating brains and minds" one of the most clinically useful concepts for understanding normal human behavior. That's why for the remainder of this book, I shall call the right and left hemispheres the right and left brains. (Four reviews of research that support that view of the brain are Galin 1974; Levy 1969; Levy et al. 1972; Wexler 1980).[2]

Section I of this chapter describes in clinically useful terms right-brain and left-brain neuropsychological research that forms the basis of RBT theory and technique. Section II of this chapter describes the major different activities of the right and left brains, explains why people rarely keep New Year's and other resolutions not to keep doing undesirable acts, and describes other clinically useful neuropsychophysiological insights.

SPECIAL VOCABULARY—SECTION I

Appositional thoughts: unspoken mental images and other neuroelectrical, computer-like, mental programs for holistic reactions to conditioned or voluntarily learned behavioral cues. Appositional thoughts occur mainly in the right brain and make up Lee's experiential world-of-not-words (Lee 1941, p. 16). (For an excellent detailed description and discussion of appositional thought, see Bogen 1969a.)

[1]Italics are my insertions.

[2]For a good discussion of a different view, see *The Integrated Mind* by Gazzaniga and LeDoux (1978). In my opinion, however, the implications for RBT are the same, regardless of which view of the mind you accept.

Mind: the functional unit (or units) of the brain that deals primarily, if not exclusively, with learning and with creating symbolic information for use in self-control. Those units form two organized mental structures: the conscious mind, and the superconscious mind defined in Chapter 4.

Cognitive Dissonance: Festinger's concept (1962) for describing the psychological discomfort that results when two or more personal beliefs, or personal behaviors and personal beliefs are in conflict. A common way people eliminate that psychological discomfort is to adopt new beliefs (that is, rationalize) so that they can comfortably maintain both their conflicting beliefs and their conflicting behaviors.

Neurologize: to make statements about presumed brain activities, based on facts that have not yet been shown empirically to have the exact cause-effect relationships that are being described.

Propositional thoughts: self-talk words and sentences that form statements which people either believe or disbelieve. Propositional thoughts occur mainly in the left brain and make up Lee's experiential world-of-words. (For an excellent detailed description and discussion of propositional thought, see Jackson 1958, p. 130.)

FOCUS ITEMS —SECTION I

1. Which brain controls which side of the body?
2. What happens in people's brains at the age of language?
3. What is the importance of language in self-control?
4. How do the right and left brains differ in their views of the world?
5. What is a split-brain patient?
6. Which brain seems to control new learning?
7. Which brain seems to maintain habitual responses?

CHAPTER 3

One Head, But Two Brains

The distributions of the nerves from each brain to the rest of the body are almost completely crossed. That means the right brain sends and receives almost all of its outgoing and incoming nerve impulses to and from the left side of the body; the left brain does the same thing for the right side of the body. Consequently, brain damage to the right brain usually shows up in the form of disability on the left side of the body, and vice versa. Keep those facts in mind when you read the following research on how the right and left brains process the same type of stimuli.

YOU MAY BE RIGHT

At some points, you may well think I am neurologizing learning theory concepts. You may even be right. But I agree with Galin (1974). So-called neurologizing is appropriate when a scientist attempts to explain objective facts in clinically useful ways that could lead to new research and improved theories. Any neurologizing I do in this chapter has those potentially valuable goals.

NEUROPSYCHOLOGICALLY RIGHT-HANDED PEOPLE

To keep this discussion factual yet simple, assume, unless it is stated otherwise, that the following deals with neuropsychologically right-handed people. These are people who are right-handed on the basis of both left brain control and performance preference, and whose left brains control their propositional thoughts.

Considerable evidence exists that most people have a genetic disposition for this type of brain function (Galabruda et al. 1978; Geschwind 1979; Geschwind and Levitsky 1968; Levy-Agresti and Sperry 1968; Wada and Davis 1977). Everything discussed here, however, will apply in the opposite ways to people who are neuropsychologically left-handed—less than 10 percent of the world's population. The neuropsychology of the remaining people (less than 20 percent of the people in the world) is too mixed and variable to be discussed here.

From birth until the age of language, the right and left brains seem to process incoming stimuli in the same non-verbal ways. In fact, if either brain is surgically removed before an infant reaches the age of 6 months, the remaining brain can almost completely take over all the functions normally carried out by both brains. Consequently, the person can become a productive adult with minimal noticeable handicaps.

After infants learn to talk, the degree of compensating neurological equipotentiality of their brains declines rapidly. But excellent clinical research (Humphrey and Zangwill 1952; Zangwill 1954; Smith 1966) indicates some neurological equipotentiality probably exists until death.

Until the age of language, infants get stimuli only from their bodies' various sensory organs and biochemical regulatory mechanisms. But with the onset of language, in addition to the use of their sensory organs, infants get the second signal system called language, or the world-of-words.

Language changes the right-brain and left-brain functions dramatically. In addition to being the body's most important stimuli-gathering organs, left brains start producing the most important stimuli for adult-level self-control: namely, words and propositional thoughts. In addition, right brains begin reacting to left brains' words as if those words were the events they represent.

For example, in bed in the middle of the night, you will react as fearfully to the sincere thought of a burglar being in your house as you would react to the reality of a burglar being in your house. Your right brain might even give you a clear mental image of a human figure climbing through a window, or opening drawers. This fact will be discussed later in more detail.

After the onset of language, a person's right and left brains often function as a relatively closed system, generating their own linguistic and other cognitive stimuli; the brains then take those self-generated stimuli and create the symbolic information used for that person's self-control. That's why the more irrelevant to external, objective stimuli people make their words and thoughts, the more irrational their self-control usually becomes.

HOW THE BRAINS REPRODUCE REALITY[3]

The right and left brains individually convert stimuli into their own unique symbolic information that each brain uses in its owner's self-control. But the mental mechanisms needed to create propositional thoughts seem to be quite different from those needed to process appositional thoughts (Bogen 1969a). That's probably the main reason why the two brains create their own relatively unique views of the world (Levy-Agresti and Sperry 1968).

The right brain specializes in reproducing Lee's world-of-not-words. Specifically, the right brain deals with spatial orientations, spatial patterns, and concrete objects; this view is synthetic, musical, pictorial, wordless, and maplike. It's an overview or holistic or comprehensive view of the world. In short, the right brain shows people the forest instead of the individual trees.

The left brain specializes in reproducing Lee's world-of-words. This view is verbal and, therefore, abstract, sequential, and deductive. In contrast to the right brain's holistic or comprehensive world view, the left brain's view is analytic or subdivisional. In short, the left brain shows people the individual trees instead of the forest.

Even though the left brain is the talking brain, both brains use words, but each in its own particular way. Jackson was among the first scientists to describe and contrast the different word processing functions of the right and left brains. In Jackson's words, "both halves [*the right and left brains*][4] are alike in so far as each contains processes for words; they are unlike in that only the left is for the use of words in speech and the right is for the other processes in which words serve" (Jackson 1958, p. 130).

Much neuropsychological research (Bever and Chiarello 1974; Bogen 1969, 1969a; Bogen and Bogen 1969; Cohen 1973; Galin 1974; Galin and Ornstein 1972; and Gazzaniga 1967, 1970) now gives firm support to the assumption that the left brain deals primarily with language or propositional thought. (For similar research evidence indicating that the right brain deals primarily with wordless, appositional thoughts, see these same references plus De Renzi and Spinnler 1966; De Renzi et al. 1969; Levy-Agresti and Sperry 1968; Levy et al. 1972; Nebes 1971).

The remainder of this chapter deals with facts mainly from these research studies. Then it describes how and why those facts support the RBT theory of behavioral learning and therapeutic behavioral reeducation.[5]

---

[3]Rational Behavior Therapy is based on the almost universal scientific assumption that an objective world of reality exists outside human minds. But people never experience the objective world of reality directly; they experience it only through the direct and indirect stimuli created by their first and second signal systems. Those two signal systems produce people's worlds of arbitrary, subjective, experiential reality. These worlds both make up people's personal lives and are the targets of psychotherapy.

[4]Italics are my insertions.

[5]The rational view is that when psychotherapy does not include drugs, electric shock or psychosurgery, any relatively permanent, therapeutic behavior changes in behavior result from therapeutic, behavioral reeducation.

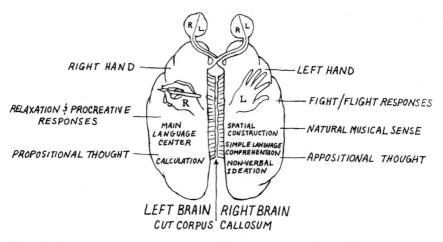

RIGHT HAND

RELAXATION & PROCREATIVE RESPONSES

PROPOSITIONAL THOUGHT

MAIN LANGUAGE CENTER

CALCULATION

SPATIAL CONSTRUCTION

SIMPLE LANGUAGE COMPREHENSION

NON-VERBAL IDEATION

LEFT HAND

FIGHT/FLIGHT RESPONSES

NATURAL MUSICAL SENSE

APPOSITIONAL THOUGHT

LEFT BRAIN | RIGHT BRAIN
CUT CORPUS CALLOSUM

3-1   Schematic Diagram of a ''Split Brain''

One of the accepted treatments for severe epilepsy is to surgically separate the right brain from the left brain by completely cutting through the corpus callosum (see brain diagram above).

The surgical operation is called a commissurotomy and the recovered patients are called split-brain patients. Careful examination of the mental functions of the right and left brains in split-brain patients probably gives us the clearest view of how the two connected brains normally produce and reproduce perceptions of reality. As you read, keep in mind that the left brain controls the right side of the body and the right brain controls the left side of the body.

By touch alone, right-handed, split-brain people can match the arcs of circles with the correct circles significantly better with their right-brain-controlled left hands than they can with their left-brain-controlled right hands (Nebes 1971). This demonstrates that the right brain handles concrete forms and spatial patterns better than the left brain does (see illustration below).

3-2   A Split-Brain Patient

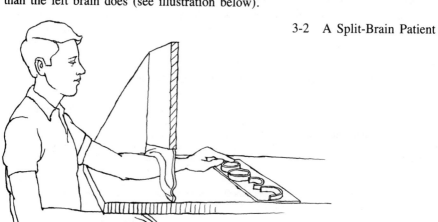

The left-brain-controlled right hands of split-brain people can write well. Writing is verbal and, therefore, is a specialized function of left brains. But only with their right-brain-controlled left hands can those people copy simple geometric figures such as cubes or triangles (Bogen 1969; Gazzaniga 1970).

Right-handed people whose left brains have been removed cannot write with their left hands; but they can still copy simple geometric figures (such as cubes and triangles) with their left hands. However, right-handed people whose right brains have been removed can still write with their right hands; but they can't copy simple geometric figures (such as cubes and triangles) with their right hands (Bogen 1969).

Those studies justify these two conclusions: (1) To copy, people must hold in their brain a holistic image of the model being copied; (2) In right-handed people only the right brain seems to have that holographic image-holding ability. The following clinical data also support the same conclusions and, in addition, clearly indicate how the two brains probably work together in their normal, connected state.

Right-handed people who have suffered certain posterior temporal, left-brain injuries have anomia for familiar objects; that is, they misname familiar objects, forget the meanings of familiar words, and lose their ability to evoke visual images in response to specific words. When these people look at simple drawings of objects, they can copy the drawings well. But they cannot draw a copy of the same drawing when they use their memory alone (Luria 1973, p. 145). Their memory-based drawings are so bizarre, it is almost impossible to recognize them. Simple line drawings of animals or objects might well turn out like this:

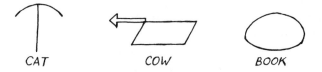

CAT   COW   BOOK

Those facts justify these three conclusions: (1) Words in the left brain function as mnemonic cues that trigger corresponding right-brain mental images of remembered or imagined objects and events. (2) Those images then serve as mental cues and pictures that trigger and control the person's behavioral responses. But people with anomia can't label objects or they mislabel objects and the parts of objects or both. (3) The inability of anomic people to draw objects from memory alone indicates that, without verbal cues from their left brains, their right brains no longer can hold or recall old holistic images of absent objects. That fact makes it impossible to draw from memory alone.

These conclusions led to these three basic clinical assumptions in RBT:

1. The only way people can change their self-control (without potentially harmful drugs or brain damage) is to change their thinking.

2. Therapeutic changes in self-control (without potentially harmful drugs, psychosurgery, or electric shock) require healthy (that is, *rational*) improvement in people's thinking.

3. People cannot *rationally* improve their thinking without *rationally* improving their choice and use of words.

If you put a familiar object (such as a ball or spoon) into the right hands of blindfolded split-brain patients, they can immediately name the object. But even if you put the same objects in those people's left hands, they *cannot* verbally name them. (In the illustration below, remember that the talking left brain controls the right hand.)

3-4 Testing Right-Brain Vs. Left-Brain Language Function

Although these people cannot name the objects placed in their left hands, they can quickly retrieve those objects from a pile of different objects of similar size and shape (Bogen 1969, 1969a; Gazzaniga 1970; Sperry 1968).

With special tachistoscopes, you can flash pictures of words to people's left and right brains individually. When you flash either words or pictures to their left brains, split-brain patients immediately read aloud the words, comply with them if they are commands, and call out the names of pictures.[6]

When you flash words or pictures to the right brains of those patients, however, they honestly maintain that they saw nothing but a flash of light. But they will respond appropriately to command words. For example, they will laugh in response to the flashed word *laugh*. But when asked why they laughed, they—that is, their now completely ignorant left brains—will honestly make up a believable story, such as accusing either the tachistoscope or you of having made them laugh. When you flash the word or picture for a ball, scissors, or some other familiar object, the patients will still claim they saw nothing; yet they can quickly retrieve the correct object from a group of other objects; but they can retrieve it only with their right-brain-controlled left hands.

If you flash an erotic picture to their right brains, these patients will blush and giggle but will still maintain they saw nothing. And when asked to explain their

[6]The data here apply only to those split-brain patients whose anterior commissures were included in their commissurotomies. The anterior commissure transfers visual information between the right and left brains.

blushes and giggles, their completely ignorant left brains will honestly make up a believable story blaming either you or your tachistoscope (Sperry and Gazzaniga 1967; Gazzaniga and Le Doux 1978, pp. 141–162). That and similar facts may mean that one left-brain function is to give people a personally meaningful (that is, believable) explanation of their conscious realities. If so, the common tendency of people to authoritatively explain things of which they are relatively ignorant becomes understandable. Also, such a left-brain function would be neuropsychological support for Festinger's theory (1962) of cognitive dissonance. In any event, this fact seems clear: *When people are sufficiently familiar with verbal or nonverbal signs and cues for habitual emotional and physical reactions, their right brains can react to those cues by triggering those people's habitual physical and emotional reactions without having any conscious or unconscious aid from propositional thoughts in their left brains.*

For a variable period of time after cerebral commissurotomy, right-handed split-brain patients cannot carry out with their left hand oral instructions such as: "Stick out your index finger," "Pretend you are using a pair of scissors," "Pretend you are turning the doorknob to open a door" (Bogen 1969, 1969a).

But these people can quickly carry out those requests with their right hands. And if you demonstrate the requested actions using your left hand, then these people can and will carry out the requested actions with their left hands.

Now consider this: These patients can readily carry out this oral instruction: "Put your right hand in your pocket and keep it there as you leave the room through the closed door there." They simply walk up to the closed door and without hesitation use their left hand to open the door and leave the room.

To understand the clinical importance of those facts (especially about pretending versus actually opening the door), remember this fact: Opening an obstructing closed door is a well-learned, automatic reaction for normal adults. The reaction is so habitual that people don't need to think about it before carrying it out. Just the cue of a closed door obstructing their path triggers the holistic door-opening behavioral program in their right brains.

In normal people, the linguistic cues "open the door" or "pretend to open the door" can and do trigger the same right-brain responses that are triggered by the external cue of the obstructing closed door. But in split-brain patients, their left brains no longer have direct linguistic influence on their right brains. The following studies will show you the clinical importance of this fact.

Dimond (1972) cites several studies that show that damage to the right brain can significantly impair people for carrying out simple, well-learned, habitual responses such as those involved in dressing oneself.

Alajouaine (1948) reported that Maurice Ravel, the famous composer, suffered left-brain damage that caused severe Wernicke's aphasia at the peak of Ravel's musical career. As a result, Ravel permanently lost most of his great ability to analyze musical notation and to play the piano by sight-reading music. But he could still play his own pre-illness musical compositions on the piano and sing songs (both from memory) almost as well as ever.

Smith (1966) reported the case of a man whose left brain had been surgically removed. Although the patient was then completely aphasic for voluntary speech, he could still recite the Lord's Prayer and sing songs that he knew well before his operation. But as with Ravel, some other person had to start the prayer or songs for him.

Bogen (1969a) points out that Penfield, in his experiments stimulating the brains of human beings, reported eliciting visual hallucinations only when he stimulated the right brains. In the same article, Bogen also cites three other large studies indicating that visual illusions and hallucinations are almost always associated with right brain activity.

The three important clinical facts here are (1) the aphasic, left-brain injured patients of Alajouaine (1948), Luria (1973), and Smith (1966) could perform old habitual acts well, but (2) they did not seem able to learn very similar new habits. And (3) to initiate their old habitual behaviors, those patients still needed externally supplied behavioral cues.

These diverse clinical research findings support four important theoretical assumptions in RBT:

1. In neuropsychologically normal people, the left brain is mainly responsible for converting stimuli into linguistic, symbolic information which it then uses to initiate and largely direct most voluntary, but still nonhabitual, behaviors, including speech.

2. After enough practice converts voluntary behaviors into reflex-like habitual reactions, the right brain, with its wordless mental images and computer-program-like behavioral maps, maintains and controls those habitual responses until people either forget or extinguish them. In RBT, we call those wordless mental images and computer-program-like behavioral maps *attitudes*.

3. In habitual reactions in normal people, the left brain, with its well-learned linguistic behavioral cues, has unique behavior-cueing influences on the right brain that are similar to behavior-cueing influences of the outside world-of-not-words. Both sources of behavioral cues trigger wordless, appositional thoughts, which the right brains use to elicit and carry out automatic, habitual reactions with minimal or no associated conscious, or unconscious propositional thought.

4. Except in Pavlovian-type conditioning, the conscious, directive influence of the left brain's propositional thoughts seem to be the essential first step in habit learning. Otherwise, the right brain does not create wordless, mental, computer-like programs of appositional thoughts. Without such right and left brain cooperation, voluntary habit learning occurs slowly, or not at all (see Razran 1961, p. 121).

There are other basic neuropsychologic facts about normal brain functions that firmly support the theory and techniques of RBT. Those facts will be described at the specific points in the case examples where I make therapeutic use of that particular RBT theory or technique.

The table on page 44, of the best-known characteristics of left-brain and right-brain activities, is based primarily on the references already cited.

This table lists left-brain and right-brain activities as if they were all-or-none features of the individual brains. In reality, though, both brains probably always retain some degree of their original equipotentiality for all those activities (see Gazzaniga and LeDoux 1978; Humphrey and Zangwill 1952; Smith 1966; Sperry 1970; Zangwill 1954).

SECTION II

SPECIAL VOCABULARY—SECTION II

Anabolic: promotes the assimilation of nutritive matter and its conversion into living substances and stored energy; restores healthy bodily functions and activities.

Catabolic: promotes the breakdown of living substances and the release of energy; the opposite of anabolic.

FOCUS ITEMS —SECTION II

1.   What is the evidence that the right brain processes holistic concepts?
2.   Why does it seem that the right brain controls habitual reactions?
3.   What is the evidence that the left brain usually initiates new learning?
4.   What is one explanation why people rarely keep New Year's resolutions not to do certain undesirable acts?
5.   Explain the neuropsychological basis for insisting that P-Cs make objectively accurate use of words, that is, say what they mean and mean what they say.

AN IMPORTANT CLINICAL FACT

Neither a camera nor the human brain can form an image of a state of nonbeing. That's probably why the right brain does not seem able to process negations directly. Statements of negation using words such as *not, none, nobody, never,* or *nowhere* often don't trigger the same specific right-brain images. That's the main reason that seldom, if ever, do even the most sincere New Year's resolutions "not" to keep doing undesirable things cause people to change permanently to more desirable behavior.

To understand the great clinical significance of that insight most quickly, do this little exercise. Mentally picture yourself driving a specific car. As soon as you get a clear image, eliminate that image by picturing yourself doing any part of your morning get-up routine. Then, as soon as you get that clear image, eliminate it by picturing yourself driving that same car again. Alternate those images until you have

LEFT-BRAIN AND RIGHT-BRAIN ACTIVITIES

Major Physiologic Responses Elicited[7]

Left Brain	Right Brain
Parasympathetic	**Sympathetic**
Feed and sex	Fight and flight
Relaxing	Tension inducing
Anabolic	Catabolic

Main Types of Information Processed

Primarily Verbal	**Primarily Nonverbal**
Words and other verbal symbols with little or no affective or nonverbal communication	Visual, feeling-tone, affective, and other nonverbal communicative cues (collectively called prosody); few nouns and adjectives.
Nonmusical (without training)	Musical (naturally)
Nonrhyming and arrhythmic sounds	Rhyming and rhythmic sounds
Nonautomatized sensory information (that is, information does not elicit a habitual response)	Automatized sensory information (that is, information elicits a habitual response)
Verbal symbols for abstract concepts (such as love, honesty) and concrete concepts	Mental picture-maps for concrete concepts/ (such as body anatomy), objective things and imaginary events
Time-relevant stimuli; deals with past, present, and future	Non-time-relevant stimuli, focused always in the here and now

Main Types of Thoughts

Propositional Thought	**Appositional Thought**
Objectively descriptive	Subjectively descriptive
Nonevocative	Evocative
Literal	Pictorial
Logical and analytic	Associative and holistic
Deductive	Inductive and synthetic
Qualified and limited	Unqualified and nonlimiting
Concrete	Rhetorical and metaphorical
Can both negate and affirm; processes negations such as not, don't, won't, can't	Can only affirm; does not process negations

[7]There is still controversy about the assumption that the left-brain and the right-brain control different physiologic responses. Evidence supporting this assumption is described in: Blumstein 1974; Dimond and Farrington 1977; Dimond et al. 1976; Flor-Henry 1979; Gainotti 1972; Gasparrine et al. 1978; Heilman et al. 1975; Lishman 1971; Monrad-Krohn 1947; Ross and Mesulam 1979; Schwartz et al. 1975; Wechsler 1973; Wexler 1980. I have not found comparable research evidence against this assumption.

pictured yourself driving that same car four times. As soon as you complete that little exercise, repeat it, but with this minor change: For the car part of the exercise, now picture yourself *not* driving that car. That is, for four times, alternate an image of you not driving that car with a scene from your morning get-up routine.

If you are like most people, your images of you driving that car were very similar to each other. That is, you were doing pretty much the same thing in the same way each time. But your images of you *not* driving the car could have been quite different. In one you might have been walking; in another riding in the back seat; in another watching TV. But even if you had the same car-related image each time, it was still an image of you in that specific state of being and NOT an image of you in a state of nonbeing. But no matter what your images were, you have still discovered why people rarely keep New Year's (or any other) resolutions not to keep doing undesirable, habitual acts. So let's take a detailed look at your discovery.

Resolutions not to keep doing something are behavioral resolutions. To keep such behavioral resolutions, people must get rid of the undesirable habit of doing the act they have resolved not to do anymore. But in psychological science as in physical science nature seems to abhor a vacuum. Therefore, people can *not* just get rid of a habit; people have to replace every old habit with a new habit.

Now, what do people have to do to form a new habit? They have to have the same mental image of themselves acting out the same new behavior, in the same way, every time they normally would act out the old, undesirable, but habitual behavior. But as your experiment with picturing yourself *not* driving a car showed, people's thoughts of themselves "not doing" things trigger images of them doing the act they resolved not to do, or images of them doing some other ever-changing acts or images of them doing the same (but usually improbable) acts.

Why do I say: "usually improbable act"? Because the images of personal actions people usually get when they think of themselves *not* doing things rarely represent acts those people are likely to do in the same way, every time they have a cue for their old, undesirable behavior. But to learn a new behavioral habit, people must have the same specific, mental images, or behavioral picture-maps of themselves acting out the new behavior in the same way, every time. In addition, the people must be willing to act in the new way every time they have a cue for the old behavior.

Now let's apply those insights to a common clinical situation. Suppose you are a typical, weight-sensitive, habitual overeater invited to a party tonight. You would sincerely resolve, "I'm not going to eat ice cream tonight." But, the aphasic patients of Alajouaine (1948) and Smith (1966), Luria's anomic patients (Luria 1973, p. 145), plus your own mental exercise above, all indicate your left brain's words only trigger images of states of being in your right brain. Therefore, the word "not" in your phrase "not going to eat ice cream" wouldn't trigger any specific image. So your right brain would do one of these two things: (1) respond only to the phrase "going to eat ice cream" with an image of you eating ice cream or (2) create an image of whatever unusual and, therefore, improbable non-ice-cream-eating be-havior you happened to think of at that moment.

To prove to yourself how sincere you are, you would repeat your "not-going-to-eat-ice-cream" resolution several times. But each time you would get the same results—usually either images of you eating ice cream or images of the same, or ever-changing, unusual and, therefore, improbable non-ice-cream-eating behaviors. Consequently, what would be the two most likely events to occur at the party?

First, when ice cream was available you probably would not get any of your unusual, non-ice-cream-eating images mentioned above. Even if you got one, you either could not or would not act it out at the party; the act would be too unusual for you to do in public.

Second, your old tendency to eat ice cream at every possible chance would be as strong as ever. Therefore, your most consistent and powerful behavioral cues at the party would be your right brain's mental picture-maps of you eating ice cream. That's why eating ice cream is what you would most likely end up doing.

Granted, with continuous repetitions of "I'm not going to eat ice cream" you might get yourself through the party without eating ice cream. But in the process, you would build up such an uncomfortably powerful urge to eat ice cream that you probably would eat ice cream, or some equally sweet substitute before the night was over. And your habit of eating ice cream at every opportunity would be as strong, if not stronger than ever.

The same logic holds for promises such as "I'm not going to get angry, de-pressed, or afraid about that again." Those left-brain ideas sound good and trigger logical, positive emotional feelings. But what specific right brain's behavioral picture-maps do these people's promises trigger? Either none, or images of unusual reactions, for which these people don't have significant habit strength or response potential, or images of the people responding with their unwanted, but habitual an-ger, depression, or fear in their usual situations. Also, the situations themselves will still be well-learned cues for these people's right brain's automatic, computer-like programs for their old angry, depressive or fearful responses. Predictably, therefore, these people will usually react with their habitual emotional responses, even though they don't want to and even though they have sincerely promised, or even ordered, themselves not to respond that way.

CLINICAL APPLICATIONS OF THOSE FACTS

Always focus on getting P-Cs to think and talk in terms of a specific new behavior they want to and will act out every time they are in the situations of their old, unde-sirable behavior. And when P-Cs say, "I'm not going to . . . ," always ask, "What will you do instead, and can you see yourself doing it every time?" Then get your P-Cs to commit themselves to some specific, effective state of being or behav-ior that will prevent their undesirable behavior every time, and one that the P-Cs are willing to act out every time.

CLINICALLY USEFUL NEUROPSYCHOPHYSIOLOGICAL INSIGHTS

The neuropsychophysiological data already presented make this fact quite clear: *The words people think trigger corresponding right brain images or sensory equivalents of what those words represent.* For example, with only their verbal thoughts, people can not only mentally picture a thick, juicy steak, but they can also mentally recreate the smell, taste, and feel of it. These facts show that people's right and left brains respond neuropsychophysiologically to words as if those words were the objects and events they represent. That's why when people's words (and, therefore, their mental images and sensory equivalents) are inappropriate for the external reality, those people's emotional and physical reactions to the external reality will also be inappropriate.

For example, if a noise in your kitchen suddenly wakes you up in the middle of the night with the thought, "*My God!* That's a burglar!" you will feel as fearful as you would feel if a burglar were really there. In addition, you might well have a mental picture of a burglar climbing through your window, even though the noise is actually the result of wind blowing through a one-inch crack in your window, rattling your venetian blinds. Clearly then, your fear, although real, would be most inappropriate for the external reality. Remember these neuropsychophysiologic facts as you read on.

You would remain panic stricken until you changed your belief from: "*My God!* That's a burglar!" to "Oh, it's only the wind blowing through the window that I intended, but forgot, to close." That example is good evidence that beliefs or more precisely, the words people use to think, are more important in their emotional control than objective facts.

Those easily observable neuropsychophysiological facts plus the other research on words in self-control described in this chapter are the basis for the consistent, systematic focus in RBT on precision in word use for analyzing and trying to solve emotional problems. New P-Cs, however, as well as inexperienced therapists, initially tend to downplay the importance of people's saying what they mean and meaning what they say.

For example, many P-Cs as well as psychotherapists have this initial response to the way I handled the Mouse Lady: "Oh, that was just semantics; you knew she didn't really believe she was a mouse. I mean, she wasn't psychotic, and she had normal vision; so she had to know she wasn't a real mouse."

For two reasons, my response is "yes and no." An objective look at the burglar example will show you clearly why that answer is accurate.

First, in the burglar example, as long as you stayed in your bedroom, all you would see would be your bedroom walls and furniture. But that would not prevent you from forming mental images of a burglar somewhere in your house, and fearfully reacting to your images. Why? Because mental imagery is *not* mediated by the same neural mechanisms as objective visual perceptions (Gazzaniga and LeDoux 1978, pp. 121–124). But as Luria's famous clinical study of a mnemonist clearly showed, mental imagery can have as great effects on people's physiological reactions as objective stimuli have (see Luria 1968, pp. 139–143).

Second, although the right brain does not usually express itself, it is neither "word-blind" nor "word-deaf" (Sperry and Gazzaniga 1967). Normally, moreover, the right brain automatically converts the left brain's verbiage into subjective, experiential realities. That's because words not only trigger images in right brains; words also have the same positive, negative, and neutral emotional value for both brains (Gazzaniga and LeDoux 1978, pp. 152–153).

For those neuropsychophysiological reasons, RBT therapists say, *"It's never just semantics* when emotionally upset people call themselves or other people names—such as S.O.B., fascist pig, or gutless mouse—that don't match objective human things. Where emotional control is concerned, *it's always all semantics."* That's because right brains automatically convert those objectively meaningless names into personally meaningful symbolic information. Then those people react emotionally to that symbolic information the way they would react if those objectively meaningless names really were the nonexistent things they refer to. That fact makes RBT's Camera Check of Perceptions and its Five Rules for Rational Thinking both neuropsychophysiologically sound and clinically valuable therapeutic techniques.

Left brains seem to be both logical in cognition and intolerant of cognitive dissonance. That's why, with just the concept of the Camera Check of Perceptions, the Mouse Lady could be led to think in an objectively logical way about her thoughts; the simple act of checking the objective accuracy of her self-image immediately caused her to improve both her self-image and her thinking. Then her emotional feelings about herself unavoidably improved rapidly. Otherwise, it would have been necessary to reconsider the possibility that the Mouse Lady had brain damage or that she was either psychotic or under the influence of drugs or both.

THE COGNITIVE-BEHAVIORAL DYNAMICS OF THE MOUSE LADY CASE

The Mouse Lady became angry at herself for being afraid to disagree with her mother. So she called herself a gutless mouse and her right brain responded by producing the neuropsychological equivalent of that hated self-image plus the intense anger that went with it. Next, the Mouse Lady's left brain logically, but incorrectly, interpreted her anger about her hated self-image as evidence that her gutless-mouse label was appropriate. Then this attractive, intelligent woman concluded, "Yep, I must be a gutless mouse because I feel like one." That belief prevented the uncomfortable cognitive dissonance that otherwise would have resulted from the conflict between her belief that she should behave like a mature adult and the fact that she habitually behaved like a fearful child.

Unfortunately for the Mouse Lady, anger is an urge to harm or destroy. Understandably, therefore, when the Mouse Lady got angry enough at herself for "being a gutless mouse," she attempted suicide.

CONFESSION

I can't prove that these cognitive-behavioral dynamics accurately reflect what went on in the Mouse Lady's left and right brains. But this analysis fits the neuropsychology of right-brain and left-brain function. In addition, that analysis led to neuropsychologically valid, as well as immediately effective, therapeutic action. That's the main, if not sole, justification for any dynamic formulation.

The Memory Aids for this chapter are on page 215.

CHAPTER **4**

PREVIEW

Rational Cognitive-
Behavioral Learning
Theory[1]

The same mental processes of learning and practice produce people's physical habits and their emotional habits. This assumption is the backbone of RBT theory and its emotional self-help concepts and techniques. For two well-written, comprehensive collections of the vast research supporting that assumption, see Mowrer 1960 and 1966.

When people learn their "life long" set of emotional habits, they give themselves an emotional education. Emotional education occurs in four stages (Maultsby 1976, 1978):

1. intellectual insight
2. practice
3. emotional insight
4. personality-trait formation

Candidates appropriate for psychotherapy want to replace self-defeating or otherwise undesirable emotional habits with more personally desirable habits. To achieve their therapeutic goals, these people must give themselves an emotional reeducation. Emotional reeducation has these five stages (Maultsby 1976, 1978):

1. intellectual insight
2. practice
3. cognitive-emotive dissonance
4. emotional insight
5. personality-trait formation

Section I of this chapter uses the example of learning to type to give you a detailed description of the first half of the Rational Cognitive-Behavioral Learning Theory of

[1]Rational Cognitive-Behavioral Learning Theory includes the basic principles of classical and operant conditioning. In my opinion, however, the theory of operant conditioning is more a theory of motivation for learning than a theory of the mental mechanisms in the learning process (see Gazzaniga and LeDoux 1978, pp. 125–129). This chapter describes a comprehensive theory of the neuropsychophysiologic mechanisms that seem to operate in the human learning process, but that traditional learning theorists have usually ignored.

physical and emotional habit formation. Section II of this chapter also uses the example of learning to type to give you a detailed description of the second half of the Rational Cognitive-Behavioral Learning Theory of physical and emotional habit formation. By the end of Section II you will have learned about the four stages of behavioral education, the Gooney Bird Syndrome, and a highly effective way to handle resistant P-Cs. You will also see that the ABCs of Rational Cognitive-Behavioral Learning Theory apply equally to physical habits and to emotional habits.

SPECIAL VOCABULARY—SECTION I

Apperceptive unit: a semi-permanent cognitive habit, produced by people repeatedly pairing the same or similar perceptions with the same or similar sincere evaluative thoughts and emotive feelings until either the perceptions alone or the sincere thoughts alone will trigger the same emotive feelings. The two main cognitive habits or apperceptive units in self-control are *beliefs* and *attitudes*. They are also the main cognitive factors in both healthy and unhealthy learning.

Apraxia: inability of people to do an act on conscious will even though they want to do the act, know how to do it, and, under other circumstances, they can do it (case examples appear on page 41).

Cognitive-Emotive Dissonance: the experience of being in a familiar situation, but having new thoughts (and possibly new actions) about it that are illogical for the emotional feelings you habitually have in that situation. This is a special variant of Festinger's (1962) concept of cognitive dissonance that's unique to RBT. RBT therapists use the term cognitive-emotive dissonance to describe the unavoidable dissonance that's unique to the third stage of behavioral reeducation, as opposed to the several other examples of dissonance Festinger describes.

Correct: as used in RBT, label for responses that most often, most accurately reflect or describe the facts of specific situations. For example, 4 is most often the most accurate response to "What is 2 + 2?" But the answer "Two plus 2 is greater than 2 + 1" is a "right" response, though not the correct (that is, the most accurate) response. RBT focuses primarily on correct emotional and behavioral responses. *Synonym:* factual. *Antonym:* incorrect or false.

Education: as used in RBT, the learning of specific behavioral responses to a specific situation, one for which the person had not previously learned a specific response.

Emotive response: as used in RBT, label for limbic-system-related responses that create the feeling part of emotions. Except for the precision required for theoretical discussions, emotive response can be used interchangeably with emotional response or emotional feeling.

Reeducation: as used in RBT, the learning of specific behavioral responses to specific situations, so that these responses will replace already learned, but undesirable, responses to those situations.

Right: as used in RBT, label for responses that are currently acceptable responses to specific questions or situations, even though those responses are incorrect. For example, until people knew and accepted the objective fact that the world is round, "The world is flat" was the "right," though incorrect, response to the question "What is the shape of the earth?" Beliefs or truths that are right, but incorrect, are the main causes of emotional distress in everyday life. *Synonym:* believed or true. *Antonym:* disbelieved or wrong.

Superconscious mind: as used in RBT, the functional mental unit that consists of learned mental mechanisms that make correct performances possible with minimal or no conscious thought. The clinical case reports of Alajouaine (1948), Bogen (1969), Humphrey and Zangwill (1952), and Smith (1966) indicate that the superconscious mind is largely a product and unit of right-brain activities. This concept of a superconscious mind is quite different from the concept described in Psychosynthesis (Crampton, 1981).

Truth: in RBT, any idea people believe. Truth, therefore, often has little or nothing to do with facts. That's probably why in American courts, witnesses are never asked to swear to the facts; they may not know them. Court witnesses are only asked to swear to the truth, or what they believe. People usually know that. In addition, truths, or personal beliefs *(but never facts)* are the most important factors in emotional and physical behavioral control. That fact will become obvious in this chapter.

FOCUS ITEMS —SECTION I

1. Can people make an unbiased perception?
2. How do the right and left brains interact when people perceive?
3. What are the four stages of emotional education?
4. If you understand how people learn to type, do you really know all you need to know to understand emotional education?
5. Understanding how beliefs influence behavior gives you what useful therapeutic insight into emotional learning?

CHAPTER 4

Rational Cognitive-Behavioral Learning Theory

SECTION I

Chapters 1 through 3 gave you the scientific basis for the theoretical constructs I shall now present. You saw, therefore, that these constructs are scientifically valid; the examples will show that these constructs are clinically useful. They are also the focus of increasing research to reconfirm and improve them. But keep in mind that these are clinical formulations, designed to help busy practitioners and inexperienced therapists give emotionally distressed people scientifically valid, yet immediately useful insights into their emotional problems. Therefore, I purposefully kept this discussion at a clinically practical level of sophistication.

Rational Cognitive-Behavioral Learning Theory is a theory of normal human behavior. It is a logical, internally consistent combination of recent neuropsychophysiologic research and basic principles derived from nine different scientific approaches to understanding human behavior (see Chapter 1). Since learning usually starts with perceptions, I shall start there now.

From birth until the age of language, human perceptions seem to be relatively passive, yet highly accurate, holographic cameralike reproductions of the external world (Pribram 1969; Bower 1974). After the age of language, however, perceiving ceases to be—if it ever was—a passive process. Instead, perceiving becomes a highly active process, heavily dependent on belief, attitudes, and old emotive and other mnemonic cues for past behaviors.

The RBT view of perceptions is based on Luria's descriptions (1973, pp. 229–244; 1976, pp. 20–47) of the direct effects language has on perceptions and apperceptions. For RBT and any other efficient psychotherapy, Luria's most important research finding was *people largely apperceive what they already believe exists* (that is, what they have a label for). Unfortunately, however, language often has names that don't represent objective human or nonhuman things; nevertheless, people react to those names as if they were the nonexistent things they represent. The Mouse Lady's case history is an excellent example.

As the studies on split-brain patients showed (see Chapter 3), after the onset of language, both brains continue to perceive reality. But, the perceptive processes are different in each brain. Basically, the left brain converts perceptions into linguistic representations of reality; the right brain, however, converts perceptions into holistic images and subjective impressions of reality. Yet, those holographic, perceptive gestalts contain much more recorded sensory input than people are normally aware of or can put into words or both. Still, probably more than any other system of mental mechanisms, the left-brain language system continuously monitors, labels, and organizes people's perceptions and other cognitive, emotive, and physical behaviors. That is why people's language system is the main component in their personal sense of conscious reality, including their self-concepts. In addition, under normal conditions people's words label and limit both the perceptions they pay attention to and the behavioral intentions and plans people have about those perceptions. But the nature of the actual behavioral response determines which brain finally controls the behaviors (Cohen 1973; Galin and Ornstein 1972; Levy et al. 1972).

People usually best learn new material that is similar or referable to what they already know. So to keep this discussion simple yet scientifically valid, let's switch now to the process of typing education. Almost everyone (even a nontypist) knows what's involved in learning to type. According to RBT theory, the same neuropsychological processes control both emotional learning and physical learning. For that reason I often use learning to type as an example to teach P-Cs what they need to learn about emotional education to solve their emotional problems rationally. That knowledge decreases therapeutic resistance; it also enables P-Cs to improve their emotional control naturally and in the fastest, yet safest way possible.

As nearly as possible, this example has been written the way I explain it to my P-Cs. Normally I begin by saying, "Successful psychotherapy, which in reality is merely emotional reeducation, requires you to do the same things that successfully learning to type requires you to do. So, let's imagine someone learning how to type."

To learn correct typing habits, Michael must first realize that typing involves learning to press the keys and space bar of the typewriter in a specific way that reproduces on typing paper the text in the typing exercise book. That realization is *Intellectual Insight,* the first stage in any education. It means knowing what people must practice to learn their desired behavioral habit.

4-1   The ABCs of Learning to Type

The second stage in any behavioral education is *Practice*. There are two types of practice—mental[2] and physical. In the beginning of new learning, the left brain initiates and directs both practice routines. That's why people must talk themselves through each step of early physical practice maneuvers.

To practice typing, therefore, Michael must first perceive and label (that is, apperceive) each letter and figure to be typed. Those letters and figures are the As in the ABCs of learning to type. Then Michael's left brain must process sincere, correct typing thoughts about those As. Michael's correct typing thoughts are the Bs of the ABCs of learning to type. They are thoughts such as "With my hands in the correct positions, if I depress the typing key under my left index finger, I will type the letter F. If I depress the typing key under my right index finger, I will type the letter J . . . '' and so forth for each letter in the alphabet.

Normally, the left brain's correct typing thoughts at B will elicit in Michael's left and right brains mental images or picture-maps for the correct typing actions. Those mental picture-maps then trigger the correct physical typing actions. Then together, Michael's self-talk and mental images of the correct physical typing actions trigger those typing actions; in addition (via the limbic systems of the first functional brain units—see Chapter 2) Michael's self-talk, mental images, and physical actions all trigger the most logical emotive reactions for those mental and physical responses. The logical emotive reactions for those responses are what make people's habitual thoughts, mental images, and physical actions come to "feel right" to them.

In terms of the ABCs of typing, those logical, or "right," emotive feelings are C-1 in the ABCs of learning to type; they reinforce the correct typing self-talk, the appropriate mental images or cognitive maps, and the correct typing actions.

---

[2]In RBT, the technique of mental practice is Rational Emotive Imagery or REI (Chapter 15 in this book). REI is an ideal technique for practicing new emotions.

Also, those "right" emotive feelings make *incorrect* typing thoughts, mental images or cognitive maps, and actions instantly and automatically "feel wrong."

The C-2 of the ABCs of learning to type are the correct, physical typing actions.

THE ABCS OF NEW TYPING LEARNING

A   The perceptions of the typing drills and typing keys
B   The correct typing self-talk
C-1 The logical emotive response for B
C-2 The logical or appropriate typing actions for B

ANALOGOUS EMOTIONAL LEARNING

Since fear of snakes is almost universal, let's use it to show the ABCs of emotional learning.[3] Even though almost everyone is afraid of snakes, hardly anyone has ever had a dangerous experience with a snake. Therefore, most people *learn* their fear of snakes through *mental practice alone*. Such vicarious emotional learning is possible because words are stimuli that can and do substitute for every real stimulus (Eccles 1958; Pavlov as quoted in Volgyesi 1954, slightly paraphrased).

From the time most people begin to talk, almost every idea they hear or read about snakes is fearful. Then, depending on how imaginative those people are, their left-brain words trigger fearful, right-brain scenes, and minimal-to-severe fear reactions. Otherwise emotionally healthy, well-educated people, for example, have left my lectures in mild panic after watching the few slides about snakes that have been mixed in with more than a hundred other nonsnake lecture slides. It's easy to imagine how those people reacted as kids, when other kids passionately told them, "Snakes are dangerous. They kill people. Oh! They're scary! They're sneaky! They bite you! You'd better watch out for snakes!"

Having the same emotional feelings again and again in response to the same type of thoughts is one of the most rapid ways to form a strong emotional habit (Mowrer 1966, pp. 117–162). Predictably, therefore, by the time most children reach the age of ten, merely the serious thoughts that a snake is close to them triggers instant fear, even though no snake is within miles.

This is an important point—remember it well. Every perception or thought activates the limbic systems via the first functional brain unit. The limbic systems respond with a positive, negative, or neutral emotive urge for action, depending upon whether the person's self-talk is positive, negative, or neutral about the perception. Without those emotive urges for actions (that is, emotional feelings) people would not know when to protect themselves. That fact makes the brains the main organs of voluntary survival and emotional comfort.

---

[3]Because human fear of snakes is so common, many people believe that it has a genetic basis. But in their recent review of the literature, Mavissakalian and Barlow (1981) failed to find any biological or genetic evidence to support that belief.

When people with normally functioning brains think the same sincere thoughts at B, about the same perceptions at A, and get the same emotive and behavioral Cs enough times, the following extremely important thing happens. Their left brains convert those repeatedly paired perceptions and sincere thoughts into semipermanent, personally meaningful, conscious, apperceptive units, or mental programs, called *beliefs* (Maultsby 1976, pp. 34–40).

FROM A, B, C to a-B, C: BELIEF-CONTROLLED REACTIONS

A Perceptions	after	No external perceptions at A
	enough	
	repeated	
B Evaluative thoughts[4]	pairings	a-B Only beliefs (that is, habitual evaluative thoughts)
C Emotive and physical reactions		C Emotive and physical reactions

In RBT, the a-B apperceptive unit represents a belief. The capital B in the a-B unit indicates that spoken, or conscious self-talk is the controlling cue in that apperceptive unit. Neuropsychologically, the words at B (in the a-B apperceptive unit) trigger in right brains holistic mental images of old, real, as well as imagined A-events. Therefore, the a-B apperceptive unit triggers the same habitual emotional and physical reactions at C as the real As and Bs triggered in the original A, B, C pairing or practice sessions.

After people form beliefs, their left brains no longer need to process old A-stimuli as single mental events. At this point, their left brain's words elicit internally stored a-B apperceptive units, which then trigger right brain controlled habitual emotional and physical reactions at C. And every repetition of that a-B, C sequence is an instance of practicing those habitual C-reactions.

FROM A, B, C TO a-B, C: BELIEF-CONTROLLED EMOTIONS
(The Snake-Fear Analogue)

A, B, C, NEW EMOTION[5]		a-B BELIEF-CONTROLLED EMOTION
A Sight, picture or thought of snake	after enough repeated	No external perception at A
B Evaluative thoughts	pairings	a-B Only beliefs (that is, apperceptive units)
1. Snakes are dangerous		1. Snakes are dangerous
2. They are scary!		2. They are scary!
3. Etc.		3. Etc.
C Emotive feelings of fear		C Emotive feelings of fear

[4]In RBT, the evaluative thoughts in the A, B, Cs of new emotional or behavioral learning are new, sincere thoughts as opposed to a-B beliefs (that is, the habitual apperceptive unit) that repeated pairings of the same As with the same Bs produce.

[5]According to my best information, Albert Ellis formulated the A, B, C model of new emotions (Ellis 1963). I derived the A-b, C and a-B, C models of habitual emotions (Maultsby 1976, pp. 34–40) from Ellis' A, B, C model.

THE VALUE AND ROLE OF BELIEFS IN SELF-CONTROL

Beliefs free people from subhuman, animallike dependence on the external world for appropriate emotional and physical behavioral cues. That's why Michael could learn to be afraid of snakes without ever having been threatened by one. That's also why, after Michael learned the correct typing beliefs, he could sit away from his typewriter, close his eyes, mentally practice typing, and still increase his typing skill. It was irrelevant that he was not actually typing. He still could imagine the correct typing scene in his mind.

Neuropsychophysiologically, imagination is all that healthy brains need to trigger the appropriate mental images necessary for both physical and emotional learning. Those same mental mechanisms enable poeple to practice daily— purposefully or unwittingly—all their emotional habits. Unfortunately, though, people rarely see their daily emotional reactions as *emotional practice*. Why? Simply because most people don't use the word practice when they think about their emotions. Yet, whether or not people realize it or admit it, every time they repeat any specific emotional reaction in specific situations, they are practicing having that emotion in those situations.[6]

That ends Section I of this chapter. Next are the Focus Items for Section II.

SECTION II

SPECIAL VOCABULARY —SECTION II

None.

FOCUS ITEMS —SECTION II

1. What are the five important facts about emotional feelings listed in this section?
2. What is the research evidence for those assumptions?
3. What conviction about emotions do new P-Cs usually have?
4. How do RBT therapists justify using the example of learning to type to explain emotional learning?
5. What is the relationship between an attitude and a habit?
6. What useful functions do attitudes serve?

---

[6]Zajonc (1980) cited an impressive list of empirical facts that (in my opinion) support the RBT view of the mechanisms of human emotions. Unfortunately, in his discussion of those facts, Zajonc failed (in my opinion) to describe useful clinical insights. Still, I think the reader may find his article interesting reading, in light of the RBT theory of human emotions.

FROM A, B, C TO A-b, C: ATTITUDE-CONTROLLED REACTIONS

A	Perceptions	after enough repeated pairings	A-b	Attitudes
B	Evaluative thoughts			No conscious evaluative thought at B
C	Emotive and physical reactions		C	Emotive and physical reactions

At the same time that left brains are forming beliefs, right brains are forming their own special form of apperceptive units called *attitudes* (Maultsby 1976, pp. 34–40).

In RBT, the A-b apperceptive unit represents an *attitude*. The small "b" in the A-b units indicates that attitudes are wordless, and therefore unspoken, superconscious forms of beliefs. And beliefs are the spoken or conscious form of attitudes.[7]

That important clinical insight enables you to help P-Cs take the magical ITs out of their emotional understanding. I'll talk more about that later.

Neuropsychologically, attitudes index or code every habitual thought, cognitive map, and mental image of the objects, events, and actions we perceive. That's why after people form attitudes, their right brains no longer perceive old external stimuli at A as single mental events. Instead, right brains then apperceive those old A stimuli as conditioned cues, coded with A-b attitudes that trigger holistic brain programs for habitual emotional and physical reactions at C. Therefore, with minimal or no conscious thought, people can react with instant, seemingly involuntary, but correct emotional and physical reactions for their old attitude-coded perceptions of old, external A-activating events.

Those instant, involuntary, yet correct reactions indicate learning has moved to the third stage of behavioral education: *Emotional Insight*. Emotional insight means consistently having the most correct emotive response at C for the currently-paired A-perceptions and B-thoughts. Emotional insight indicates that these specific A-perceptions and B-thoughts have been paired enough times with the same emotive response for the right brain to have taken that emotive response and used it as an "emotive rope" to tie those separate A, B, C components into a behavioral gestalt. During practice (stage two in behavioral education) the left brain used those separate As and Bs to direct and control the early learning process. But the right brain's behavioral gestalt indicates a behavioral habit has formed. People commonly describe that new behavioral state with ideas like: "Now I've got the feel of it; now I see it; now I feel I know how to do it."

The "emotive ropes" or "emotive bindings" (commonly described as "feeling right") that hold behavioral gestalts together are probably the main bases of prosody and dysprosody. Prosody and dysprosody are the nonverbal affective components of vocal and so-called body language. Monrad-Krohn (1947) and Ross and

---

[7]That may sound like a tautology to some. But it's no more tautologous than saying, "Ice is the solid form of water; and that makes water the liquid form of ice."

Mesulam (1979) discuss in instructive detail the essential role prosody plays in effective interpersonal communication and the severe emotional problems dysprosody causes. I mention these concepts here as another example of the essential contribution that the silent right brain makes to effective linguistic communication.

Correct prosody means advanced learning, indicative of having acquired a new behavioral habit. Primary control of the new response has then shifted from conscious, spoken, left-brain thoughts to the corresponding wordless, superconscious, right-brain attitudes.

Let's assume Michael has now gained emotional insight into typing. Now he can merely apperceive the letters and figures at A, and instantly type them correctly at C, without consciously thinking anything at B. In fact, if Michael were to start thinking first at B now, before he reacts at C, he would necessarily decrease his typing speed and his typing errors would increase.

FROM A, B, C TO A-b, C: ATTITUDE-CONTROLLED EMOTIONS
(The Snake-Fear Analogue)

	A, B, C, NEW EMOTION		A-b ATTITUDE-CONTROLLED EMOTION
A	Sight, picture or thought of snake ⎫ after	A-b	Sight or picture of snake
	⎬ enough		
	⎪ repeated		
B	Evaluative thoughts ⎭ pairings		No conscious evaluative thoughts at B
	1. Snakes are dangerous		
	2. They are scary!		
	3. Etc.		
C	Emotive feeling of fear	C	Emotive feeling of fear

Here's an important therapeutic insight; remember it well. People's wordless, superconscious attitudes create the illusion that magical, external HEs, SHEs, ITs, and THEYs are in control of their emotions. Fortunately, though, those illusions are just that: *illusions*. Otherwise psychotherapy would be a waste of time and money.

Every time Michael automatically makes the correct finger movement at C, without having to think first at B, his right brain's limbic system triggers the neutral-to-positive emotive responses associated with his correct-typing motions. Like most people, Michael labels these emotive responses *feeling right*.

Here's why emotional insight is so important for habit maintenance. When Michael doesn't get that "right" feeling with a typing motion, he knows instantly that he has made a mistake; he doesn't need to see it; he "feels" it. That's why Michael now describes any unusual feeling about a typing motion or idea, with thoughts such as: "That feels wrong; or it doesn't feel right."

This is an excellent place to show you how to help P-Cs *take the popular magical IT out of emotional understanding*. To begin, ask P-Cs, "Can you imagine

4-2   Attitude-Triggered Responses

yourself seriously accusing IT, the typing page, or THEM, the letters on the typing page (at A) of making Michael's fingers type correctly at C? Of course not! That would mean you admittedly believe in magic. You certainly are not that naive. You know that people make their own fingers move in both correct and incorrect typing, even though their typing rate is too fast for them to be able to think first, and type second. Right?'' My P-Cs have all responded with: ''Yes'' or ''Right.''

Continue with: ''Then here are the two very important therapeutic insights to make here: (1) It would be naive, magical nonsense to believe some external IT, HE, SHE, or THEY can make Michael's fingers involuntarily type. (2) And it is just as much naive, magical nonsense to believe some external IT, HE, SHE, or THEY can make Michael's gut involuntarily move—that is, without his cooperation, cause his (or anyone else's) emotional feelings.''

That explanation is all most P-Cs need to make this third important insight: Whether people are typing or having emotional feelings, it's their attitudes (their wordless, superconscious, A-b apperceptions) that trigger their seemingly automatic, instantaneous, involuntary emotional and physical reactions at C.

At this point, perceptive trainees often ask: ''But if attitudes are wordless and superconscious, how can you get people to change them?''

My answer is always: ''*Easily!* Just show them how to convert their wordless attitudes back to their belief form.'' Here's how: First, point out that attitudes and beliefs are simply different forms of the results of the same A-perceptions and B-thoughts having been processed differently by the right and left brains. Once people understand this, they usually have no trouble seeing that beliefs are simply the word forms of attitudes, and that attitudes are simply the wordless forms of beliefs.

Long before their therapy, most P-Cs have learned that their attitudes and beliefs are intimately related. So they are already well prepared for the next step in converting an attitude to its spoken belief form.

Second, tell P-Cs to ask themselves and then honestly answer this question: *''By reacting as I did, what ideas did I react as if I sincerely believed?''*

Third, give P-Cs a common yet instructive example of their attitudes in action. A good example is, "Suppose you were driving your car and a child suddenly ran across the road in front of you. You would immediately slam on the brakes and feel afraid, all without taking time to think anything first. By reacting that way, you would have reacted as if you had sincerely thought: 'I'm about to have a terrible accident; I'd better stop immediately.' Right? Well, those ideas would have been your attitudes. They are the logical and correct ideas you would have thought, had you taken the time to think something before you slammed on the brakes; this fact makes those ideas the wordless or unspoken form of your safe-driving beliefs.

"Your wordless, or unspoken beliefs, exist in your superconscious mind as attitudes. Superconscious attitudes enable a person to react to external situations, instantly and seemingly involuntarily, but with correct, learned reactions (such as fearful auto-braking) without the person needing to think conscious thoughts about the situations beforehand.

"Now suppose that while driving, you see two children running down the sidewalk parallel to the street. You would probably maintain your speed and continue to feel calm about doing it. And again, you would react without consciously thinking anything. Why? Because your controlling attitudes then would be your unspoken, superconscious, mental equivalent of beliefs such as, 'There is no danger, I have no reason to slow down or feel afraid.' Those personal examples show you clearly the essential role that attitudes play in rapid, logical, correct emotional and physical self-control."

THE VALUE AND ROLE OF ATTITUDES IN SELF-CONTROL

Attitudes give people preprogrammed, superconscious, wordless plans for immediate, yet correct reactions. Suppose, for example, that drivers had to take the time to think the above auto-braking thoughts before they reacted. They would probably hit the child every time.

ANOTHER CLINICALLY USEFUL INSIGHT

Attitudes are what make actions as well as ideas instantly feel right or wrong without conscious analysis. Here are the neuropsychophysiological reasons: Attitudes are a form of right-brain knowledge. Normally, the left brain has the same knowledge the right brain has; and they both react to it by producing similar emotional feelings. Sometimes, however, left brains seriously entertain new ideas about old familiar events. During those same moments, the left brains cannot trigger their old emotional reactions to those old events. But the old events themselves (or their neuropsychological equivalents) still elicit from the silent right brains the same old habitual, attitude-triggered emotional reactions. Because the left and right brains are then reacting with different emotional responses to the same old events, it *seems* as if the left brain is disagreeing with the right brain's knowledge.

That situation is cognitive-emotive dissonance. It's analogous to the situation wherein the left brains of split-brain patients incorrectly comment on right-brain knowledge. In such cases, right brains trigger negating emotive and physical reactions (Sperry and Gazzaniga 1967, p. 112; Gazzaniga 1970, p. 107) that patients experience as "feeling wrong."

Normally, left brains react to "feeling wrong" (that is, cognitive-emotive dissonance) by rejecting their new ideas. That is how (and why) attitudes save time when people are not interested in either learning anything new or taking any new actions in old situations. Imagine what would happen if people had to think their way through every daily routine; it would be almost lunchtime before they complete their morning get-up activities.

To avoid confusion about this discussion, remember these five important facts about emotional feelings.

1. Attitudes are the wordless forms of beliefs; normally, therefore, attitudes and beliefs trigger the same type of emotional feelings about the same events.

2. Believing an idea makes it true for the believer. That's why people never accept as true (or as being a fact) an idea they believe is incorrect—*even though the idea may be a fact.*

3. People's oldest or strongest attitudes, beliefs (or personal truths) trigger their experiences of feeling right or wrong about new ideas or actions. That's why, if people think more about their emotional feelings than they think about their thoughts, they won't learn any new behaviors. In RBT we call that type of thinking "gut thinking."

"Gut thinking" causes the Gooney Bird Syndrome. Gooney Birds fly backwards. (See Figure 4-3, p. 64.) They are not interested in where they are going; they are only interested in where they came from.

Gooney Birds can fly safely *only as long as what they believe really is all they need to know.* But much of what P-Cs believe is the main cause of their emotional problems. To benefit from psychotherapy, therefore, P-Cs have to replace their self-defeating beliefs with new, self-facilitating beliefs. But "gut thinking" prevents that therapeutic change. That's why RBT therapists systematically discourage "gut thinking" during psychotherapy.

The other two facts to remember are:

4. Just because an idea feels right, or wrong, that fact does not prove the idea is correct, or incorrect.

5. A person's "right" or "wrong" feelings about an idea prove only that the person believes or doesn't believe the idea. Therefore, as a basis for action, "right" and "wrong" feelings are no more reliable than the beliefs and attitudes that trigger them.

The fourth state of all behavioral education is *Personality-Trait Formation*. This happens when people have practiced a habit so much that it becomes one of their

4-3   A Gooney Bird Flying Backwards

predictable behavioral characteristics. People reach this stage merely by consistently acting out their emotional insights.

RESEARCH SUPPORT FOR RBT's ATTITUDE THEORY

Having a clear idea of the RBT theory of superconscious, attitude-triggered emotions and actions is basic for taking the mystery and the magical IT out of emotional understanding. So, let's briefly review the main research support for this useful clinical insight. The best place to start is with Bogen's (1969, pp. 102–105) case studies of apraxia (inability, without paralysis, to perform familiar acts) in split-brain people.

Remember, the right brain controls the left hand; but the right brain doesn't process language well, at least as spoken words. The left brain controls the right hand and specializes in processing language as spoken words.

For varying lengths of time after surgery, the right brains of "split-brain" people cannot comply with the verbal request "Stick out your *left* index finger." But they can easily comply with the verbal request "Stick out your *right* index finger." On the other hand, their right brains *can,* and will, enable these people to stick out their *left* index finger if someone shows them, by visual demonstration, that this is the desired response. Similarly, those people can use scissors correctly if you put the scissors in their left hands. But if you ask them to use their left hand to pretend they are using scissors, they can't do it. And of course, they can do both tasks with their right hands.

Now, if you ask those people to pretend they are opening a door with their left hands, they can't do that either. But those people will approach a closed door with their right hands in their pockets, and without hesitation, automatically open the door with their left hands, and leave the room.

Those experiments indicate that the left brains of split-brain people retain their presurgery ability to initiate and direct behavior. Those experiments also indicate that the right brains of split-brain people maintain their nonverbal A-b wordless behavioral programs or mental images and cognitive picture-maps for their presurgery, habitual actions. On external cue, therefore, these split-brain people can perform their old habitual right-brain acts as readily as they did prior to surgery. But the verbal influences of their left brains on their right brains have been surgically eliminated; so, these people cannot respond with their left hand to the linguistic cues ''Pretend to open a door'' or ''Pretend to use a pair of scissors.'' However, those people's ability to perform the real actions correctly is proof that: (1) their right brains still have both the cognitive picture-maps or brain programs for those behaviors and (2) their right brains still have the ability to trigger those reactions on appropriate external cues. In the cited examples, appropriate external cues were the closed door blocking departure from the room, scissors placed in the left hand, and the left hand of another person demonstrating, visually, the hand motions to be mimicked.

Neuropsychologically, the activity of the right brains of those split-brain people was probably the same as the activity that occurs in Michael's right brain when, on external cue, he seemingly types automatically, slams on the brakes in his car automatically, or jumps back automatically from a snake or another dangerous object without first thinking about the reaction.

People who are normally mute due to left-brain damage or left-brain loss can still sing songs and recite poems and prayers that they had thoroughly learned (that is, had made into seemingly automatic, A-b, attitudinally triggered reactions) while they still had normal left brain function (Alajouaine 1948; Bogen 1969; Humphrey and Zangwill 1952; Smith 1966). But after their brain damage, these aphasic people have to be primed with external cues to get them started; that is, some other person has to start the song or prayer (see Chapter 3). Those external cues trigger their right brains' A-b, superconscious, attitudinal programs or mental picture-maps for the complete responses.

Righthanded, split-brain people are not able to write at will or from dictation with their left hands; but they may still be able to sign their names with their left hands. Also, patients with left hemispherectomy can utter old habitual obscenities when frustrated. Why? Because writing one's own name and uttering obscenities are usually automatized, involuntary, A-b, attitudinally triggered, right-brain-controlled habitual reactions; they don't require left-brain propositional thought (Bogen 1969, pp. 96–101).

Ravel, Alajouaine's famous aphasic patient (1948), retained excellent piano playing and singing skills; his skills, however, were only for musical pieces he had thoroughly learned before his left-brain damage. After his left-brain damage, Ravel did not seem able to learn any new musical pieces. Neither Bogen (1969) nor Humphrey and Zangwill (1952) nor Smith (1966) reported any new voluntary learning in their aphasic patients.

The data presented in this chapter clearly indicate the left brain is primarily responsible for initiating new learning and the right brain is primarily responsible for maintaining old habits.

A USEFUL THERAPEUTIC MANEUVER

Even after a graphic, detailed, nonmagical explanation of how their emotions work, a few P-Cs will still resist believing that merely changing their minds (that is, their beliefs), will—or even can—change their powerful emotions. But the following simple maneuver usually gets these resistant P-Cs to discover their error for themselves; then they clearly see the following two helpful facts:

1. They already know that changing their minds can instantly change their emotions; they just ignore that fact and thereby deny themselves the emotional benefit of knowing it.

2. They usually have already proven to themselves that they know Fact 1, but they ignore that fact, too.

Interacting With A Resistant P-C

Me: Have you ever been in this situation? You are angry because you believed an important situation is not the way you wanted and believed it should be. Then, while you are still angry, you discover you are mistaken; the situation really is the way you wanted it to be.

P-C: Yes, I've had that embarrassing experience.

Me: Good. Everybody has probably had it at some time or other; so now tell me, would you go on being angry after you discover your mistake?

P-C: Of course not.

Me: But how could you stop being upset if IT, the external situation, was what made you upset in the first place? Since the external situation would not have changed at all, how could you calm down?

P-C: I would see that I had made a mistake and that it would be silly to stay angry.

Me: Right! You would see that you had made a mistake, and you would change your mind about the situation. At first, you would have the incorrect belief or attitude that the situation wasn't the way it should be. And your incorrect belief or attitude that such situations (or such ITs) can and do upset you, would have triggered your anger. It's irrelevant that your perception of IT in this case would have been inaccurate and imaginary. After people learn to talk, what they perceive most and best is what they already believe or imagine exists. That insight is so useful, I shall repeat it. After people learn to talk, what they perceive most and best is what they already believe or imagine exists. So because you would have believed the situation wasn't the way it should be, you would have initially perceived it that way. Only later, after an objective look, would you have perceived the situation accurately. Now let's see how you would have gotten yourself to calm down. For as long as you can remember, you have had the attitude that it's silly to be upset when things are both the way you want them to be, and how you believe they should be. So you would have immediately replaced your initial attitudes—(1) that you should be angry about the situation, and (2) that this situation makes you angry, with your equally sincere attitude that you shouldn't now be angry because there's nothing to be angry about. So, simply changing your mind from "It makes me angry because it shouldn't be this way," to "Everything is the way I want it and the way it should be," you would have immediately changed your emotions. That's how and why you would have calmed yourself down as soon as you discovered your mistake.

Author's Note

At this point, nonpsychotic P-Cs see clearly how it would have been their beliefs and attitudes all along (and not the external situation) that would have triggered—as well as changed— their emotional feelings. That insight enables even the most resistant P-Cs to begin accepting this fact: Their own personal beliefs and attitudes are triggering their present emotional distress.

At that point in RBT, psychotherapy largely becomes an experience of RBT therapists' directing and monitoring the rational efforts of P-Cs to discover and learn rational beliefs and attitudes with which to replace their irrational beliefs and attitudes.

EMOTIONAL REEDUCATION AND BEHAVIORAL REEDUCATION

Emotional reeducation and behavioral reeducation follow the same A-B-C sequence of learning and have the same stages of learning emotional education and behavioral education have. But in addition, emotional reeducation and behavioral reeducation have an extra stage called cognitive-emotive dissonance.

Cognitive-emotive dissonance exists when people are in a familiar situation, but they are having new thoughts (and possibly new actions) that are illogical for the emotional feelings these people habitually have in that situation.

Cognitive-emotive dissonance is the unavoidable third stage of therapeutic change; but new P-Cs usually don't understand it at all; instead, they fear it. That's why it's important to teach your P-Cs how to recognize and handle cognitive-emotive dissonance rationally; otherwise, it will confuse and discourage them. In Chapter 13 you will learn how easily you can help your P-Cs move rapidly, smoothly, and pleasantly through cognitive-emotive dissonance into desirable emotional insight.

The Memory Aids for this chapter are on page 217.

PART THREE

Strategies and Techniques of RBT

Part Three consists of eight chapters. They are:

The RBT Intake (Chapter 5)
Behavioral Groupings in RBT (Chapter 6)
How to Start RBT (Chapter 7)
From the Unlikely to the Here and Now (Chapter 8)
Therapeutic Interactions in RBT (Chapter 9)
The Remainder of Mrs. Morrsey's Therapy (Chapter 10)
Rational Thinking as the Ideal Tranquilizer (Chapter 11)
Helping P-Cs Discover What's Rational for Them (Chapter 12)

With excerpts from actual case histories, these chapters demonstrate and explain the strategies and techniques that make RBT a comprehensive, short-term, cross-cultural, drug-free cognitive behavior therapy that produces long-term results. When you thoroughly understand the contents of any part of this section, you will be able to put it to immediate clinical use.

CHAPTER **5**

The RBT Intake

Mrs. Morrsey was born and raised in the eastern mountains of Kentucky. When she was 15 years old, she married her first husband. After eighteen years of marriage, her first husband ran off with a new 15-year-old girlfriend. Mrs. Morrsey immediately divorced him; then as a single parent working two jobs, she raised her four children (three sons—then aged 15, 13, and 11—and a 2-year-old daughter).

When I first saw Mrs. Morrsey she was 37 years old and married for the second time. She had met her second husband two years after her divorce. They had courted for a year and married seven months prior to this intake interview. Immediately after the marriage, the second husband, his 15-year-old daughter, Mrs. Morrsey, and her children all started living together.

After they had lived harmoniously for about a month, Mr. Morrsey's daughter ran away and Mr. and Mrs. Morrsey began to fight regularly. During the three days before Mrs. Morrsey's intake sessions, she had attempted suicide three times. Her oldest son, home on a weekend pass from a nearby army base, interrupted her third suicide attempt and brought her to our emergency psychiatric walk-in clinic.

SPECIAL VOCABULARY

None.

FOCUS ITEMS

1. What good does it do to have people in emotional crisis fill out a pre-intake form?
2. Why do RBT therapists keep psychotherapy in the here and now?
3. Why do intelligent people who have miserable pasts continue to be miserable in the present?
4. What are the first five general principles of RBT intakes?
5. What is the rational view of the influence of past experience on people's present behavior?

CHAPTER **5**

The RBT Intake

Intake Principle 1: Use a standard pre-intake form to get the P-C's identifying data, including name, age, sex, marital status, children, work, and the presenting problem.

Pre-intake forms help you and can also help your P-Cs. The information on the form enables you, in your initial contact, to have a greater sense of the individual people who are your new P-Cs. You are then more likely to see them as people with problems rather than as problems with people. And your P-Cs will be more likely to react toward you with openness and trust than with reservation and suspicion.

Keep your forms simple. As much as possible, use the fill-in blanks and checklist formats.

What if people can't read, or if they just refuse to fill out the forms? Instantly, you will have two useful pieces of information. In the first case, you will know *not* to assign your illiterate P-Cs the otherwise routine bibliotherapeutic readings used in RBT. In the second case, the P-Cs will have let you know right away that they need special attention. This information will signal you to start gathering data immediately for making three important clinical decisions:

1. What special attention do these P-Cs need?
2. Are you able and willing to give them that special attention?
3. Is it best for you to accept these P-Cs for treatment or to refer them elsewhere?

Remember, though, a good pre-intake form is not an evaluational short-cut. Instead, a good pre-intake form is only an aid to good clinical evaluation.

Pre-intake forms can aid P-C evaluation in two important ways: (1) Pre-intake forms enable P-Cs to tell you immediately about personal problems they may be too ashamed of to mention verbally. (2) Pre-intake forms can also be therapeutic distractions for P-Cs. For example, in a later chapter you will observe Mrs. Morrsey saying that filling out our pre-intake form caused her to stop and think for the first time about something important: If she killed herself, her little girl would have no real parent to take care of her. So even before I had talked to Mrs. Morrsey, the pre-intake form had already helped her decide to go on living for her daughter's sake.

Granted, living one's life solely for a child is not the ideal basis for emotionally healthy living. But I enthusiastically reinforce such altruism if the alternative is suicide.

If people are to receive RBT, it doesn't matter why they have decided to go on living; if you can get them to cooperate in RBT, they will quickly start living for emotionally healthy reasons. Then their ever-increasing personal satisfaction will be the reinforcement that leads them on to therapeutic success.

Intake Principle 2: Focus primarily on the here and now.

All life takes place in the present. Therefore, the present is the only time people can have or solve problems. That's why RBT (and any other efficiently effective psychotherapy) is here-and-now psychotherapy. That is also why rational intakes give you immediate, clear-cut answers to two important questions:

(1) How are P-Cs experiencing their lives now? (2) What seem to be the motivating forces in the P-Cs undesirable behavior?

BASIC RBT THEORY OF HUMAN MOTIVATION

What are the main motivations of behaviors that are appropriate for psychotherapeutic changes? Those motivations are: Hope for something, fear of something, anger about something, or some combination of those three emotions. In taking a history, therefore, look for evidence of self-defeating hope, anger, or fear as motivational factors in your P-Cs' presenting problems. Then formulate your behavioral dynamics in terms of what your P-Cs seem to be hoping for, and/or afraid of and/or angry about.

MRS. MORRSEY'S INTAKE INTERVIEW[1]

Me: Mrs. Morrsey, I'm Dr. Maultsby. I understand that you've been depressed quite severely for about a week now, and you even tried to kill yourself a couple of times over the weekend, is that right?

P-C: Yes, sir.

---

[1]Narrated, excerpted audio and video tapes of the actual RBT sessions with Mrs. Morrsey are available for professional teaching and training purposes.

Me: Tell me, when did you first start getting so depressed?

P-C: Friday, I guess.

Me: Friday, what happened?

P-C: I worked all day and my husband was drunk. He kept on drinking and drinking; and Saturday I was at work and called him to come get me because I was sick. He was drunk, and had been driving the car all day, drunk. Then he started calling me all kinds of names and what have you; and when we got home, it was just a big fight. I took it as long as I could; then found all the pills I could and took them.

Me: Then what happened?

P-C: I don't even remember; I don't remember anything else until Sunday.

Me: And what happened on Sunday?

P-C: Got up Sunday evening and the same thing started all over again, his drinking, cussing, arguing. They thought they had poured out all my pills, but I found some more and took them, and then I got me a razor blade, and my son caught me with the razor blade. I just got to where I couldn't take it anymore.

Me: What was it exactly you didn't think you could take anymore?

P-C: When you've been depressed for so long, things just begin to add up on you and you just don't care anymore.

Intake Principle 3: Get a clear view of the world as your patient-clients experience it.

One of the best ways to get your P-Cs' view of the world is to ask them if they can remember when they were relatively satisfied with their lives. If they can, ask them to start there and describe the chain of events that led to this intake visit. If they don't remember when they were relatively satisfied with their lives, ask them to describe a typical day of living with their problem now. That description will usually give you a clear idea of what the main problems are.

Almost always, P-Cs' main problems will be negative emotions that are excessive, poorly handled, or both. But everyone has his or her own special ways of creating personal emotional misery. So, the more clearly you understand each P-C's special cognitive habits, the better you'll be able to help them help themselves to happiness.

After P-Cs choose a problem for therapeutic focus, I often give them this homework assignment: "On three separate days, write down the very first answers that pop into your mind for these three questions"

1. Is there anything at all that's good about your problem?
2. What desirable things do your problems stop you from doing?
3. What aspect of your problem are you most fearful or angry about?

I use the P-Cs' responses to decide which emotion—hope, fear, or anger—seems to be the main driving force in their present problem.

In nonpsychotic suicidal depression, P-Cs usually see themselves as over-whelmed emotionally by some external HE, SHE, or IT. Fortunately, that is almost never the objective reality. Teaching P-Cs their Emotional ABCs is one of the fastest ways to help them see that obvious fact. Once they see it, they are ideally ready to take the first step toward rational hope and rapid drug-free relief.

But this point in Mrs. Morrsey's intake was not the time to introduce the Emotional ABCs. I needed more history to make an accurate behavioral grouping of her depression. In RBT, the behavioral grouping of the presenting problem largely determines whether or not people are appropriate for RBT; it's also the main factor in deciding whether or not to treat P-Cs inside or outside a hospital, with or without drugs.

Me: When did things, in your mind, start to add up on you?
P-C: Seems like it all really started back in February.
Me: That's about six or seven months ago.
P-C: That's when my husband's daughter ran off to live with her grandmother. She just couldn't get along with my boys, and I couldn't afford to give her what she had been used to having. Seems like that's when it all started, all his drinking so much, fussing and fighting. *(Mrs. Morrsey started to cry softly.)*
Me: I see, had he been drinking before that?
P-C: Just a beer once in a while, but it wasn't anything like this; it's seven days a week now. He hides his bottles; I find them under the mattress and I find them in the drawers.

Intake Principle 4: Allow P-Cs reasonable freedom of expression; but stay in control of the session.

At first, Intake Principle 4 may seem like contradictory advice. But look at it like this. Mrs. Morrsey seemed quite concerned about her husband's drinking. I thought, therefore, it might be helpful later if I already knew her views of her husband's drinking habits. So I let her briefly describe them. But when I heard all I wanted to hear, I immediately switched the focus of the interview back to her.

Me: What kind of work do you do?
P-C: I'm the fountain manager at the Mall Pharmacy. I've been there for nine years.
Me: I see, that's very good. Now tell me, when you say fighting, do you mean physically fighting or just arguing back and forth?
P-C: No, I mean fighting. See. *(She showed me bruises.)* I've got the bruises here.

A COMMON QUESTION

"Isn't a person's past important in RBT?" Answer: Yes, a person's past is very important. Present problems are the algebraic sum of everything that did (and did not) happen in the past. But psychoemotionally, people's pasts affect them in the present largely through their memories of them. Fortunately, though, whether or not people realize it, if they have healthy brains they choose which memories they focus on. Therefore, they alone choose how much of and which of their past events affect them now.

Why then do many intelligent people waste their potentially happier present and passionately relive their miserable past? They do it mainly out of emotional ignorance. Those unhappy people simply don't know they have other emotional choices. Consequently, they naively believe their miserable past forces them to have miserable feelings now.

Fortunately, they are wrong—they don't have to be emotionally miserable now, just because they have emotionally miserable pasts. The here-and-now, self-help focus in RBT can enable people to prove that fact to themselves quickly, without the hazards of legal or illegal drugs.

The other main reason why intelligent people waste their potentially happier present, making themselves miserable about their miserable past is this: they don't believe they have a more pleasant past that's worth remembering. In RBT though, such P-Cs quickly learn the following obvious fact:

TODAY IS EVERYBODY'S PAST OF TOMORROW[2]

By emphasizing that fact, RBT therapists quickly get P-Cs interested in giving themselves instant happier pasts to remember and enjoy any time they choose to do so. How? Simply by showing P-Cs how to give themselves a happy day, every day.

Remember: *Today is everybody's past of tomorrow*. By rationally living their lives today to their satisfaction, cooperative P-Cs create an instant happy past for themselves to remember and enjoy at will. The past of today is just as real and legitimate to remember and react to as the past of yesterday, last year, or the last decade.

If P-Cs cooperate, RBT keeps them optimally enjoying their happy todays every day. As a result, they don't waste much time reliving their pasts, even though their pasts are then happy pasts. But that too is all right. People's pasts never get tired of waiting; their pasts are always there to be remembered and relived as miserably or as happily as people desire to relive them.

---

[2]The following insights about people's pasts were taken from a cassette tape in the *"Create Your Own Happiness"* kit (Maultsby 1982).

THE RATIONAL VIEW OF THE PAST

RBT therapists don't completely ignore P-Cs' past histories. But we get only enough past history to give us an accurate, as well as clinically useful, gestalt of the present problems. Such past histories give factual answers to the following nine questions:

1. What was the P-Cs' family structure?
2. How did the P-Cs experience growing up in their families?
3. What behavioral, medical, social, financial, or other problems did P-Cs and their parents have?
4. How many siblings were there?
5. How did the P-Cs feel about and get along with their siblings?
6. What are the P-Cs' school, work, military, romantic, sexual, social, and medical histories?
7. What are the P-Cs' past and current medical diagnoses?
8. What are the P-Cs' legal and illegal drug-taking histories?
9. What are the P-Cs' past and present suicidal or homicidal thoughts, plans, and actions?

A well-structured pre-intake form will give you the answers to most of those questions, especially the less relevant ones, before you see new P-Cs. Then you will be free to take the most thorough here-and-now history in the shortest possible time.

WHO IS APPROPRIATE FOR RBT?

To decide rationally if a person is appropriate for RBT (or any nondrug therapy) you must be able to answer "yes" to this question: "Does the case history mainly reveal the logical but undesirable results of self-defeating learning by a normally functioning brain and mind?" In addition, you must be able to answer "no" to this question: "Does the case history reveal significant evidence of the logical but undesirable results of behavioral control by an unhealthy brain and mind, independent of self-defeating learning?"

At this point in Mrs. Morrsey's intake, I thought I had enough information about her to say confidently that her suicidal depression was probably the logical but undesirable result of self-defeating learning by a normally functioning brain and mind. That assessment made her an ideal candidate for RBT. Once you read "Behavioral Groupings in RBT" (the next chapter), you will see clearly these two important therapeutic points: (1) Why that assessment could be made rapidly, yet accurately. (2) Why drug-free, out-patient psychotherapy could be started immediately.

The Memory Aids for this chapter are on page 218.

CHAPTER 6

Behavioral Groupings in RBT

In RBT, therapists divide human behavior into two basic groups—the not-learned and the learned behaviors. But human brains normally control both groups according to the same A, B, C sequence of behavioral control. First, people's brains form perceptions—labeled A, the activating event. Then their brains process those perceptions, using the people's sincere self-talk—labeled B, their evaluative thoughts. Their evaluative thoughts trigger real, logical, and correct emotional feelings and physical reactions—labeled C, the consequences of B.

For example, let's look at the fear created by the unhealthy brains and minds of alocholics in DTs (delirium tremens). This fear is real, logical, and correct for the alcoholics' sincere, evaluative thoughts at B (about the hallucinated wild animals they perceive at A).

RBT therapists refer to problems caused by unhealthy or functionally impaired minds and brains as not-learned behavioral problems. Such problems indicate qualitative abnormalities in the anatomy or biochemistry of the brain. People who have these problems need medical evaluation and medical treatments designed to restore their brains to healthy functional states. Only then (if at all) are people with not-learned behavioral problems appropriate for RBT or for any other type of nonmedical therapy.

Now let's look at the ABCs of the fear created by the healthy, normally functioning minds and brains of people who have flying phobias—that is, people who are afraid to fly on regularly scheduled commercial airplanes.

Just like the fears of delirious alcoholics, the phobics' fears at C are real, logical, and correct for their sincere evaluative thoughts at B (about the real and imagined events they perceive at A about flying).

Both examples of fear work according to the same A, B, Cs. But neither fear is in response to objectively dangerous situations. And the appropriate treatment for each fear is drastically different. Delirium tremens needs medical care in a hospital. But many phobics need only three to twelve office sessions of RBT.

RBT therapists refer to the problems caused by healthy minds and brains as learned behavioral problems. Such problems indicate learned, self-defeating, cognitive habits are forcing these people's healthy brains to control their emotional and physical behaviors in self-defeating ways. The book *The Neurological Foundation of Psychiatry* (Smythies 1966) provides a detailed review of the numerous well-done research studies that support the validity of the grouping of not-learned versus learned described here.[1]

SPECIAL VOCABULARY

Delusion: a strongly believed, incorrect idea that is not based on primary group or secondary group teaching and that has no basis in fact, but that a person refuses to change in spite of obvious factual evidence against it. Delusions usually indicate psychosis or some other serious brain disorder.

Empathize: as used in RBT, imagining accurately another person's situation without experientially sharing or simulating any of that person's emotional and/or physical experience. The ability to empathize with P-Cs increases the therapist's effectiveness.

Hallucination: a perception that has no objectively real or consciously imagined stimulus. Hallucinations usually indicate psychosis or some other serious brain disorder.

Practice: repeatedly pairing the same perceptions with the same sincere evaluative thoughts and emotional reactions, physical reactions, or both.

Statistically credible history: a history that is common in the lives of people in general, or of people in a specific culture or subculture.

Sympathize: as used in RBT, experientially sharing or simulating a person's emotional experiences, physical experiences, or both, with or without accurately imagining the events that caused those experiences. Sympathizing with P-Cs almost never aids therapy; but sympathizing very often decreases therapists' effectiveness and leads to professional burn-out.

FOCUS ITEMS

1. What is the treatment of choice for not-learned behavioral problems?
2. What are the three main characteristics of learned behavioral problems?
3. What are the ABCs for practicing behavioral problems?
4. Why does RBT seem to be an ideal psychotherapy for psychosomatic disorders?
5. Who are the most logical therapists for people who have psychosomatic disorders?
6. What are five major signs of a not-learned behavioral problem?
7. What are three major signs of a learned behavioral problem?

---

[1]After deciding which behavioral group best fits your P-C's problem, use the Diagnostic Criteria from DSM-III of the American Psychiatric Association to identify the appropriate diagnostic label.

CHAPTER 6

Behavioral Groupings in RBT

After RBT intake, the first question the therapists want to answer confidently is, "Is this person's problem learned or not-learned?"

Not-learned behavioral problems are inappropriate for RBT, or any other nonmedical therapy. But the fear examples in the preview showed that not-learned behavioral problems can have the same A, B, C components that learned behavioral problems have. That is why the two groups of problems can look alike, even though they need drastically different treatments.

EIGHT MAJOR SIGNS OF NOT-LEARNED BEHAVIOR

As you do your intake interview, systematically look for these eight major signs of not-learned behaviors:

First, the P-Cs are often disoriented in time, place, or person.

Second, the P-Cs often have a history of sudden onset, or a sudden exacerbation, of undesirable behavior without plausible external precipitating events.

Third, the P-Cs show no evidence of voluntary mental control over the onset, intensity, or degree of incapacity caused by their undesirable behavior.

Fourth, these P-Cs often have paralysis or persistent muscular weakness, and frequent or intractable headaches with and without a history or evidence of head trauma.

Fifth, the P-Cs often have a recent history of convulsions, amnesia, loss of consciousness, blurred vision, or recurrent or persistent vertigo.

Sixth, the P-Cs often have poor recent memory and are inappropriately distractable.

Seventh, the P-Cs often have delusions, hallucinations, or some other thought disorder.

Eighth, the P-Cs often have inappropriate or otherwise pathologic affect.

FOUR MAJOR SIGNS OF LEARNED BEHAVIOR

Looking for these four signs will help you identify P-Cs whose problems are the result of self-defeating learned behaviors:

First, these P-Cs give you a statistically credible history for their culture or sub-culture. In addition, mild forms of their problems will be common in the everyday lives of most normal people. Therefore, you will be able to empathize with these P-Cs.

The case history may reveal one or two features reminiscent of signs of not-learned behavioral problems; but those features will be isolated findings against an otherwise uniform background of inaccurate perceptions and irrational beliefs, feelings, and actions.

Second, with learned behavioral problems P-Cs give a history or show observable evidence, or both of some voluntary control over the onset of their undesirable behaviors, the intensity of these behaviors, the degree of incapacity they cause, or all these factors.

Let's stop here and apply this second sign to people with flying phobias. Many of these people will fly after they convince themselves they "just have to fly." They say things like "I'm scared to death of flying, but I've just got to take this trip."

Usually these people have effective ways of keeping themselves tolerably fearful while flying; a common way is pretending they are riding in a car, instead of flying in an airplane. However, most flying phobics who "just have to fly" simply drug themselves into semi- or total unconsciousness with alcohol or other tranquilizers. They then sort of sleepwalk, or just plain sleep, through the trip.

None of these maneuvers alone cures flying phobias. But these maneuvers do show that phobics can favorably influence their fears. This fact completely separates the healthy minds and brains of phobics from the unhealthy minds and brains of delirious alcoholics. You will never see delirious alcoholics voluntarily decreasing their DTs because they "just have to take a trip."

Third, the main presenting complaints in learned behavioral problems are usually self-defeating negative emotions. By far the most common of these negative emotions are self-defeating fear, anger, depression, or some combination of them.

Fourth, the case histories of learned behavioral problems don't usually reveal definite hallucinations or delusions. But these case histories will reveal evidence that the P-Cs have been and still are unwittingly practicing irrational cognitive, emotive, and physical behaviors.

UNWITTINGLY PRACTICING IRRATIONAL BEHAVIORS

New P-Cs don't usually realize they have been and still are practicing their problems when they come for psychotherapy. But, unwitting practice influences self-control just as directly as does conscious practice (Lacey and Smith 1954; Lacey et al. 1955; Menzies 1937; Razran 1935, 1949, 1949a; Staats and Staats 1957, 1958). In addition, unwittingly practiced emotional responses more readily generalize and are more difficult to extinguish than are consciously practiced emotional responses (Lacey and Smith 1954; Lacey et al. 1955).

The Key Insight

The large majority of people with flying phobias have never been in a real crash, or even a near-crash of an airplane. In fact, many flying phobics have never even flown. But none of them were born being afraid to fly. So how did they get their flying phobias? They learned them through diligent practice, using the same A, B, Cs of practice involved in practicing and learning any habit.

The ABCs of Behavioral Practice

A   Repeated similar perceptions, that is, activating events
B   Similar positive, negative or neutral beliefs repeatedly associated with A
C   Similar, emotive reactions, physical reactions, or both, repeatedly elicited by B in response to A

Flying phobia can be used to show you the ABCs of voluntarily but unwittingly practicing an irrational behavior. Almost any emotional or behavioral problem, if it is appropriate for psychotherapy alone, will accurately fit this cognitive model for emotional and behavioral learning.

When people with flying phobias think about flying, what do they perceive in their imagination at A? Usually, it's something like this:

Often, for as long as these people can remember, they have always had similar fearful images and thoughts about flying. Their fearful images and thoughts are the a-Bs of the ABCs for practicing their flying phobias. And their fearful B-thoughts trigger real, logical, and correct fearful emotional feelings that make an airplane crash seem certain. So these people logically, but irrationally refuse to fly. Their fearful feelings and their physical refusals to fly, or both, are the Cs of the ABCs of voluntarily but unwittingly practicing their flying phobia.

Their fearful feelings make refusing to fly feel like the right thing to do. That's because those fearful feelings are real, logical and correct for the fearful mental images and equally fearful thoughts that triggered them. But phobics either don't know, or they consistently ignore, the next fact: Their fearful images and thoughts do not apply to the objectively probable safe outcome of commercial flights. So, as long as flying phobics insist on ignoring the objective probability of a safe flight and focus on the remote possibility of a crash, it makes compelling sense to them to refuse to fly.

It's irrelevant that flying phobics often say "I know my fear is silly; I really shouldn't be afraid." They immediately cancel the potentially helpful effects of those rational ideas with "But I just feel that the very plane I get on will be the one that crashes."

The key irrational thought that keeps flying phobias active is "I just feel that the very plane I get on will be the one that crashes." When healthy brains process such sincere fearful thoughts, without any equally sincere but negating, or calming, follow-up thoughts, fearful feelings have to result.[2] And every time people repeat those ABCs of flying phobias, those people are voluntarily but unwittingly practicing their fear of flying.

This series of facts makes it obvious that flying phobics should feel just as afraid as they do feel. If phobics didn't feel so afraid, one of the following two situations would have to exist. Either their minds and brains would not be interacting properly with their bodies; or, they would have to be joking or lying when they say "I just feel that the very plane I get on will be the one that crashes." But if they were joking or lying, they would happily, or at least calmly, fly without drugging or distracting themselves.

THE PSYCHOSOMATIC BEHAVIORAL PROBLEMS

Psychosomatic behavioral problems seem to be partly learned and partly not-learned. Much recent research indicates the main mechanisms of these disorders are faulty cognitions (that is, inaccurate perceptions, sincere but irrational evaluative thoughts, or both) that trigger such severe emotive reactions that organ dysfunction

---

[2]For excellent, detailed research demonstrating the power of belief and the validity of ascribing maximal importance to vicarious emotional learning based on people's sincere evaluative thoughts, see the studies of Gatchel et al. (1979) and Paul (1966, 1967), describing lasting therapeutic learning achieved by people treated with placebo treatment.

and sometimes even tissue damage result (Grace and Graham 1952; Graham et al. 1958, 1962; Holmes 1978; Schwager and Cox 1978). That's why RBT therapists say that psychosomatic disorders are behavioral problems that are partly learned and partly not-learned.

Other research (Maultsby and Graham 1974; Schwager and Cox 1978; Holmes 1978) indicates that counseling techniques with the rational, cognitive-behavioral focus are ideal therapeutic additions to the medical treatment of psycho-somatic disorders.

A CASE HISTORY OF INCORRECT BEHAVIORAL GROUPING

Some years before unleaded gasoline and forced busing, an inner-city elementary school in a large city had classes continually disrupted by a small group of children. But for these children the punishment that was usually effective for their classmates was ineffective. Fortunately, a student teacher noticed that the unruly children all lived in the same area. Subsequent home visits revealed houses painted with lead-based paints and streets strongly scented with the exhaust fumes of the leaded gas from the heavy auto traffic.

Blood tests for lead showed that most of the children had abnormally high levels of lead in their blood; in one-third of the tests the lead levels were toxic. Those findings led to appropriate medical treatments for lead toxicity and appropriate changes in the children's home environments. Predictably, those nonpunitive maneuvers led to rapid, noticeable improvement in the children's classroom behavior, without further punishment.

That case history demonstrates the tremendous value of just thinking about the possibility that behavioral problems may be not-learned problems. Remember: Psychotherapy, counseling, punishment, and positive and negative reinforcements affect only learned behavioral problems.

A WORD OF CAUTION

Don't expect to make accurate diagnoses for every P-C after one, or even two, intake interviews. Your P-Cs probably won't have read this chapter, and therefore, most of them won't know which signs to tell you about first. In addition, some P-Cs may have one or two questionable signs of both not-learned and learned behavioral problems. When in doubt, get a medical consultation or at least get the advice of an experienced colleague.

In rare cases, a consultation will either be impossible to get, or it won't be helpful. What then? Give those P-Cs a therapeutic trial of daily RBT for one or two weeks. Appropriate P-Cs who cooperate will usually show evidence of behavioral improvement within a week, and almost always within two weeks, of daily RBT. And a two-week delay in getting a medical evaluation will usually be safe for P-Cs whose symptoms are too vague to merit an immediate not-learned behavioral grouping.

What if P-Cs' behavioral signs are unchanged or worse after two weeks of daily RBT? Refer such P-Cs for neurological or complete medical evaluation.

BEHAVIORAL ASSESSMENT OF MRS. MORRSEY

Mrs. Morrsey was alert and oriented for time, place, and person. There were no signs of intoxication of any type and no reasons to suspect a significant medical disorder. But most important, she had the four major signs of learned depression.

First, she gave a statistically credible history. I could easily empathize, as opposed to sympathize, with her.

Second, although she had been practicing her depression for six months, she had not missed one day of work. That seemed to be evidence in favor of significant, voluntary control over the intensity and disabling power of her depression.

Third, she had logical, externally directed anger (toward her husband), self-directed anger, and an overwhelming sense of helplessness. That triad is present in up to 80 percent of learned depressions; but that triad is almost never present in not-learned depressions.[3]

Fourth, Mrs. Morrsey's history failed to reveal any significant evidence of a not-learned depression. But her depression fit easily into the ABCs of learned depressions.

She had frequent (if not daily) *perceptions* at A of her husband drinking excessively and abusing her verbally and often physically.

She frequently (if not daily) had these sincere *evaluative thoughts* at B: "My God, how did I get into this mess? I must be some kind of idiot. How could I have been such a fool? I can't stand this. My life is a living hell, and there's nothing I can do about it. Nobody cares about me. Not even the police will help me. It's just not worth it. I'd rather be dead. Not even hell can be this bad."

When people's healthy minds and brains frequently and sincerely process such thoroughly depressive, suicide-implying ideas, those people inevitably *feel and act* suicidally depressed at C. Otherwise, they would lose their personally meaningful sense of reality and psychoemotional congruence. When those losses are sudden and intense enough, even normal people will "flip out" into temporary psychotic states.

Operational Assumptions

Mrs. Morrsey certainly had an objectively undesirable life situation; I wouldn't have wished it on anyone. But her situation at A was not depressing her at C; instead, she was depressing herself with her depressive thoughts at B. In addi-

---

[3]The other 15 percent to 20 percent of people with learned depressions usually have this triad: (1) a longstanding belief in their own inadequacy as a human being; (2) an overwhelming sense of helpless inability to correct their imagined inadequacy; and (3) intense self-directed anger about their imagined inadequacy.

tion, she was the only person who could stop doing that. That's the typical situation in learned depressions.

Those facts make antidepressants useless for learned depressions. There are no healthy, antidepressive beliefs in any antidepressant pill. So giving antidepressants to P-Cs like Mrs. Morrsey is both a waste of money and potentially harmful.

The most immediately therapeutic thing therapists can do for people like Mrs. Morrsey is teach them their Emotional ABCs. The next chapter will show you how Mrs. Morrsey learned her Emotional ABCs in less than fifteen minutes.

The Memory Aids for this chapter are on page 219.

CHAPTER 7
How to Start RBT

By now, I hope you accept this fact: *Thinking is the single most important thing people do.* Yet you will rarely ever see P-Cs who are concerned about the way they've been thinking lately. Almost always, they will only be concerned about the way they've been feeling lately. That's understandable.

Before most people learn their Emotional ABCs, they tend to be "feelers" rather than "thinkers." Worse yet, they want to feel better without thinking better. But the only way people can feel better without thinking better is through brain damage or drug use. That fact is the main reason why legal and illegal drug abuses are America's main health and social problems—Americans naively insist on trying to feel better without thinking better. That's why your new P-Cs usually will be overtly or covertly expecting that therapeutic miracle. But unless you can walk on water, you won't have any such therapeutic miracles to give them.

Rational Behavior Therapists don't worry about not being able to perform miracles. The A, B, C model of emotions is a quick way to get new P-Cs past their irrational therapeutic expectations and to enable them to focus on this obvious fact: *For people with healthy brains to replace any emotional feelings, those people must first replace the sincere thinking that triggers or maintains those feelings.*

SPECIAL VOCABULARY

Anticipatory attention: ideal psychological readiness to accept therapeutic advice.

FOCUS ITEMS
1. Why was Mrs. Morrsey an ideal candidate for RBT?
2. What is the main reason nonpsychotic people make themselves feel emotionally miserable?
3. Why are even educated people usually afraid to consult psychotherapists?
4. Why do new P-Cs often refuse to describe their main problems during their intake interview?
5. What is a good way to reassure new P-Cs about their sanity?
6. Why does knowing their Emotional ABCs help P-Cs feel better immediately?

CHAPTER **7**

How to Start RBT

Mrs. Morrsey neither had brain damage, nor did her depression need drugs. But she was more emotionally miserable than she wanted to be. Those conditions made her an ideal candidate for RBT.

Me: Now listen, I'm going to try to help you get over your grief and depression; and once you're feeling better emotionally, you'll be able to handle your problems with your husband yourself. Would you like to feel better emotionally as soon as possible?

P-C: I sure would.

Me: Well, are you willing to give up the idea of killing yourself and start working at getting yourself together? You see, I can't work with you if you are dead.

P-C: Yes, that's true.

Me: Tell me, where do you think your feelings of depression come from? You look like you feel miserable. Where do you think those miserable feelings are coming from?

P-C: I just don't know.

Author's Note

I like to get that response! The admission of ignorance is the first step in rapid learning. People are not usually interested in learning what they think they already know.

Me: Well, that's what I'm going to teach you right now, where your emotions come from. You see, all emotions—depression, love, sadness, or what have

88

you—all emotions are created by the person who feels them. That means you are creating your own depression right now. Did you realize that?

P-C: I guess so; what I've done, I've done myself.

Me: That's right. But you don't have to kill yourself to stop depressing yourself. But before you can stop doing something, you have to first realize that you are doing it; then you have to see how you are doing it.

Author's Note

If you were looking at the videotape of this session, you'd now see Mrs. Morrsey establish eye contact with me for the first time. That indicated to me she was hearing something new, something she hoped she could use immediately to help herself.

From that point on, Mrs. Morrsey seemed to be more and more involved, just waiting for my next idea. In short, she seemed to be giving me anticipatory attention. And that fact brings me to

AN IMPORTANT THERAPEUTIC INSIGHT

Nonpsychotic people don't want to feel emotionally miserable; they do it mainly because they don't believe they have any other emotional choices in their present situation.

Me: Do you know how you can stop feeling so bad right now?

P-C: Right now, no!

Me: All right, that's what I'm going to teach you—how you can start making yourself feel better right this minute. Well, maybe not this minute, but certainly within the next hour or so. You see, every time normal people have an emotional feeling, they first have to become aware of something. We call whatever it is they are aware of A, their perception, or what they pay atttention to. Now, the main job of your brain is to keep you alive. But that job has two parts. First, your brain has to make you aware of things; and second, based on your personal beliefs, your brain instantly and automatically groups the things you notice as being either positive, negative, or neutral, for you and your survival. Now the positive, negative, or neutral thinking you use to evaluate your perceptions is B, in the ABCs of Human Emotions. And it's always your beliefs at B about what you notice at A that instantly trigger your gut or emotional feelings, which we call the C in the ABCs of Human Emotions. Now those are the ABCs of your emotions, my emotions, and every other normal person's emotions.

Author's Note

Did you notice the emphasis that the Emotional ABCs apply to all normal people? I did that to help Mrs. Morrsey relax. Almost without exception, new P-Cs are mildly panic-stricken during their intake sessions. Regardless of their education, new P-Cs are usually afraid that needing to see a mental health professional means one of two things: (1) they (that is, the P-Cs) have gone crazy, or (2) they are about to go crazy.

Those fears are the main reasons new P-Cs often don't talk about their main problems during intake. They think, "My God! If I tell them all that, they'll know I'm crazy."

Most emotionally distressed, but otherwise sane people hate and fear the idea of being discovered to be crazy. As a naive form of self-protection, therefore, they often do one of two things: They avoid psychotherapists, or they try to get therapeutic help without revealing the main reason they need it. Quite often, therefore, new P-Cs refuse to talk about their main problem until they believe their therapist is convinced that they are not crazy.

Most experienced psychotherapists know those facts well. But even experienced therapists often don't have a logical explanation for why so many educated people have those irrational fears about their sanity. So let's look at the rational explanation. To most people, crazy behavior means undesirable behavior that they want to control completely, but which they don't seem able to control at all. In addition, most people believe only crazy people have persistent crazy behavior.

Now what causes most people to seek psychotherapy? Their own persistent undesirable behavior that they want to control completely but that they don't seem able to control at all. So even though new P-Cs rarely mention it, usually they are anywhere from minimally anxious to frankly panic-stricken about the possibility of being crazy. A common, veiled plea for reassurance by mildly panic-stricken P-Cs is, "I just don't understand myself, I know what I'm doing is crazy, but I just can't stop it. Isn't that the craziest thing?"

The old truism "only sane people worry about being crazy" is rarely enough to reassure these emotionally distressed people. To be ideally reassuring, you must give them immediately useful insights into their main problem, even though they may not yet have told you what it is. Such insights show P-Cs what they can do to start helping themselves immediately.

If possible, your insight should make it obvious that the P-C's main problem is similar to the problems most normal people have. But to be ideally reassuring, your insights must also show P-Cs that their problems are both logically understandable and solvable. In the minds of most P-Cs, only sane people have logically understandable and solvable behavioral problems.

Teaching new P-Cs their Emotional ABCs is the easiest and fastest way I've found to help P-Cs quickly reassure themselves appropriately. That's especially so, when they can be gotten to personalize their Emotional ABCs. Next is an effective way to do that.

GETTING P-Cs TO PERSONALIZE THE EMOTIONAL ABCs

Usually, new P-Cs immediately understand the A, B, C model of emotions. But the A, B, C model is still a new way of thinking about emotions that conflicts with P-Cs' old emotional beliefs. So the Emotional ABCs don't feel right at first. This scientific explanation of their emotions, therefore, is often not enough to counteract the popular emotional magic that fills the minds of most new P-Cs.

Getting P-Cs to personalize their Emotional ABCs is a good way to get them past their old beliefs about emotions, which prevent therapeutic learning. The more dramatically, yet pleasantly, you get them to personalize their Emotional ABCs, the more likely they will remember and use them. The rattlesnake supposition (presented on page 91) is a particularly effective way to get P-Cs to do that helpful personalizing.

Me: Suppose you were to look down now and see a rattlesnake slowly crawling.

7-1   The Rattlesnake Supposition

Author's Note

That was a very informative response. As usual, the rattlesnake supposition was so unexpected and so irrelevant to Mrs. Morrsey's real situation that she thought it was funny, and for the first time in the session, she smiled. But she also assumed I had a serious purpose, so she gave me a serious answer.

That behavior revealed four important facts about Mrs. Morrsey: (1) She was appropriately cooperative. (2) She was appropriately distractable. (3) Her "I'd be scared!" revealed appropriate reality orientation. (4) Her genuine smile revealed that her depression had the mercurial quality characteristic of learned depressions. Those facts virtually guaranteed that she had a learned (that is, neurotic or reactive) depression, as opposed to a not-learned depression. So I could proceed confidently.

Me: Where do you think your fear would come from?
P-C: I guess it would come from inside you and the snake, too.
Me: No, it wouldn't come from the snake; that's where people make their mistakes; they believe their fears and other emotions come from outside of them, but they don't; your emotions always come from inside of you. Now, remember what I told you. Every time you have an emotion, you are first of all aware of something. So you would have looked down, and seen a rattlesnake; the snake would be A. Now, how have you learned to evaluate the situation of a rattlesnake being close to your foot? In your mind, what kind of situation is that?
P-C: Kind of scary!
Me: Right! That's why you and any other sane, normal person, would feel afraid. Now, do you see how your fear would have come directly from what you

would have thought about your situation? First, you would have seen the rattlesnake moving toward your foot, and because you have learned that rattlesnakes are dangerous, you would have instantly, but correctly, labeled that situation, "A dangerous situation to be in." And that's why you would have instantly had a real, logical, and correct feeling of fear, right?

P-C: Yes, sir.

Me: But suppose while you were jumping up on the chair out of the way, you were to see me reach down, pick up the snake, wind it up and show you that it was just a toy snake. Would you go on being afraid?

P-C: (Smiling) No.

Me: Why not?

P-C: Because you would have proved to me that it wasn't real.

Author's Note

It is probably apparent that Mrs. Morrsey was an ideally cooperative P-C. But less cooperative P-Cs also respond as Mrs. Morrsey did to the rattlesnake supposition. Their response provides a golden opportunity to ask them, "Do you know what you have just done? You have just proven to yourself that you already know, without realizing it, that you can and do change your emotional feelings instantly, anytime you sincerely think your emotions are unrealistic or otherwise inappropriate for your situation."

IMPORTANT CLINICAL INSIGHT

Usually, people with healthy brains only maintain emotions they believe are appropriate at the moment.

When I first made that insight, I thought it was an original discovery. But one of the many counseling ministers taking intensive training in RBT informed me, "that insight is over two thousand years old. Proverbs 21:2 clearly says: 'Every way of people is right in their own eyes.' "

That experience opened my eyes to this surprising fact: Many scientific principles of normal human behavior were described over two thousand years ago in the Bible. I now use Biblical descriptions to get religious-minded resistant P-Cs quickly past their resistance. Usually such P-Cs readily accept scientific principles of human behavior that happen to be paraphrased in Bible verses. Consequently, I value quite highly the numerous Biblical references that counseling ministers continually give me.

At this point trainees often ask, "Did Mrs. Morrsey reverse her depression as fast as she indicated she would have reversed her snake fear?" Answer, "No." Here are the reasons she could *not* have done so. As it is with most children and adults, reversing an inappropriate fear of a toy (or any other obviously mislabeled perception) was already one of Mrs. Morrsey's well-learned emotional habits. So making that reversal *did not put her in conflict with any of her other strongly held beliefs.*

But what about these ideas? "You are depressing yourself; you don't have to be any more depressed than you want to be; you alone can and will have to stop depressing yourself." *Those ideas were in direct conflict* with Mrs. Morrsey's life-long beliefs that some external HEs, SHEs, ITs and THEYs in the outside world caused her emotions against her will. It takes a little time and rational practice to resolve such conflicts in favor of rational, and therefore, healthy emotional control. Now let's rejoin our conversation about the toy snake.

Me: All right, and what would have happened to your fear?
P-C: It would be gone.
Me: Right, it would have disappeared. But what would have had to have happened first, to make your fear disappear? You would have had to have changed the things you believed about the snake. Your first ideas would have been "It's dangerous; it might bite me;" or "It might kill me." So you would have felt a real, logical, healthy, feeling of fear. But after you would have seen me pick up the snake and play with it and show you that it wasn't real, what would have happened to your fear?
P-C: My mind would be at ease.
Me: Right! And when your mind is at ease?
P-C: Your emotions are at ease.
Me: Right! Now, do you see how your emotions follow directly from what you think and believe about what you perceive and pay attention to?
P-C: You're saying it's your beliefs that make you scared.
Me: That's right and it's also your beliefs that make you feel depressed, happy, love, hate and all the other emotions you have.

Author's Note

The videotape of this session reveals the pleasantly dramatic emotional learning experience the rattlesnake supposition gives new P-Cs. In addition, that rattlesnake supposition usually gives P-Cs a clear view of the following four sets of helpful emotional facts.

1.   Emotions include more than just feelings. Emotional feelings are just one third of a new emotion; and for useful self-understanding, emotional feelings are the *least important* factor. That's because emotional feelings are completely dependent on the positive, negative, or neutral evaluative thoughts that people believe at B about what they perceive at A.

2.   Neither HE, nor SHE, nor IT ever causes people's emotions. Instead, people themselves create, maintain, and eliminate their own emotions with what they believe about the HEs, SHEs and ITs in their worlds.

3.   People can change their undesirable emotions quickly and safely without drugs, electric shock, or brain damage. All they have to do is change what they perceive or believe, or both. Then their undesirable emotional feelings will have to change. Emotional feelings simply cannot maintain themselves by themselves; people always have to support their emotional feelings with logical sincere beliefs.

4.   People themselves are the only ones who can change or get rid of their emotional feelings without drugs, electric shock or brain damage. That fact makes it both inappropriate and incorrect for people to blame, or try to get someone else to accept responsibility for, their positive, negative, or neutral emotions.

HOW THE EMOTIONAL ABCs HELP P-Cs FEEL BETTER IMMEDIATELY

The Emotional ABCs give emotionally distressed people a valid, readily believable, and quickly useful way to think about themselves. Immediately, P-Cs can make this reassuring insight: Their former bewildering and seemingly uncontrollable emotional feelings are the understandable and controllable reactions of the normal, sane people that they hoped they were but were afraid they weren't.

The A, B, C emotional model also shows P-Cs how and why they can make themselves feel better immediately with just their undiseased, undrugged brains. And most P-Cs immediately start doing it.

TWO COMMON QUESTIONS

First, what if Mrs. Morrsey had responded to the rattlesnake supposition with an apathetic "You mean a snake like the ones that have been eating on my brain for the last two months?" Answer: I would have stopped my explanation of the Emotional ABCs, changed my diagnosis to a not-learned, psychotic depression, and hospitalized her immediately. Suicidally depressed psychotics are too unreliable to treat on an outpatient basis.

The other common question is, What if Mrs. Morrsey had responded to my rattlesnake supposition with "I just might let it bite me." Answer: I would have interpreted such a response to mean that she was not yet sure she wanted to go on living. In such cases, I reverse roles with the P-C in the rattlesnake supposition. I say, "Okay, just for the sake of our discussion, imagine how I would feel if I were to look down and see a rattlesnake slowly moving close to my foot."

That maneuver is effective because if P-Cs have learned depressions, they appropriately empathize with me in the rattlesnake supposition. Then they make the same emotional insights about me that Mrs. Morrsey made about herself. Consequently, these P-Cs personalize the Emotional ABCs, even though it is my foot, instead of theirs, in the rattlesnake supposition. Then I help these P-Cs apply to their current situations the four sets of helpful emotional facts listed earlier in this chapter. After that discussion, I focus on helping these P-Cs improve the accuracy and appropriateness of their perceptions and thoughts about their current situations. So far, I've always succeeded in getting such P-Cs to decide that suicide is not the best solution to their problems.

WHY ACCEPTING THE EMOTIONAL ABCs IMMEDIATELY HELPS P-Cs

"I have no choice about the emotions I feel." That widely popular, though irrational, belief alone causes up to 25 percent of the emotional distress of most people. That's why just learning their Emotional ABCs can cause an immediate 10 percent to 25 percent drop in people's emotional distress. The Emotional ABCs show people clearly that much emotional distress is a personal choice. After people make that insight, they usually start thinking of commonsense ways to help themselves emotionally. Consequently, an immediate 10-to-25 percent drop in emotional distress is almost automatic.

What about the remaining 75-to-90 percent of people's emotional distress? That distress is usually habitual, and to eliminate it, people need more knowledge than just the Emotional ABCs. That's why habitual emotional distress is the most logical main focus of all psychotherapy. This fact underscores the great need for a research-supported model for habitual emotions.

As a physician, I have always viewed psychosomatic disorders as medical problems caused by unhealthy emotional habits, in people predisposed to somaticize their emotional distress. So I combined the psychosomatic research data of Grace and Graham (1952) and Graham et al. (1958, 1962) with Ellis's A, B, C model (1963) of emotions. That combination made possible the A-b, C and a-B, C models of habitual emotions described in Chapter 4. After many years of continuous clinical testing, those models still are the most clinically useful ones I have found for giving people a complete as well as immediately helpful understanding of all their emotional experiences.

NEUTRAL EMOTIONS

The Emotional ABCs describe all emotions—the positive ones, the negative ones and the neutral ones. Most P-Cs readily accept this description for their ABCs for their positive and negative emotions. Unfortunately, though, many P-Cs incorrectly believe that their positive and negative emotions are their only real emotions. Such P-Cs mislabel their neutral emotions *no emotions*. That mislabeling can be a source of therapeutic resistance, especially with self-defeatingly hostile or depressed P-Cs.

Nonpsychotic P-Cs almost never get self-defeatingly hostile or depressed about things they want to feel good about; nor do they want to be nonfeeling, that is, to have no emotions at all. Consequently, many of these clinically hostile or depressed P-Cs will refuse to work at therapy; they incorrectly believe their only emotional choices are to feel good about what they are hostile or depressed about, or to have no emotions at all.

In my experience, disappointed lovers who are hostile, or depressed, or both most commonly show that type of therapeutic resistance. After I tell them, "I can certainly understand how anyone would probably be upset about a romantic disappointment like yours," I happily add, "but the good news is, you don't have to feel that miserable about it." Rather than reciprocating my elation, however, they angrily ask, "Are you saying I should feel good about the way so and so treated me? Never! You'd have to be crazy to do that."

Those P-Cs believe they have to go on feeling miserable about their situation, or feel good about it, or be crazy, or have no emotions at all. None of the latter three options is acceptable to them; so, they temporarily opt to go on feeling miserable.

But I quickly add, "Yes, I agree; you'd have to be crazy to want to feel good about that. That's why I would never suggest it. I'm just suggesting that you can exercise your other emotional choice to feel less miserable and less miserable until you have neutral emotions about it. It's only after you develop neutral emotions about it that you can and will quickly forget it."

P-C: But I don't want to lose my feelings; I like my emotions.

Me: I understand that; but you see, neutral emotions are real emotions too. It's just that you don't notice them; but that does not mean they are not there. Also, it is medically impossible for a healthy person to lose their emotional feelings. It doesn't matter how quickly you make yourself feel less miserable, you are never going to lose any of your ability to have emotions; I guarantee that. Now tell me, how does your left cheek feel right now?

Author's Note

That last question is second only to the rattlesnake supposition for getting P-Cs' anticipatory attention. During the first few seconds of their surprise, they realize they hadn't noticed any feeling there; but now that they think about it they see they can and do feel their left cheeks. Then I Add:

Me: See, until I asked you about it, you weren't noticing the feelings in your left cheek; but did that mean you didn't have any feelings there, or that you just weren't noticing your left cheek's real feelings?

P-C: Yeah—I wasn't noticing them.

Me: Okay, now if you want to compare that with no feelings, think about the last time you visited the dentist and received a local anesthetic that spread to the whole left side of your face. Then you really didn't have any feelings in your left cheek; but were you aware, or unaware that there were no feelings?

P-C: I was very much aware of it.

Me: Right. But you were aware of having no feelings there. The same thing is true of your emotions; there's a big difference between not noticing your emotions and not having emotions. Your neutral emotions are finely balanced states of emotions in which you don't notice any particularly positive or negative ones. But you are still having real emotional feelings. That's the state we physicians call physiologic homeostasis; it's the state of maximal productive function and where most healthy people spend most of their time. So don't confuse yourself by incorrectly thinking that the opposite of emotional misery is emotional happiness; it isn't—it's the absence of emotional misery. So any time you want to, we can start working at making you less miserable and less miserable until you don't feel any more misery than you want to feel. And I can assure you that you don't have to worry about happiness slipping up on you and grabbing you when you are not looking. That just can't happen. Now, wouldn't you like to feel a little less miserable than you are feeling now?

Author's Note

I've never had a P-C answer "no" to this question. But if one ever does, I'll calmly invite the P-C to show me how remaining as emotionally miserable as he or she seems to be will help the situation any better than it would be helped if they felt less miserable.

It's never facts or events that upset people emotionally. This fact is the backbone of RBT. RBT therapists make consistent therapeutic use of this fact by keeping their dialogues with P-Cs as factual as possible. That maneuver immediately gets P-Cs involuntarily moving toward less emotional misery, and less emotional misery, and ultimately into the neutral emotional state. In the neutral emotional state, P-Cs are maximally free to plan and pursue their most rational emotional and physical goals. So remember to emphasize this fact: Neutral emotions are real emotions, too.

THE NEUROPSYCHOPHYSIOLOGY OF RBT STRATEGY

Next is one of the most important therapeutic strategies in RBT. In therapy sessions, RBT therapists refuse to use, or reinforce, the common sloppy and often irrational thinking of everyday life. Instead, we insist on communicating in the most objectively factual terms possible.

Here are the two neuropsychophysiological reasons for that strategy: (1) Facts are neither good nor bad, upsetting or calming; it's beliefs and attitudes that make facts appear to be good, or bad, or upsetting or not upsetting. Therefore, when emotionally upset people concentrate objectively on facts (as opposed to their beliefs and attitudes), their left brains usually trigger most of the emotional responses. (2) Left brains favor relaxing or calming emotions (see table in Chapter 4).

Take for example frustrated parents who claim: "My kids are driving me crazy; I can't get them to do anything." I usually respond with, "Wouldn't it be more accurate to say that you are more upset than you want to be about your kids, and more often than you desire, your kids disobey you?" After they think objectively about it for a moment, they more calmly respond with, "Yes, that's exactly what I mean."

By getting parents to process those factual thoughts, their right brains respond with relatively neutral mental images; such images are least likely to trigger in the right brain inappropriate flight/fight reactions. That's why RBT therapists rarely use profanity in therapy sessions; they also get their P-Cs to translate their profanity into objectively factual terms. And RBT therapists neither use nor agree with emotionally charged but objectively meaningless adjectives such as *terrible* or *awful*.

Here's how you can handle P-Cs who claim that they can't stand something they obviously have been putting up with. Point out, "Since you haven't died or disappeared yet, you obviously can stand it. Granted, you stand it miserably; but you still stand it. And anything you can stand miserably, you can probably stand less miserably. So until you are able to change that admittedly undesirable situation, let's work at standing it less miserably. Okay?"

Please keep the above neuropsychophysiological facts and logic in mind as you read on. Otherwise, it may *appear* that the language-related therapeutic points made in this book are "just a matter of semantics." Hopefully though, Part Two of this book made these two facts clear: (1) *Where emotional and physical self-control is concerned it's never just semantics; it's always all semantics.* (2) *Thinking, in the form of self-talk, is probably the single most important factor in healthy, drug-free, emotional and physical self-control.* That's why RBT therapists insist that P-Cs make their semantics as healthy as possible.

The Memory Aids for this chapter are on page 221.

CHAPTER 8
From the Unlikely to the Here and Now

Trainees in RBT often ask, "Since the first rule for Rational Behavior Therapy is obvious fact, why use such an unlikely example to teach P-Cs their Emotional ABCs?"

That question means, "Could you have taught Mrs. Morrsey her Emotional ABCs by using the obvious facts in her depression?" Yes, I could have said, "When your drunk husband is beating you up, that's A, your perception. You are aware of that. Then at B, you evaluate that situation with sincere thoughts such as: 'I can't stand this. My life is a living hell. I'd be better off dead.' Right? Well, that's B, your thoughts. Now when normal people sincerely think ideas like that at B, they have to feel depressed at C; otherwise, their brains and bodies won't be interacting in a normal, healthy way."

But if I had done that, what most probably would have happened? Those painful memories probably would have triggered as much continuous crying in the last half of the session as they had already triggered in the first half. Crying, however, is usually more of a barrier than an aid to rapid therapeutic learning. In RBT the focus is on the most rapid therapeutic learning possible. That's why I didn't want Mrs. Morrsey to cry any more.

Instead of giving Mrs. Morrsey stimuli to cry, I wanted to teach her how to feel better emotionally in the fastest, yet safest way possible. That meant teaching her the Emotional ABCs as fast as possible. In my experience, P-Cs learn their Emotional ABCs fastest when the therapist uses unlikely yet dramatically instructive teaching examples that clearly show the direct relationships between their emotional As, Bs, and Cs. Those criteria make the rattlesnake supposition hard to beat.

Section I of this chapter shows you how to help depressed P-Cs apply the Emotional ABCs to their own situations; how to use the Five Rational Questions clinically; and how to introduce P-Cs to rational bibliotherapy. Section II of the chapter includes a discussion of the concepts of the emotional white lie and the misleading rhetorical question.

SPECIAL VOCABULARY—SECTION I

Emotional Self-Defense: any technique people use to control their emotions to their satisfaction.

Rational Bibliotherapy: use of emotional self-help articles and books that are based on RBT theory.

FOCUS ITEMS—SECTION I

1. How can you ensure that P-Cs transfer their emotional insights from the snake, or any other unrealistic supposition, to their personal problems?
2. What two ways did the pre-intake form help Mrs. Morrsey?
3. What are the three essentials for consistently successful bibliotherapy?
4. Why do Rational Behavior Therapists encourage P-Cs to look for points they disagree with in their bibliotherapeutic readings?
5. What is the therapeutic value of the Five Rational Questions?

CHAPTER **8**

From the Unlikely to the Here and Now

SECTION I

Some P-Cs won't automatically transfer their emotional insights from the rattlesnake supposition to their emotional problems. A few will be too distressed to see the analogy without help; a few others will think that because the snake example is so simple and unlikely, those ABCs couldn't possibly apply to their real, complex emotional problems. Fortunately, those P-Cs are both wrong and easy to correct. Just help them translate the ABCs of their rattlesnake fear to the ABCs of personal events in their everyday lives. At first, though, it's usually best to use events that are less emotionally charged than those of the P-C's presenting emotional problems.

I never can tell beforehand who will and who won't automatically transfer the ABCs of the snake example to their emotional problems. Also, preventing P-Cs from forming antitherapeutic conclusions is preferable to later correcting those conclusions. So, immediately after explaining the ABCs of the snake supposition, I routinely lead P-Cs through a transfer of their ABC insights to themselves. That maneuver prevents P-Cs from incorrectly thinking the ABCs don't apply to them.

AN IMPORTANT CLINICAL INSIGHT

There are no objectively trivial emotional problems.

Every time people get more upset than they want to be, that's a significant problem. I routinely confirm that fact while discussing the problem. But I also point out that undesirable emotional distress is usually a personal choice; so, it is avoidable. That's why psychotherapy can help distressed P-Cs help themselves in the fastest and safest way possible.

Next you'll see how the significance of Mrs. Morrsey's problem was confirmed without commiserating with her, or otherwise encouraging self-pity. Then you will see how she was helped to transfer her insights from the snake example to her emotional problem.

Me: Now, how does the rattlesnake example relate to you and your present situation? Very easily. In the first part of the session, you told me how badly your husband has been treating you; and I agree with you. That is a real undesirable life situation. I wouldn't wish that situation on anybody. But you mistakenly believe that because you have such a completely miserable life situation at A, you have to feel completely miserable about it at C. Fortunately, that's a mistake. You *don't* have to feel miserably depressed and want to kill yourself just because you're in a miserable situation. I'll bet the biggest part of your bad feelings is coming from the bad names you have been calling yourself at B. I'll bet you've been saying things like: "You're an idiot or stupid fool for getting into this situation."

P-C: Yes, I've done that, too.

Me: Right! Well, if you believe you're a stupid idiot and that stupid idiots deserve to die, or at least deserve to suffer, how are you going to feel?

P-C: Miserable.

Me: Right, and if you feel miserable enough, you end up wanting to kill yourself, right?

P-C: Yes, sir.

Me: But when the intake form got you to stop blinding yourself with mistaken ideas about having nothing to live for, you clearly saw that you have your daughter to live for; and that belief immediately made you feel better, right?

P-C: Yes, sir.

Me: Beautiful. Now do you see what you've just done? Without even realizing it, you have just applied the Emotional ABCs to your problems, and proved that your emotions work just like everyone else's emotions work. You improved your thinking, and your emotional feelings immediately improved; that's exactly the way healthy brains and bodies interact. Now, if you just keep on thinking in that improved way, you will go on feeling better and better, even though your situation with your husband doesn't improve at all.

Author's Note

That short exchange did two valuable things. First, it gave me a good chance to show Mrs. Morrsey that her emotions were not only understandable, but that they also work just like everybody else's emotions work. Most emotionally distressed people feel very reassured when they see evidence that their emotions work just like everybody else's. That knowledge helps them convince themselves they are not crazy.

Second, that exchange provided two excellent opportunities to help Mrs. Morrsey personalize her Emotional ABCs using highly meaningful events in her life. The first opportunity was to apply her Emotional ABCs to her insight that she could live for her daughter. The second opportunity was to show Mrs. Morrsey which rational changes in her Bs would cause therapeutic changes in her depression at C, even though her undesirable, though accurate, perceptions at A remained the same.

Me: Now the big insight I want you to get today is that you can't control your husband's drinking, or any of the other bad things he does. But what you can do is improve your feelings about yourself; and the first step in doing that is to stop calling yourself bad names that don't even apply to you, and that don't do anything for you, except make you feel bad. If you stop doing that, you will quickly start feeling better; and once you are feeling better emotionally, you will be able to think more clearly about the best way to stop your husband from abusing you. Do you see what I mean?

P-C: Yes, sir.

Me: Granted, you may have made some stupid mistakes; but that fact does not mean you are a stupid person. Making stupid mistakes is what I, you, and all sane, intelligent people do repeatedly. So, that can't be a good reason to get suicidally depressed. Okay, I see our time is up. We'll stop here and let you listen to the tape of this session. That repetition will help you fix your Emotional ABCs firmly in your mind. The better you remember them, the better you can use them to stop yourself from feeling so depressed. Okay?[1]

P-C: All right.

Author's Note

At the end of that half hour, Mrs. Morrsey looked noticeably less depressed than she looked at the beginning. But that fact did not mean she was over her depression. RBT works rapidly, but not instantly. No psychotherapy works instantly.

After people practice emotional responses for six months, these responses begin to come under the person's right-brain attitudinal control. Mrs. Morrsey had practiced her depression for six months; so it was partly under the control of her wordless, depressive attitudes.

Attitudinal control of a response indicates habit formation. That's why Mrs. Morrsey couldn't get rid of her depression in just one half-hour-long RBT session, or even two or three. Getting rid of emotional habits requires emotional reeducation. Granted, people can start their emotional reeducation instantly; but like all reeducational processes, emotional reeducation occurs gradually, in the five stages described in Chapters 4 and 13.

[1]Normally, intake sessions cover only historical data. Therefore, I don't usually have patient-clients listen to the audio recordings of their intake sessions. No, therapy tape recording and listening is *not* essential for rapidly effective RBT; but it usually helps. So, if P-Cs have tape recorders and can ensure that no one except them will listen to their tapes, I let P-Cs carry the tape of each session home for tape listening between sessions. But I record each new session over the previous session's tape; that keeps therapy tapes from accumulating.

How fast is "gradual"? In Rational Behavior Therapy, gradual can be as fast as three to five sessions. Normally, though, ten to thirty sessions is the usually expected range.

A COMMON QUESTION

What if Mrs. Morrsey had appeared more, rather than less, depressed at the end of her intake session? I still would have stopped the session after I had described her Emotional ABCs; then I would have had her listen to the part of the intake tape that dealt with the Emotional ABCs.[2] Immediately after that tape-listening session, I would have given her another half-hour session of RBT. But in that next session I would have helped her put the most distressing aspects of her situation into the A, B, C format. Finally, I would have used the Five Rational Questions to get her to see how her own inaccurate perceptions, or irrational beliefs, or both, were causing her emotional distress.

THE FIVE RATIONAL QUESTIONS

1. Is my thinking here factual?
2. Will my thinking here best help me protect my life and health?
3. Will my thinking here best help me achieve my short-term and long-term goals?
4. Will my thinking here best help me avoid my most undesirable conflicts with others?
5. Will my thinking here best help me feel the emotions I want to feel?

Three honest "no's" reveal unhealthy, irrational thinking that must be changed before unhealthy emotional feelings will change without drugs, or electric shock, or brain damage.

THERAPEUTIC VALUE OF THE FIVE RATIONAL QUESTIONS

I can't think of any objectively rational reasons for any nonpsychotic P-C to be suicidally depressed. Therefore, I am confident of being able to get most such P-Cs to see that their suicidal desires are irrational. I've never failed yet. But, being only an FHB (fallible human being), I'm sure I will fail some time in the future. When I do, I'll hospitalize that P-C.

---

[2]If the session had not been recorded, I would have had her do the bibliotherapeutic reading, described later in this chapter. If she had been illiterate, I would have had her just sit and rethink the session for a half hour. Then I would have continued as described above.

THE END OF RBT SESSIONS DOESN'T STOP THERAPEUTIC PROGRESS

Mrs. Morrsey was going to go back home after she had listened to the tape of her session. But home was where she had been physically and verbally abused and depressed for six months. The process of emotional conditioning ensured that just the thought of going home would be a powerful cue for her old, depressive feelings. Having her listen to the tape of her session, however, helped ensure that she thoroughly understood that she alone controlled how depressed she felt. Still, she (like all new P-Cs) would benefit from having an effective technique of emotional self-defense to get her through the night without drugs.

IMPORTANT THERAPEUTIC INSIGHT:

WHEN P-Cs KEEP THEIR MINDS FILLED WITH THOUGHTS BASED ON RATIONAL BIBLIOTHERAPY, THEY CAN'T BE MAKING THEMSELVES EMOTIONALLY MISERABLE.

Rational Bibliotherapy is the use of written, emotional self-help materials that are based on RBT theory. When therapists use this valuable technique systematically, their P-Cs will be reading helpful restatements of therapeutic insights that they will have discussed in their most recent RBT session. This review of insights makes Rational Bibliotherapy an excellent emotional self-defense against unhealthy, negative emotions between therapy sessions. For that reason (and the reason described next), I routinely use Rational Bibliotherapy with all literate P-Cs.

Rational Bibliotherapy is probably the simplest yet most effective way to get P-Cs actively involved in psychotherapy immediately. My research indicates consistently successful bibliotherapy has three essentials: (1) short, well-illustrated, pleasant examples of therapeutic concepts and techniques in action in everyday life events; (2) daily, specific goal-oriented reading instructions; and (3) consistent bibliotherapeutic follow-up at each therapy session.

Appendix B contains an example of the bibliotherapeutic material we use routinely at the RBT Center. Mrs. Morrsey was introduced to Rational Bibliotherapy in this way:

Me: Here's a little book entitled *You and Your Emotions*. I want you to take it home and read Chapter 1 at least twice before I see you tomorrow. Chapter 1 is also entitled "You and Your Emotions"; it uses lots of cartoon illustrations to show you exactly how your Emotional ABCs work in everyday life. Read it at bedtime, and in the morning as soon as you wake up. It's very short, so even if you are a slow reader, you can read it in twenty minutes or so. Now the first time you read the chapter, read just to understand it. But the second time you read it, look for things you disagree with, and things you don't think apply to you. Write all those points down, because they are the first things I will want to discuss with you tomorrow. Okay?[3]

P-C: All right.

Author's Note

The most common question here is "Wasn't telling her to look for things to disagree with just inviting therapeutic resistance?" No, not really. Having P-Cs look for things to disagree with only invites them to let you deal immediately with the natural therapeutic resistance almost all new P-Cs bring to psychotherapy.

In the minds of almost all new P-Cs, failure to be somewhat resistant to psychotherapy would be to admit they really need psychotherapy. But they irrationally fear that admitting they really need psychotherapy would mean they are crazy. So, as a magical form of self-protection against being crazy, some new P-Cs initially refuse to admit, even to themselves, that they really need psychotherapy.

That fact explains why virtually every new P-C comes to psychotherapy secretly, but anxiously hoping to learn they don't really need it. By instructing them to look for things to disagree with, therefore, you will quicky accomplish two important therapeutic goals:

First, you will virtually ensure that P-Cs read the bibliotherapeutic material thoroughly. If they weren't looking for something to disagree with, thorough reading would imply they expected to learn something really helpful. In their minds, however, finding something really helpful would mean they really need help, which could mean they are crazy. But that's the very finding they want to avoid. Those facts make new P-Cs anxious to find something in the reading to disagree with.

Second, you will get your P-Cs to talk freely about their resistance, without making an issue of it. That enables you to get P-Cs appropriately involved in therapy in the shortest time possible.

At this point, new trainees worry, "But what if they find something to disagree with and prematurely end therapy?" Answer: Some P-Cs may prematurely end therapy. But they won't do it because they have found a valid point of disagreement.

Genuinely rational bibliotherapeutic materials (see Appendix B) describe research-tested principles of normal human behaviors. In addition, those materials explain those principles with such typical, everyday-life examples that P-Cs can easily identify with them. That's why all the disagreements I've ever seen P-Cs have, have been due solely to their emotional and behavioral ignorance, or to their misinterpretations of their bibliotherapeutic readings or both.

This book provides you with all the knowledge you will need in order to be able to replace your P-Cs' ignorance and misinterpretations with useful, research-tested facts. After you confidently though compassionately correct your P-Cs, they will increase their faith in you. At the same time, your P-Cs will decrease both their

---

[3]Appendix B contains a copy of my article "The Professional's Guide for Using Rational Bibliotherapy" and a copy of the printed daily reading instructions I give to all P-Cs. You have my permission to reproduce those instructions at will for use in your therapy and counseling.

fear of psychotherapy and any therapeutic resistance they may have. Then rapid, smooth therapeutic progress results.

Granted, a rare P-C may continue to disagree in spite of your competent, factual explanations. But in my experience, such P-Cs are determined to find some reason—any reason—to drop out of therapy as soon as possible anyway. So, you have everything to gain and nothing to lose by inviting P-Cs to look for areas of disagreement in their bibliotherapeutic readings.

Next is an extremely helpful reading instruction for P-Cs in acute emotional distress, especially if they have been thinking of suicide.

Me: Also, anytime you start to feel like you are losing emotional control, immediately read the chapter again. If the reading doesn't immediately help you control yourself better, call me. Here is my card. Now, can I trust you to go home overnight?

P-C: Yes, sir.

Me: You're not going to go home and kill yourself are you?

P-C: *(Smiling)* No, you can trust me.

Author's Note

Always give your suicidally depressed P-Cs reliable, quick telephone coverage. But if you have them doing rational bibliotherapeutic reading, they only rarely will feel bad enough to call you.

The only time P-Cs have called me is when they have not done the suggested reading. At those rare times, I first determine that the P-Cs are no worse off emotionally than they were when I saw them earlier. Then I say, "Okay, I'll hang up now, and let you do your assigned reading. Then if you still want to talk, call me back, and we'll talk."

Almost never do I get a second call; I've never lost a P-C and I've always been able to handle that rare second call in fifteen minutes or less.

SECTION II

SPECIAL VOCABULARY—SECTION II

Lies: statements the speakers don't believe.

Misleading rhetorical question: a statement of a hidden personal belief or attitude in the form of a question. For example, an angry "Why in the devil did you do that?" hides the attitude (that is, the unspoken belief) "You shouldn't have done that."

Emotional white lie: an obviously incorrect statement that makes the speaker feel as if the lie were an obvious fact. For example, the Mouse Lady (in the Introduction) said, "I'm a gutless mouse." That idea was an obviously incorrect statement that made that intelligent, attractive woman feel as if it were an obvious, self-hate-worthy fact.

FOCUS ITEMS —SECTION II

1. What might have happened if Mrs. Morrsey had not been told the rest of the emotional story?
2. Is the RBT theory of how people learn both rational and irrational beliefs and attitudes reasonable to you?
3. What example will you use to teach your P-Cs how to convert their unspoken attitudes to their spoken belief forms?
4. What's a good way to avoid eliciting a crying response while helping P-Cs apply their Emotional ABCs to their daily life events?
5. What two reasons best explained Mrs. Morrsey's reluctance to talk insightfully about the hypothetical suicidal situation?
6. Why is the misleading rhetorical question an important concept?

Normally, I start my RBT sessions by reviewing what P-Cs have done to help themselves since the last session. I ask, "Did you listen to the tape recording of your last session? Tell me your reactions to listening to it." If the P-C didn't listen to it, I say, "Tell me how you talked yourself out of that simple way to help yourself." As they reply, I actively look for irrational thinking to correct, and for therapeutic insights that I can honestly reinforce the P-C for having made. Then I ask about their bibliotherapeutic readings and any written notes they may have made.[4] Mrs. Morrsey didn't have a tape recorder. So I began her second session by asking about her bibliotherapy.

MRS. MORRSEY'S SECOND RBT SESSION

Me: Did you do your emotional self-help reading?

P-C: Yes, sir.

Me: Great! Did you find anything that you don't agree with, or that you don't see how it can help you?

P-C: No, sir. I found a lot I can use to help myself.

Me: Good! Give me an example of what you learned.

P-C: Well, I used to think that when I get mad it's just that something made my temper flare up. But I understand now that it really doesn't have to happen.

Me: That's right! If you have a flare up in temper, you make it happen. It never does anything to you emotionally. You always do everything emotionally about it. That's why you always have a choice about your emotions.

Author's Note

The main therapeutic goal in the first RBT session was to teach Mrs. Morrsey her Emotional ABCs. That brief exchange showed me that she had not only learned her Emotional ABCs, she had begun to apply them to herself. That's the most reliable evidence that a P-C is cooperative.

But your cooperative P-Cs will be the ones who quickly discover the next potentially confusing fact. Their Emotional ABCs do not explain well all of their daily emotional experi-

[4]See "Your Daily Reading Instructions" in Appendix B.

ences. And remember, most P-Cs initially resist accepting responsibility for their negative emotions. Understandably, therefore, they immediately decide, "There must be more to my emotions than just ABC." And they are correct; that's why this is usually the first point of potentially significant therapeutic resistance with inadequately informed P-Cs. Fortunately, though, this potential therapeutic resistance can be easily prevented by telling your P-Cs the rest of the emotional story before they discover there is more of it to hear. Usually the best time to tell P-Cs the rest of the emotional story is as soon as they seem to understand their Emotional ABCs. That means as soon as your P-Cs can correctly explain to you the A, B, C model of new emotions. It's neither necessary nor recommended that you wait until P-Cs accept their Emotional ABCs. You will now see how I told Mrs. Morrsey the rest of the emotional story.

Me: Yesterday, when we were talking about emotions, I said that what you think and believe about what you perceive makes you feel the emotions you feel and do the things you do. But I'm sure that lots of times you get upset so fast, you don't have time to think anything. Right?

P-C: Right, that happens to me a lot and I just can't understand it, because most times I know I'd be better off if I just ignored things more and not get so mad.

Me: Right! Well, let's see if I can help you understand better what really happens when you get angry even though you know you'd be better off if you stayed calm. Look at it like this. All your life, what have you always thought every time you have ever seen or heard about snakes?

P-C: That they bite you; so you should stay out of their way, or kill them.

Me: Right! You have always thought in terms of how dangerous they are, and how bad it would be if they bite you. And when you thought those thoughts, you usually felt, or at least imagined how frightened you'd be if you suddenly came face to face with a snake. Right?

P-C: Right.

Me: Now, every time you have thought those fearful thoughts and felt even the slightest bit afraid, or even imagined how afraid you might feel, you were practicing the ABCs of being afraid of snakes. And because you have a normal brain, after you had practiced those ABCs enough times, your mind caused your brain to change your fearful self-talk ideas into your fearful attitudes about snakes.

And once normal people get fearful attitudes about something, they don't have to think any more at B before they feel afraid at C. All they have to do then, is just become aware of the thing at A, and BAM! They feel afraid, long before they could have thought anything at B. For example, what do you think you would do tonight, if while you're watching TV, your little girl were to slip up behind you and drop a big five-and-dime-store rubber snake in your lap? I'll bet you'd almost jump right out of your skin, without time to think anything, right?

Well, it wouldn't have been the snake that frightened you. You alone would have frightened you with your fearful attitude about snakes. And you know something else? You learned that fearful attitude the same way you learned the correct car-driving attitude—by simple, mental repetition, or mental practice.

Author's Note

Remember, an important theoretical assumption in RBT is that people learn their emotional beliefs, attitudes, and habits by using the same ABCs of behavior practice they use when they learned their behavorial beliefs, attitudes, and habits. Since Mrs. Morrsey knew how to drive, I spent about five minutes reviewing with her the ABCs of her driving practice, that resulted in her learning her correct car-driving beliefs and attitudes. That explanation was analogous to the explanation of the ABCs of learning to type, given in Chapter 4. (The typing example could have been used here instead of the car driving example; almost all P-Cs readily understand either example.)

After discussing correct car-driving attitudes, I switched back to the snake example. As is usually the case, Mrs. Morrsey easily understood both the spoken a-B, belief-controlled form of her driving, and her fear of snakes. Then to help her take the universally confusing, magical, HEs, SHEs, ITs, and THEYs out of her emotional understanding, I also showed her how to convert the unspoken, A-b, attitude-controlled forms of her driving and emotional reactions to their spoken, a-B, belief forms.

Me: Now, tell me, if you were to have time to think something before you jump tonight when your daughter drops that snake in your lap, which of your beliefs would make it still seem logical to jump up immediately?

P-C: That it might bite me.

Me: Right! "It might bite me, it might kill me." These are the unspoken, and therefore, unnoticed, superconscious, personal attitudes you, and most sane people, have about snakes suddenly appearing in their laps. And those would be the attitudes that would trigger your automatic fear reaction, before you realized it was a rubber snake. And if you didn't change those attitudes, you would either run, or try to kill the snake, or both. Now, let's apply those insights to your home situation.

Author's Note

Almost without exception, your P-Cs will thoroughly understand their attitudes about snakes and cars. But to make sure you get your therapeutic points across, always get your P-Cs to refocus on their emotional problems, before the session ends.

But what if you don't want to risk a crying response? Then use the indirect "as-if" maneuver demonstrated in the next excerpt.

Me: Suppose we were talking about my neighbor and I said, "You know, Mrs. Jones came home the other day and found her husband drunk as usual, and he beat her up again. But for the first time in her life, she tried to kill herself. And you know, she said that she just can't understand why she did it, because she had always thought of herself as being too afraid of dying to ever try to kill herself. But she said she did it without thinking."

Now by trying to kill herself, Mrs. Jones was acting as if she were thinking what? What attitudes do you think could have made her try to kill herself without taking time to think about why she was doing it?

P-C: That's hard to say. There isn't any of it that makes any sense.

Me: Oh, I disagree, it all makes sense. Granted, much of it is the sense of nonsense; but there is always logical sense in every voluntary action. But you may never see the sense in it, especially if you don't change your unspoken attitudes back to their spoken belief forms. Do you follow me?

P-C: I'm not sure.

Me: Well, do you think she might have thought, "Boy, I'm so happy, I feel like going out and buying myself a new dress?" Do you think she might have thought that?

P-C: (Laughing) No, I'm sure she wouldn't have thought that.

Me: All right, what do you think she might have thought that would have made it seem logical to her to kill herself? Do you think she might have thought that it was just great to be alive?

P-C: No, she wouldn't have believed that either.

Me: Well, if she wouldn't have believed those ideas, what do you think her beliefs might have been? Just use your imagination.

P-C: She might think, "What have I got to live for?"

Me: Okay, she might think: "What have I got to live for?" Anything else?

P-C: But you really don't stop and think about it.

Me: Right! That's a beautiful insight. You ask yourself the question: "What have I got to live for?" But do you answer that question?

P-C: No, at least I didn't.

Author's Note

Did you notice how reluctant Mrs. Morrsey was to talk insightfully about that hypothetical situation? Many inexperienced therapists would interpret that seeming reticence to be therapeutic resistance. But I thought her seeming reticence was really confusion, both about how to describe her attitude-triggered emotions and about how to discuss the emotional consequence of having posed, and left unanswered, the misleading rhetorical question, "What have I got to live for?"

Like most people, Mrs. Morrsey had never been questioned before about her misleading rhetorical questions. So she didn't quite know how to respond. To help you understand most clearly Mrs. Morrsey's confusion, let me first explain the RBT view of the nature of rhetorical questions versus real questions.

Real qeustions are sincere requests for information; that's why, even if the answer is, "I don't know," people almost always answer real questions.

A rhetorical question is not a real question; instead, a rhetorical question is the camouflaged statement of a personal belief in the form of a question. It is a dramatic, oratorical device that lets speakers subtly restate a personal belief, to give it added emphasis and emotional impact.

A rhetorical question is misleading when it triggers a different emotional response from the response that the most objective answer to the question would trigger. For example, an impassioned patriot might ask, "Should we stand and fight like fearless men, prepared to die if need be, so that our beloved Mother Country might live; or, should we turn and run with our tails between our legs like frightened dogs?"

That seemingly sincere request for information is really a camouflaged, emotion-charged statement of this belief: "We should stand and fight like fearless men." The important insight here is this. The beliefs that are hidden in unanswered rhetorical questions trigger specific reactions in the speakers as well as in the listeners. But those reactions are usually different from the reactions that the objective answers to the rhetorical questions would trigger. That's why it is so therapeutic to get P-Cs to answer every question they pose to themselves. Even if the answer is: "I don't know," I still try to get my P-Cs to say it.

To see the immense emotional value of that emotional self-help maneuver, let's imagine what would be the most objective answer to our patriot's question, "Should we stand and fight like fearless men?" The most objective answer to that question would be: "I don't know if we should or not. It depends on how much each of us values his life versus his country's freedom. So let's each do our own individual analysis, and decide for ourselves individually what we should do." The calm emotions that objective answer would trigger would be quite different from the intense emotions that the patriot's unanswered rhetorical questions most probably would trigger.

Clinically, one of the most common misleading rhetorical questions P-Cs distress themselves with is "How could I, he, she, or they, have done such a stupid thing?" The hidden belief usually is "I, he, she, or they shouldn't have done such a stupid thing." That belief triggers anger and undesirable mental images of self and others. But let's see what would happen if people were to answer that question objectively.

Probably the most objective answer to "How could I have . . . ?" is "Easily. I did it so easily I didn't even realize I had done it until after I did it." That objective answer usually makes it difficult for people to get undesirably angry at themselves or at any other error-making FHBs (fallible human beings) about their objectively stupid acts.

Usually, though, speakers don't bother to answer their rhetorical questions. That's logical; rhetorical questions are not really questions—they're really statements of personal belief hidden behind question marks. And beliefs don't trigger answers; they only trigger the most logical emotional and physical reactions to themselves. Now let's rejoin Mrs. Morrsey.

Me: Right! You didn't answer your question because it wasn't really a question. It was what we call a misleading rhetorical question. In other words, it was a fake or pseudo-question hiding a strong, but unspoken belief. I think the belief hidden in your rhetorical question was "I've got nothing to live for." And that belief triggered emotional feelings and physical actions that were real, logical, and correct for a person who really didn't have anything to live for. But was it a fact that you had nothing to live for?

P-C: No, sir. I have my little girl to live for. But I didn't see that then.

Me: Right! That's why you need to answer all of your questions. Because if you don't answer them, they may make you feel and react as if obvious lies are really obvious facts. We call those kinds of lies *emotional white lies.* They can cause you a lot of emotional trouble.

The Memory Aids for this Chapter are on page 222.

CHAPTER **9**

**Therapeutic
Interactions in RBT**

At this point in RBT training seminars, someone usually points out, ''You haven't said anything about the therapeutic relationship in RBT; why not?'' My research on the therapeutic relationship in RBT (Maultsby 1975) indicated an interesting fact. There is good reason to doubt there is an objective thing in RBT that can be reliably recognized as a specific ''therapeutic relationship.'' Instead, it seems more logical to talk about therapeutic interactions; that means interactions between therapists and P-Cs that help P-Cs help themselves.

That research finding led me to conclude that consistent therapeutic interactions in RBT have three essential features: (1) efficient teaching of effective self-help concepts and techniques to P-Cs; (2) a friendly competent therapist; and (3) a cooperative P-C.

SPECIAL VOCABULARY

Sign: something that represents something else.
Symbol: a sign that's understood.
Thinking: the mental processing of symbols. For humans, words are the most common symbols used in conscious thought.

FOCUS ITEMS

1. What are the two basic ways people can try to do things?
2. Is it appropriate for people to try to control their emotions by refusing to think?
3. What influences do people's words have on their thoughts and emotional feelings?
4. What about self-distraction as a self-help maneuver?
5. Is it risky to switch therapists when treating suicidal depression with RBT?
6. Why could Dr. W. confidently assign Mrs. Morrsey to read Chapter 2 in *You and Your Emotions?*

CHAPTER 9

Therapeutic Interactions in RBT

I was unavailable for Mrs. Morrsey's third session. My assistant, Dr. W., conducted the session for me. When colleagues use RBT, their P-Cs can readily adjust to new therapists and continue their therapeutic progress. That valuable feature of RBT makes it an ideal technique for clinics or group practices where therapists frequently change, or where other events sometimes require therapists to have sessions with P-Cs they don't usually treat. That feature also indicates the "therapeutic interactions" in RBT are both ideally flexible, yet therapeutically stable.

MRS. MORRSEY'S THIRD RBT SESSION

Dr. W. began the session by briefly summarizing my notes on the first two sessions. That showed Mrs. Morrsey that Dr. W. knew about her case and was ready to pick up where I had left off. When Dr. W. asked, "How have you been doing?" Mrs. Morrsey said, "Better, I guess. I'm trying not to depress myself as much. I don't want to get like I was last week."

Mrs. Morrsey's responses revealed these two important points: First, she now saw that she had created her own depression. Second, she was trying to use her new knowledge to help herself.

In RBT, we recognize two basic kinds of trying: rationally trying and irrationally trying. Rationally trying is the only kind that's worthwhile. Unfortunately, though, new P-Cs often act as if they believe any old trial at self-help should do just fine. That fact brings me to an important clinical rule in RBT.

114

NEVER ACCEPT WITHOUT QUESTION P-Cs' REPORTS OF THERAPEUTIC SUCCESS OR FAILURE. ALWAYS ASK P-Cs TO TELL YOU EXACTLY WHAT THEY DID.

Why ask for the details of reported therapeutic success? Because accidentally, P-Cs sometimes get positive results from irrational self-help efforts. Always point out and correct irrational self-help efforts—they are never consistently helpful; in addition, their positive results often turn into negative results. Then P-Cs get confused and discouraged and want to blame RBT for their negative results, rather than blaming their irrational self-help efforts.

Equally carefully, examine every report of therapeutic failure; each will give you golden opportunities to remind your P-Cs of these two important points: (1) RBT works only when P-Cs use it *correctly*. (2) People receiving psychotherapy (or any other treatment) always get the therapeutic results that are logical and correct for what they actually do.

You will be amazed at how many highly intelligent people act as if they don't know that second fact. On the other hand, I have never had a P-C report therapeutic failure who also described the correct use of the appropriate, rational self-help concept or technique. I don't believe you will have any such P-Cs either.

At this point, the most common question is, "But what if a P-C uses the appropriate rational self-help maneuvers correctly and still doesn't improve?" I've never seen or heard of such a P-C. But if I were to discover one, I would immediately reassess the accuracy of my diagnosis. As I pointed out earlier, RBT is not appropriate for all emotionally distressed people. That's why accurate intake evaluation is so important.

A COMMON IRRATIONAL ATTEMPT AT SELF-HELP

Mrs. Morrsey's tentative "Better, I guess. I'm trying not to depress myself as much" didn't tell Dr. W. much about the type of self-help trials she had been making. So he asked her: "How do you try not to depress yourself?" She said, "I try to keep doing things like working or talking to my little girl, instead of thinking."

On the surface, Mrs. Morrsey's idea about not thinking made logical sense. The Emotional ABCs clearly show that if people don't think depressive thoughts, they don't usually feel depressed. That's why trying to stop thinking is a common, but irrational attempt at self-help.

It's almost impossible, however, to remain alert and not think. People's brains must maintain a certain level of noticeable cognitive activity; otherwise, they fall asleep. So, if people choose to stay awake, they almost certainly must think. They can only choose *what they think and how they think about it.*

A few of your P-Cs will try to stop thinking altogether; but because that's an impossible feat, they will fail and get upset about their failure. So, advise them, "Don't try to stop thinking; just make sure that what you think is rational."

Other P-Cs will mislabel self-distraction as trying not to think. That irrational habit is also a common cause of therapeutic problems. And here are the reasons why.

HARMLESS AND HARMFUL SELF-DISTRACTIONS

There are essentially two kinds of self-distractions: (1) those due to insufficient personal interest in the current topic of thought; and (2) self-distractions motivated by fear. Self-distractions due to insufficient personal interest usually are emotionally harmless. But the powerful, negative-reinforcing mechanisms that maintain fear-motivated self-distractions usually convert those self-distracting maneuvers into anxiety-laden, compulsive, magical rituals. That's why fear-motivated self-distractions often harm people more than they help them.

Dr. W. wanted to help Mrs. Morrsey protect herself from that fate. So he reinforced her for her self-help efforts; then he pointed out:

T[1]:   But when you are working, or talking with your little girl, you're thinking, aren't you?
P-C: Yes, but those things don't depress you.
T: Right! Those thoughts aren't associated with depression.

Author's Note

Things never upset people; people always upset themselves about things. *The Emotional ABCs make this fact obvious. When to start systematically pointing that out to your P-Cs, however, is a matter of clinical judgment. I usually start by the third session. Until then, though, I do as Dr. W. did, which is to consistently use rationally accurate therapeutic formulations.*

For example, Mrs. Morrsey said, "Yes, but those things don't depress you." That statement showed she had not yet integrated the A, B, C model of emotions into her usual way of thinking. Such integration rarely occurs instantly or automatically; the life-long belief in the magical IT, HE, SHE, and THEY is just too strong to permit that. But after the second or third session, when P-Cs say, "It upsets me," I routinely start responding with statements such as, "I think it's you who upset you about it; and fortunately, you don't have to do that."

But until I'm sure P-Cs understand their Emotional ABCs, I simply restate their irrational ideas rationally as Dr. W. did by saying, "Right! Those thoughts aren't associated with depression." Thereby, Dr. W. gave Mrs. Morrsey the rational view and avoided engaging in a silent agreement with her irrational perception.

In the exchange that followed, Mrs. Morrsey described an episode of depression she had handled with self-distraction the morning before. She had gotten up to fix breakfast. She then started thinking about her oldest son and began to cry. To get in better control of her emotions, she woke up her children and talked with them.

---

[1]T stands for the substitute therapist.

Dr. W. used that event to give Mrs. Morrsey detailed, useful insight into (1) how she had created that depressive episode; and (2) how she had eliminated it. During his explanation, Dr. W. took the second step in teaching people how to eliminate undesirable emotions as fast as possible. He introduced Mrs. Morrsey to the Five Rules for Rational Thinking.

T: It was great that you remembered your Emotional ABCs and realized that you didn't have to keep on depressing yourself. But in the future, instead of distracting yourself by waking people up to talk to you, a better way to keep from depressing yourself is to check your thinking to see if it is based on obvious facts, and if it will help you protect your life or health, and if it will help you avoid conflicts with others, and if it will help you achieve your goal of not being depressed; and if it makes you feel the way you want to feel. If your thinking doesn't do those things, then change it to rational thinking. Rational thinking is based on obvious fact; and it *will* help you protect your life and health; and it *will* help you avoid the conflict of waking people up; and it *will still* help you achieve your goal of feeling less depressed immediately. To see how easy it is to recognize irrational thinking, let's check the thoughts that caused your depression yesterday morning. What thoughts were you thinking?

P-C: I got to thinking that my son wasn't ever going to want to come to see me anymore, because I acted so crazy last weekend.

T: Okay, now is that thought based on any kind of facts? Did he say that? Has he ever missed coming to see you before? If he cared that little about you, would he have insisted on bringing you to the hospital?

P-C: No, and he has called me every day to see how I am.

T: So your thinking disobeyed rational rules number one, two and five. It wasn't based on fact; it depressed you, and that could lead you to suicide; and it certainly made you feel more miserable than you wanted to feel, right?

P-C: It sure did. That's why I stopped it by getting the kids up.

T: That was good; but the Five Rules for Rational Thinking will let you stop such irrational depressions even faster and better just by checking and improving your thinking.

P-C: Yes, I see what you mean; because what if I'm by myself?

T: That's right; what if you don't have anyone to wake up? You'd be up a tree! But you always have your brain with you, right? So, you can always stop and think a little better, right?

P-C: Yes, sir, I think I can now.

Author's Note

Merely reciting the Five Rules for Rational Thinking does not ensure that P-Cs will remember and apply them in their daily lives. That's why Dr. W. carried Mrs. Morrsey through a step-by-step application of the Five Rules to as many other everyday events as time permitted.

At the end of that session, Dr. W. assigned Mrs. Morrsey to read Chapter 2 ("This is Rational Thinking") in You and Your Emotions *(Maultsby and Hendricks, 1974). He could do that confidently because standard RBT routine normally includes teaching P-Cs the Five Rules for Rational Thinking between the third and sixth sessions.*

A COMMON ERROR NEW P-Cs MAKE

New P-Cs often confuse the common concept of positive thinking with rational thinking. To help Mrs. Morrsey avoid that therapeutic trap, Dr. W. used humorous but instructive everyday events to show her clearly the important difference between positive and rational thinking.

In saying "common concept of positive thinking," I mean the popular *misinterpretation* of the Reverend Norman V. Peale's idea. Dr. Peale has a *rational* concept of positive thinking. But popular misinterpretation of his concept is, "Whether or not the person believes the idea, any old positive thought should produce a miracle." Of course, that doesn't happen. And that's why so many people often distrust any idea that seems similar to positive thinking. But the following two differences make it easy to separate the common concept of positive thinking from rational thinking.

First, rational thinking is factual and objectively probable. It can be positive—that is, sound good, but it doesn't have to. That's because rational thinking recognizes that some situations just don't deserve a positive thought.

On the other hand, the common concept of positive thinking is, "It doesn't have to be factual or objectively probable; it just has to sound good and that makes it a good way to think."

The second main difference between rational thinking and misconstrued positive thinking is this: Rational thinking is the most mentally and emotionally healthy way to think. Therefore, rational thinking makes people feel better emotionally because it maintains, as well as improves, their mental and emotional health.

On the other hand, the common concept of positive thinking has no built-in safeguards for emotional health. So, although positive thinking may be emotionally healthy, it doesn't have to be. Therefore, rational thinking gives people all the advantages and benefits of positive thinking plus the safeguards for emotional health that unqualified positive thinking doesn't have.

MRS. MORRSEY'S FOURTH RBT SESSION

Now let's see how P-Cs usually react to having a different therapist.

Me: Well, Mrs. Morrsey, it's been exactly a week since I first saw you, and, as I recall, you spent a good fifteen minutes of that first session crying. But today you look remarkably different. Do you feel any different?

P-C: Yes, sir. I feel completely different.

Me: Let's see, you've had three therapy sessions; two with me and one with Dr. W. Tell me, does it make any difference to you that you see me sometimes and Dr. W. other times?

P-C: No, sir.

Me: Do you learn from him as well as from me, and vice versa?

P-C: Yes, sir.

Me: Well, good! That's what we expected would happen. Tell me, how are you different now, compared to when you came in a week ago?

P-C: Most of my feelings now are good feelings, and before, everything looked bad. But I'm thinking different now and I have different feelings at home; and everything is different.

Author's Note

We shall cover more of this session in the next chapter.
The Memory Aids for this chapter are on page 223.

CHAPTER **10**
The Remainder of Mrs. Morrsey's Therapy

Here's another common observation new trainees make: "In RBT the therapists seem to talk a lot." That's really a polite way of saying, "I believe RBT therapists talk too much." But of course, we RBT therapists disagree. We believe we talk just enough—just enough, that is, to give emotionally distressed people the greatest therapeutic help in the shortest possible time.

But what is the reality? Obviously, no one can say for sure. How much or little it's best for therapists to talk is a matter of clinical judgment. Still, RBT therapists believe good clinical judgments are almost never completely arbitrary.

The rational rule is this: Say everything that could be immediately helpful to your P-Cs. Then check yourself objectively. Ask your P-Cs to explain the therapeutic insights you have just covered. Their explanations either will reveal useful understanding or they won't; if they do, you've talked enough. But if your P-C's explanations don't reveal useful understanding, you need to talk some more; if you don't, your P-C won't be able to apply your therapeutic insight correctly. Then therapeutic progress will decrease, or it may even stop.

Among the fears therapists have, fear of saying something P-Cs don't want to hear is second only to fear of being accused of talking "too much." That's why I remind new RBT therapists that RBT is as scientific as surgery. Therefore, there is no reason to abandon valid therapeutic insights just because P-Cs don't like them or don't want to admit they exist. "Would you," I ask, "want a surgeon to abandon the diagnosis of appendicitis, just because you didn't like the idea of having surgery? Would you expect, or even want, the surgeon to say, 'Okay, what if we try constipation?' "

Insights based on RBT theory are as immediately useful clinically as surgical diagnoses. So here's what I recommend when P-Cs say: "I don't like to think that," or "I can't or won't accept that explanation." Simply admit the obvious. Say, "Of course, I could be wrong; so let's see how you explain your self-defeating behavior."

Your P-Cs either will or won't be able to give you a clinically valid explanation of their undesirable behaviors. If they can give you a clinically valid explanation, then immediately put it to therapeutic use. But if your P-Cs can't give you a clinically valid explanation, invite them to show you the advantage of clinging to their useless contrary beliefs, instead of giving a therapeutic trial to your insights. Invariably, your P-Cs will fail on this point; then they usually will cooperate.

But what if they don't give up? Suppose the P-C says, "I know you're probably right. But I just can't accept it." That rarely happens; but when it does, I simply remind myself that RBT theory is as scientifically valid as surgical theory. Then I calmly use the P-C's case history to illustrate two or three examples of RBT insights in action in their daily lives. I then predict that those situations will not change until the P-Cs are willing to change their thinking. "But," I always add, "there's no rush; you haven't died from those problems yet. So chances are they are not fatal. I can wait until you decide to deal with them rationally. In the meantime, let's consider a situation you are willing to work on rationally right now."

I haven't given up on my original point, however. I routinely tape record my sessions for later P-C listening. If my insights are valid, I expect nonpsychotic P-Cs to see that fact when they later listen to the recording of the session. In addition, they will also see how useless, if not absurd, their alternative opinions are. That's the main reason I invite my P-Cs to see if they can think of more plausible explanations or solutions than the RBT ones, for the self-defeating behaviors in their personal problems.

SPECIAL VOCABULARY

Useful understanding: the ability to explain how to use an idea to solve problems in everyday life, even if the problems don't exist now.

FOCUS ITEMS

1. What is a good way to introduce P-Cs to Rational Self-Analyses (RSAs)?
2. Why is it especially important to reinforce depressed P-Cs for their drug-free, self-help efforts?
3. What are the three most common possibilities when P-Cs seem to show rapid therapeutic progress?
4. What are three reliable signs indicating P-Cs are ready for discharge?
5. What is the main reason nonpsychotic people willingly suffer undesirable emotions?
6. What was objective evidence that Mrs. Morrsey had optimal emotional health at her nine-month follow-up sessions?

The Remainder of Mrs. Morrsey's Therapy

MRS. MORRSEY'S FOURTH RBT SESSION (Continued)

From reviewing Dr. W.'s notes, I knew that he had handled Mrs. Morrsey's self-distraction by teaching her the Five Rules for Rational Thinking. That was fine; but Dr. W. did not have time to cover the issue of self-distraction. Early in Mrs. Morrsey's fourth session, therefore, I explained to her the important difference between rational and irrational self-distractions. Then I checked on whether or not I had talked enough:

Me: Do you think you have the difference clear in your mind?
P-C: I think so.
Me: Okay, give me an example of a rational versus an irrational self-destruction.

Author's Note

Mrs. Morrsey's explanation revealed only partial understanding. So I described a hypothetical, but realistic work situation in which I irrationally distracted myself from depressive thoughts. Then I asked, "What probably would have happened when I stopped distracting myself?" She said, "You'd get depressed again." I said, "Right." Then I described another hypothetical work situation in which I rationally distracted myself and asked her:

Me: What do you think would probably happen when I stopped distracting myself?
P-C: You wouldn't get depressed.

Me: Right! Now do you see the difference?

P-C: Yes, When you rationally distract yourself, it really doesn't matter to you if you keep on thinking about it or not.

Me: Right, very good. Now for your next reading assignment, I'll want you to read Chapter 3 in *You and Your Emotions*. It describes the ABCs of Rational Self-Analysis. Like always, I want you to read it once a day, every day, until I see you again. In addition, I want you to write a self-analysis of that depressive episode you talked about with Dr. W.

P-C: All right.

Me: So unless you have something more important you want to talk about now, I'd like to spend the rest of this session talking about how to do written Rational Self-Analysis. Okay?

P-C: Fine.

Author's Note

The remainder of session four was spent in telling Mrs. Morrsey about written Rational Self-Analysis (RSA). As usual, I began by asking her not to worry about how her writing looks, or her grammar, or her spelling. I emphasized that I was not going to read her RSAs. She was going to read them to me.

Remember to emphasize those important facts to your P-Cs. Otherwise, many of them will resist doing RSAs, purely out of fear of possible embarrassment about things such as illegible writing, poor spelling, and nonstandard grammar. So, emphasize that their RSAs are for their eyes only.

Next, I debunked the common, but incorrect idea that self-analysis is hard to do. I pointed out that every personal belief people have about themselves is a type of self-analysis. Next, I got her to clearly see that her main problem had been her making too many irrationally depressive self-analyses for her own good. Then I told her the good news.

So far as I could tell, she still had at least as much brain power as she had when she depressed herself; that was all the brain power she needed to stop depressing herself. I also complimented her for the drug-free, therapeutic use of her brain power that she had already made.

Next you will find excerpts from Mrs. Morrsey's fifth and final RBT session, two weeks after her first session.

MRS. MORRSEY'S FIFTH RBT SESSION

As usual, the session began with a request that Mrs. Morrsey describe her continued self-help efforts and therapeutic progress. I can't emphasize too much the importance of that simple, yet highly therapeutic maneuver. It's the best way to help P-Cs, especially depressed P-Cs, stay appropriately motivated for self-help.

When depressed people think about their problems, they tend to be irrationally perfectionistic. If they are not completely *un*depressed, in their minds, they are still completely depressed; therefore they conclude they haven't made any progress. That unrealistic idea blinds them to obvious, though gradual, therapeutic progress. Without regular, objective, positive feedback from significant others and, *most im-*

portant, from themselves, depressed P-Cs can easily talk themselves into giving up their self-help efforts. Then they ask for drugs or to be left alone in suicidal peace.

Fortunately, Mrs. Morrsey did not present any of those therapeutic problems. So let's rejoin her in her final RBT session.

Me: Well, Mrs. Morrsey this is your fifth therapy session. You've had three with me and one with Dr. W. Now when I first saw you thirteen days ago, you had tried to kill yourself twice over that past weekend. What do you think about living now?

P-C: I see I've got a lot to live for now.

Me: That's great! But tell me, these thoughts you had when you got depressed, were they really valid, rational ways to think or not?

P-C: No, not when you stop and really think, you see they're not.

ESTIMATING THERAPEUTIC PROGRESS

That response indicated one of three possibilities. First, maybe Mrs. Morrsey had learned it wasn't rational to be depressing herself, even though her marriage was objectively undesirable. Because of that insight, she had stopped depressing herself. If that were the case, then she was well down the road toward healthy freedom from emotional slavery to her husband. Therefore, she was ready for discharge.

The second possibility was that maybe Mrs. Morrsey's answer reflected a temporary flight into health. Therefore, if I discharged her then, she would quickly revert to depression, and possibly suicide.

The third possibility was that maybe Mrs. Morrsey was so grateful for my obvious interest in her that she was just trying to reward and please me by saying what she thought I wanted to hear, even though she was just as suicidally depressed as ever. If so, and I discharged her, she would see the discharge as an unfair, personal rejection. Later, she might attempt suicide, both out of rage at me for abandoning her and out of rage at herself for having trusted me.

If the first possibility were probable, then immediate discharge from therapy was most appropriate. But if either of the other possibilities were probable, she needed more therapy. So the important question then was, How best to decide which possibility was the most probable?

OBVIOUS FACT

All things rational usually start with obvious facts. It was a fact that Mrs. Morrsey certainly looked undepressed and happy. Also in favor of an ideal therapeutic response, and therefore discharge, was her indefatigable yet thoroughly appropriate therapeutic cooperation to date. She could not have cooperated more appropriately if she had been a paid actress.

But the reality still remained: ''All that glitters is not psychotherapeutic gold.'' So, with cases like this, the recommended practice is to focus on time-honored basic principles. The one I use most at this point in therapy is

WHEN IN DOUBT, RECHECK WITH YOUR PATIENT-CLIENTS

Patient-clients are the only legitimate experts on themselves. Adequately treated P-Cs either will or they will not have internalized the basic principles of rational emotional control you will have tried to teach them. If they have internalized those principles they will demonstrate it in the following three reliable ways.

1. They will look emotionally healthy. Mrs. Morrsey certainly deserved an A-plus for looking emotionally healthy.
2. They will describe objective, behavioral evidence of healthy self-control.
3. They will have a realistic plan for coping to their satisfaction with their lives in the future.

I hadn't yet had time to check Mrs. Morrsey for the second and third signs of readiness for discharge. So I used the remaining twenty-eight minutes of her fifth session to probe for behavioral evidence of healthy self-control and a realistic plan for rationally coping to her satisfaction with her life in the future. Next is one of many such therapeutic probes.

Me: Suppose you go home tonight and your husband is drunk and he has torn up the house; how are you going to keep yourself from being depressed?
P-C: His drinking? I just don't let it bother me anymore.
Me: Oh? How do you keep from being bothered?
P-C: (She pointed to her head.) I don't get it up here.
Me: Did you realize you had that choice before you came to see us?
P-C: No, sir, I didn't. I just thought my life was one way and that was it.

Author's Note

Mrs. Morrsey described there the main reason most normal people willingly suffer undesirable emotions: They believe they don't have any other emotional choices. Learning the Emotional ABCs corrects that incorrect belief immediately. That's the main reason teaching people their Emotional ABCs is so rapidly helpful. The Emotional ABCs show emotionally distressed people their six other emotional and behavioral choices: (1 & 2) People can calmly or even happily accept the obvious facts of their situation and ignore them; (3 and 4) People can calmly, or even happily, do what they can to improve their present situation; (5 and 6) People can calmly, or even happily, get out of their present situation. [1]

Me: Are you still going to sit passively and let your husband beat you up and break your ribs and so forth?

---

[1]Except for problems with procrastination and irrational fears about personally desirable acts, people seldom are interested in learning to be happy about the things they currently feel miserable about. But they still have that emotional choice.

P-C: No, sir! Not any more, I'm not. I've just told him, the next time he comes home drunk, I am going to take the kids and leave until I think he's sobered up.

Author's Note

During one of several probes of Mrs. Morrsey's apparent therapeutic progress, she told me how she had already used her new knowledge of rational self-control to help her teenage son handle a recent romantic crisis. Such voluntary disclosures are quite reliable evidence of ideal therapeutic progress. Then, near the end of this session she said:

P-C: Just like yesterday, he [her husband] went out and bought a half pint. I know he wanted me to say something, but I didn't; I just walked on out and took the car to the car-wash. When I got back, he was okay, and he hadn't even drunk half of it.

Me: How did you feel about that?

P-C: (*With a big smile*) I felt pretty good about it; I didn't fuss like I know he wanted me to, and the house was peaceful for a change.

Author's Note

During each probe of her apparent therapeutic progress, I pointed out to Mrs. Morrsey the various elements of her Emotional ABCs and the Five Rules for Rational Thinking that her responses had revealed. Since all her responses favored discharge, I discharged her at the end of this session.

The videotapes of Mrs. Morrsey's therapy sessions quickly became one of the most popular series of video teaching tapes the RBT Center distributes. And almost immediately, people began to ask for follow-up data on Mrs. Morrsey. Next are excerpts from her nine-month follow-up.

MRS. MORRSEY'S NINE-MONTH FOLLOW-UP

Me: Well, Mrs. Morrsey, it's nice to see you again. You're looking well. Are you feeling as well as you look?

P-C: Yes, sir.

Me: Well good, so bring me up to date; what's happened since I last saw you? Have you been depressed?

P-C: No, sir.

Me: Are you and your husband still together?

P-C: No, sir.

Me: Oh, when did that come about?

P-C: It'll be a week tomorrow.

Me: A week tomorrow. Now as I recall, when you stopped depressing yourself, he stopped drinking so much, right?

P-C: Yes, sir, for a little while. But he just decided he wanted to go back to drinking. He got him a good job, but last Sunday he got fired from his job for drinking.

Me: Uh huh. Well, when he went back to drinking, did he go back to his old, ah . . .

P-C: (*Smiling*) Mean habits?

Me: Yes, did you just passively let him beat you up and get depressed again?

P-C: No, we didn't have any more of that. I just ignored him.

Me: Oh? How did you keep him from beating you?

P-C: I just took the kids and we'd leave until he sobered up.

Me: Oh, that's right; that was your plan. So you followed through on it.

P-C: I sure did.

Me: I see, so you didn't get upset about his drinking this time. Okay, so how do you feel about his leaving?

P-C: I feel just fine about it. It's for the best.

Me: I see, but what if he decides he wants to come back?

P-C: No, it wouldn't work.

Me: Well, it seems you've learned that you are all you have and you are all you need to be happy.

P-C: That's right.

Author's Note

Mrs. Morrsey happily reported that her children were all doing well. Then she proudly described how she had recently insisted that her second adult son move out of her house and into his own apartment. He had been ignoring her rule against having his girlfriend sleep over with him. So Mrs. Morrsey decided he was "old enough to be on his own." She proudly pointed out that this son respected her much more after she put him on his own than he did before.

Me: And how are things with your youngest boy and your little girl?

P-C: There's no problem with him, and my little girl is fine; she likes school and everything.

Me: That's good; so how are things at work?

P-C: Just fine. I enjoy my work.

Me: Well, it seems to me that you have your life pretty much under satisfactory as well as rational control. So how would you describe yourself now?

P-C: (*Smiling*) I don't know. All you can say is I'm happy now.

Author's Note

Mrs. Morrsey also reported having helped a female coworker through a brief romantic disappointment. That woman had told Mrs. Morrsey she was thinking about killing herself, if she and her old boyfriend didn't get back together.

Former RBT patient-clients commonly report being able to help friends through minor daily conflicts. Such reports indicate that RBT not only helps people help themselves; it also helps them have healthy influences on their emotionally distressed friends. So it really does pay to have rational friends.

10-1   It Pays to Have Rational Friends

THE MOST IMPORTANT FOLLOW-UP REPORT

For me, the most important follow-up report Mrs. Morrsey made was this. Even though her husband returned to abusing alcohol, and she and he later separated, she didn't depress herself again. In fact, during the prior nine months, the only time she had missed any time from work, or had taken any medicine (aspirin) had been when she had the flu. And her three-year follow-up was equally positive.

TRADITIONAL VERSUS RATIONAL VIEW OF THERAPEUTIC OUTCOME

Traditional psychotherapists talk a lot about ''superficial'' versus ''deep'' therapeutic change. To me, such talk is interesting but nonoperational and, therefore, meaningless. For me, it's much more useful to talk about helping people achieve optimal emotional health.

THE RATIONAL VIEW OF OPTIMAL EMOTIONAL HEALTH

Optimal emotional health is fairly objective and easy to describe objectively; it exists when people are living their lives in personally satisfying, socially accepted ways in all their life's areas. According to those criteria, Mrs. Morrsey certainly gave ample evidence that RBT had helped her achieve optimal emotional health. And she achieved it with only five half-hour sessions of RBT over a two-week period of time.

With traditional psychotherapy, it often takes longer than two weeks just to establish the so-called therapeutic relationship. In addition, it takes at least that long for most popular antidepressant drugs to begin to have an effect. And in the relatively few nonpsychotic cases where antidepressants seem definitely effective, the experts recommend six to eight months of maintenance drug therapy (Weissman 1979). Those facts make it important to remember: *The rationally used, healthy, undrugged brain is the fastest, safest, and most reliable antidepressant and tranquilizer that exists.* That's why RBT is a comprehensive, short-term, drug-free psychotherapy that produces long-term results.

The Memory Aids for this chapter are on page 224.

Mrs. Morrsey had about a sixth-grade education. Yet she was an excellent candidate for RBT. But a sixth-grade education often excludes people as psychotherapy candidates for the most popular, traditional psychotherapies. Many trainees, therefore, wonder how educated P-Cs react to RBT.

Almost without exception, well-educated P-Cs have these two reactions. First, they are pleasantly surprised to see how they can readily understand their emotions and learn to control them better. They have always wanted to take better charge of themselves; but before, they hadn't seen how it was possible. Second, just as quickly as uneducated P-Cs, the educated ones get enthusiastically involved in therapy. That fact shows that formal education is usually irrelevant to improving emotional control. In reality, emotionally distressed university professors usually are as emotionally ignorant as junior high school dropouts like Mrs. Morrsey. That's the main reason they are emotionally distressed; they are emotionally ignorant. Consequently, never has a well-educated P-C complained to me about either the straightforward logic of RBT, or the simplicity of cartoon-illustrated Rational Bibliotherapy I routinely use (see Appendix B).

A WELL-EDUCATED P-C

Professor Nelson was a professor of economics. At 33 years of age, he was already a well-published authority on his business speciality, a popular tenured professor, and an important administrator in his academic department. In addition, he was in great demand as a consultant to industry. Among his industrial clients, Professor Nelson had the well-earned reputation of being a no-nonsense, reality-oriented, trouble-shooting problem solver for ailing companies.

Unfortunately, before people learn their Emotional ABCs and the Five Rules for Rational Thinking, they rarely make this important insight: *Solving emotional problems rationally is just as logical and straightforward as rationally solving problems in business, or in any other area of life.* It's most unfortunate, therefore, that most high schools have not yet begun to teach courses in Rational Self-Counseling (Maultsby et al. 1976). If Professor Nelson had been able to take even a

EMERGENCY ROOM

11-1   A Worried Professor

one-semester high-school course in Rational Self-Counseling, I doubt that I or any other psychiatrist, would have ever needed to treat him.[1]

I first saw Professor Nelson as an emergency psychiatric consultation. He sat nervously fingering his hair with small circular motions; occasionally he would jerk out several strands at a time. That was the first time I had ever seen a person actually pulling out his hair. In addition, he looked like the picture of intense emotional misery. But his only request was for a refill of his two-year-old prescriptions for an antidepressant and a tranquilizer, both prescribed by another psychiatrist.

This episode of emotional distress had begun a few days previously when Professor Nelson had discovered a mound of snow on the roof of his house. He immediately began to worry about the possibility of expensive roof damage being done that might not be covered by his insurance. His ever increasing anxiety quickly began to interfere with his work, and it decreased his sleep to "about two hours a night."

Here's how Professor Nelson described his experience of the night before I first saw him: "I went into absolute panic last night when I was in bed and heard this creaking and groaning of the wood overhead. I just knew I was getting all kinds of damage to the house. Then this morning it got to the point that I couldn't stand it; so I came to the emergency room for medication and they referred me to you."

Section I of this chapter compares treatment strategies for irrational worry with that for irrational depression. It demonstrates how people create emotional distress by mislabeling their emotional feelings as thoughts.

Section II of the chapter demonstrates the clinical application of the therapeutic insight that solving emotional problems rationally is just as logical and straightforward as solving any other problems in life, and the clinical application of the therapeutic challenge sane people rarely refuse.

---

[1]For information about teaching Rational Self-Counseling in schools, write to the RBT Center, College of Medicine, University of Kentucky, Lexington, KY 40536.

SPECIAL VOCABULARY—SECTION I

None.

FOCUS ITEMS—SECTION I

1. What usually makes acute worry easier to control than acute depression?
2. Is rational thinking really as fast and safe as tranquilizers in calming people down?
3. Under what condition would it have been logical to consider a not learned disorder for the professor?
4. Why did I use the professor's presenting problem to teach him the Emotional ABCs, when with Mrs. Morrsey I used the rattlesnake supposition?
5. What is the significant difference between thoughts and emotional feelings?
6. Why make a therapeutic issue of that difference?
7. How did RBT theory give me quick insight into the dynamics of Professor Nelson's anxiety?

CHAPTER 11

Rational Thinking as the Ideal Tranquilizer

What is a basic difference between irrational worry and irrational depression? Worried people are usually reacting to an imagined feared event that hasn't yet happened and probably won't. But depressed people are usually reacting to an undesirable event that has already happened and can't be changed. That fact usually makes it easier to get worried people to stop irrationally worrying themselves than it is to get depressed people to stop irrationally depressing themselves.

TWO IMPORTANT CLINICAL FACTS

First, rational thinking can usually calm worried people down much faster and safer than any tranquilizer can. Second, like all new P-Cs, worried people need to start therapy by learning their Emotional ABCs. But with worried P-Cs, I usually explain the Five Rules for Rational Thinking in the same session that I explain their Emotional ABCs. In addition, I initially focus more on getting worried people to see their irrational thinking than on getting them to understand their Emotional ABCs.

Tranquilizers and RBT

Normally, I don't prescribe drugs for nonpsychotic P-Cs. But I was to leave town the day after I first saw Professor Nelson. In addition, I knew that if I didn't prescribe the professor's drugs, he could and would get some other physician to do it. On the other hand, a worry problem is so ideal for RBT, I didn't want to lose him. So I made one of my rare therapeutic trade-offs.

Me: Okay, because I'm leaving town tomorrow, I'll give you your tranquilizer. But I want you to know that drugs are not the solution to your problem. So, in addition to giving you your tranquilizers, I'm going to try to get you to see that your undiseased, undrugged brain is the fastest and most powerful tranquilizer you can have; and medical science has not yet been able to improve on it. Now there's no reason to think you have a brain disease is there?

P-C: No.

Me: I agree; and since that's the case, whether you realize it or not, you are creating virtually all of your own anxiety. And if you'll let me, I'll show you exactly how you are doing it, and how you can start stopping it immediately, without drugs. First off, virtually all of your life, I'll bet you've been what could be called a "worry wart."

P-C: That's right; very much so.

Me: Well, you're not going to reverse in one session the results of all those years of practicing being a "worry wart." But you can start reversing it today, even during this session.

Author's Note

It's very important to tell all P-Cs what's realistic for them to expect from therapy; but it's doubly important with worriers. Worriers usually are either overt or covert magical thinkers; therefore, they are committed miracle seekers. In addition, they get irrationally disappointed and discouraged when therapists don't give them a miracle immediately. That's why they demand, and most physicians usually give them, the "magic pills" called tranquilizers.

How did I know the professor was a "worry wart"? Clinical experience. I've never seen a person in panic about a noncatastrophic event who wasn't a "worry wart."

What if the professor had said, "No, normally, I rarely worry about anything." Then I would have been concerned about a possible physical illness, such as hyperthyroidism, hypoparathyroidism, or drug abuse. But unless I could get more evidence of a not-learned disorder from his history than I had so far, I still would have managed him the same way.

Me: The first thing I'm going to do is teach you the ABCs of your panic. And the ABCs will show you how to stop your panic immediately. Now, the creaking of your roof last night, we'll call A. That's what you were aware of. Then you had sincere, evaluative thoughts called B, about your perceptions at A. And it was B, your sincere evaluative thoughts, about the creaking of your roof at A, that caused C, your emotional panic.

Author's Note

Professor Nelson's presenting problem was used to teach him the Emotional ABCs. But to teach Mrs. Morrsey the Emotional ABCs, the rattlesnake supposition was used. Here's why.

Irrational worriers know or strongly suspect they are overreacting. In addition, the event they are worried about hasn't yet happened, and they want evidence that it won't happen. So even though irrational worriers may be as emotionally upset as depressed people, the worriers' problems are not as emotion-charged as depressed people's problems. So I don't recommend using depressed P-Cs' presenting problems to teach them the Emotional ABCs. With worriers, on the other hand, using their presenting problems is a highly effective way to get them focused therapeutically on their exaggerated reactions.

Me: Now tell me, what specific thoughts did you have about your roof creaking?

P-C: Well, actually the first thing I said was, "What could that creaking noise be? It's probably just the wind; don't worry about it." Then I went to the bedroom window and looked out; the trees were not moving; there was no wind; and then I said, "Holy cow, what else could it be? It has to be that snow cap thing up there, and a number of things could happen. One would be a total collapse of the roof from too much weight. Another possibility is its moving and tearing off the shingles and creating a leak." And then I thought, "What are my options in this situation?" I said, "Nobody in their right mind would go up on that roof as it is now." Then I said, "In the morning I will call the insurance agency, and then the builder and ask him if he can do anything."
I couldn't get the insurance agent on the phone; so I pulled out my policy, and what really set me off was a clause there saying that collapse of a roof due to snow or ice is not covered under the insurance policy. I called the builder and he said he's not sure what was making the noise, but at night roofs will pop and moan, as he called it. Then he said he would be out there this afternoon and look at the structure. He said the trusses should be able to support that weight, but he didn't know what was going to happen to roofs around here if we get much more snow. That's when I couldn't take it anymore; so I came over here.

Author's Note

After that strightforward, factual description of those objective events, you may wonder, Was the professor really in irrational panic, or was he just reacting normally to objectively undesirable facts of life? We can't know for sure until we look at his evaluative thoughts at B.

Me: Okay, those are the facts, but facts don't upset people. It's what people think and believe about the facts that upsets them. Now what sincere, upsetting thoughts did you think about those facts?

P-C: The one that's really causing me panic is the feeling, My God, we can't afford to live right now; how can I possibly afford an uninsured repair?

Author's Note

In RBT, therapists don't make arbitrary judgments about the rationality of P-Cs' reactions. Instead, we use the Five Rules for Rational Thinking to help P-Cs decide for themselves whether or not their reactions are rational. But, before I show you how I did that, let's look at how the professor demonstrated one of the most common ways people unwittingly confuse themselves and intensify their emotional distress: They inaccurately call their sincere thoughts, or beliefs, about their situation their emotional feelings about it.

When I asked Professor Nelson about the upsetting thoughts he had been thinking, he said, *"The one that's really causing my panic is the feeling that 'My God, we can't afford to live right now; how can we possibly afford an uninsured repair?'"* What he called an emotional feeling was really one of his sincere but irrational thoughts, mislabeled a *"feeling,"* plus a misleading rhetorical question.

To understand clearly the following explanation, recall or reread the discussion in Chapter 3 about how the right and left brains habitually interact. The main point to remember is this: *The attitudinal form of beliefs triggers in right brains specific, habitual emotional feelings. So, what happens when left brains seriously entertain new ideas that conflict with an old attitude? In that instance, right brains have knowledge (in the form of the old attitude) that conflicts with the left brain's new ideas.*

Neuropsychophysiological research shows that right brains trigger negative reactions to left-brain ideas that conflict with right-brain knowledge. That fact is the basis of the next bit of RBT theory: Mislabeling personal beliefs as "feelings" is one of the common ways emotionally distressed people confuse themselves so much that they reject the very facts they need to focus on to eliminate their distress rationally.

The facts Professor Nelson needed to focus on to eliminate his panic were: *(1) He was quite easily affording to live right then; and (2) he could afford to pay for an uninsured repair.* But by sincerely saying, *"I feel we can't afford to live now and we can't possibly afford an uninsured repair,"* Professor Nelson made it seem unnecessary to question the validity or rationality of those beliefs. Why? Because emotional feelings are always real, logical and correct. That's why emotional feelings need no outside confirmation or supporting evidence; emotional feelings are their own evidence and proof. That's also why people in general, and emotionally distressed people in particular, prefer to base their actions on personal beliefs they mislabel emotional feelings, instead of on their admitted beliefs.

People know that even their sincerest beliefs sometimes prove to be incorrect. That's why people usually want outside supporting evidence before they accept new ideas or opinions as beliefs. But if those people mislabel their new ideas emotional feelings, they will confidently accept and act on those new ideas without outside evidence. That habit is the main reason people repeatedly act out incorrect new ideas to their self-defeating ends.

IMPORTANT CLINICAL INSIGHTS

To see clearly the clinical value of RBT theory, it's important for you, the reader, to know this: At this point in the interview, I didn't know whether or not Professor Nelson's beliefs about his finances were irrational. All I knew was these two facts:

(1) Professor Nelson's rhetorical question: "How can we possibly afford an uninsured repair?" probably was hiding his belief that they couldn't afford it. But he had not yet described any objective evidence that he couldn't afford an uninsured repair. (2) Instead of correctly saying, "I think and believe; therefore, I feel as if . . . '', emotionally distressed people merely say, "I feel . . . " At such times, though, people are most likely to be doing "gut thinking," and least likely to be doing the "brain thinking" that Mother Nature seems to have uniquely programmed human beings to do.

"Gut thinking" causes the "Gooney Bird" syndrome. In Chapter 4, however, you saw the main hazard of the "Gooney Bird" syndrome: It prevents new learning.[2] That's why RBT therapists systematically discourage "gut thinking" in psychotherapy. So good RBT technique alone was sufficient to justify my getting Professor Nelson to separate his beliefs from the emotional feelings they had triggered. And as you shall see, that maneuver immediately helped the professor start looking at the obvious, helpful facts that his focus on his emotional feelings had prevented him from seeing.

But don't get the idea that "gut thinking" is all bad; it most certainly is not. "Gut thinking" enables people to make correct decisions instantly, without having to think through the relevant facts. For example, the only time most people give specific thought to any aspect of their morning get-up routine is when they purposefully or unwittingly include something new in it. Then, if they haven't scheduled a little extra time, they immediately fall behind their usual schedule. So, if people are sure that what they already know, believe, and do is the best thing for them to know, believe, and do, "gut thinking" is great. It saves them time, protects them from the fear of making mistakes, and lets them act confidently in their old habitual ways.

"Gut thinking" only causes problems when what people already know, believe, and do is self-defeating. Usually, though, that is the reality in emotional distress. And unfortunately people's "guts" can't do rational thinking. That's why "gut thinking" keeps emotionally distressed people doing the same self-defeating things, and makes them feel right doing it.

Now, let's see how I used those insights to help the professor stop confusing himself and complicating his problem. First, I pointed out to him that his thought "My God, we can't afford to live right now" was not a feeling; it was merely his belief. And it was his fearful attitude about his belief that he could not now afford to

---

[2]Janis (1972, pp. 75–78) gives readers a frightening, though objective look at how "gut thinking" and the "Gooney Bird" syndrome helped make Pearl Harbor the worst military disaster in American history. Yet never before had we had such a complete, preattack intelligence picture of our enemy. Janis's factual report firmly supports this insight: Had the Naval High Command been thinking rather than "feeling" that a surprise attack couldn't happen there, they might have objectively checked their thoughts against their continuous intelligence facts. But "gut thinking" makes it seem unnecessary to look at facts. That's why it was clear to Admiral King, head of one of the Navy's inquiries, that "at Pearl Harbor there was an *unwarranted feeling* of immunity from attack."

live, then, that had triggered his intense fear. But instead of rationally checking the rationality of his fear, he was actively supporting it with irrationally fearful self-talk.

Professor Nelson's attitudes (that is, his unspoken beliefs) seemed to be "It's awful that we can't afford to live now. I can't stand it." But the professor mislabeled as his feelings, not only his fearful beliefs but also his fearful attitudes about his fearful beliefs. That confusing maneuver made it seem to him that he had nothing to check, or even to think about. Like all emotionally naive people, the professor irrationally assumed his emotional feelings at C were real, logical, and correct for, and caused by, the external situation he perceived at A, instead of by the ideas he believed at B about what he perceived at A.

The misleading practice of calling beliefs and attitudes feelings is so widespread in our society that even you, the reader, probably do it sometimes. If so, you are probably thinking, "Okay, I agree with that analysis, but how does that practice cause people to confuse themselves?" Easily!

As I explained to Professor Nelson, human emotional feelings are always real, logical, and correct, but only for the thoughts and attitudes that trigger them. Like most people, however, the professor knew that even his sincerest thoughts were sometimes unrealistic, illogical, absurdly inappropriate, and completely incorrect. Therefore, like most people, the professor knew that it's a good idea to check the rationality of his thoughts before acting on them.

At this time, however, the professor was emotionally distressed. Emotionally distressed people want fast answers that are easy, obvious, and seem certain. Checking the rationality of one's thoughts takes time and effort. Remember, moreover, people know they might even make mistakes while checking the rationality of their thoughts.

Feelings, on the other hand, either exist or they don't. So, when people inaccurately call their thoughts their emotional feelings, they don't see anything that needs to be checked. To most people, checking feelings would seem as unnecessary as checking to see if the sun they were looking at were not really the sun. Because feelings are always real, logical, and correct, they are their own proof; they don't need outside confirmation.[3] That's why people believe it is logical and realistic to act without question, on thoughts they inaccurately call feelings.

But as is often the case in emotional distress, the thoughts the professor inaccurately called feelings were the opposite of the facts. That's why he could not correct his panic until he corrected his obviously incorrect as well as mislabeled thoughts.

Before you find out how the professor was quickly taught to make those insights, please read the *Focus Items for Section II*.

---

[3]That is, feelings don't need confirmation of the reality of their existence. But the rationality of any given feeling for their current situation is the important consideration new P-Cs rarely, if ever, make. They just assume that the reality of their feelings guarantees the rationality or, in their minds, the rightness of their feelings for their current situation.

SPECIAL VOCABULARY—SECTION II

None.

FOCUS ITEMS —SECTION II

1. How can you reliably separate an emotional feeling from a personal opinion, thought, or belief?
2. What irrational cognitive mechanism blinded the professor to his other options for getting his roof repaired?
3. What common barrier to rational emotional control did the professor demonstrate?
4. How can an obvious lie make you feel as if it were an obvious fact?
5. What is the therapeutic challenge sane people rarely refuse?

What's the best way to help P-Cs stop confusing their beliefs with their emotional feelings? In my experience, the best way begins with teaching P-Cs

HOW TO RECOGNIZE EMOTIONAL FEELINGS

Emotional feelings are almost always named by one word nouns, such as love, hate, sad, happy. Therefore, when people say, ''I feel that,'' or ''I feel as if . . . ,'' or any time a ''that'' or an ''as if'' is implied after ''I feel,'' the beliefs that follow are just that—beliefs, and not feelings. To ensure that those beliefs are rational, people must check them with the Five Rational Questions.

THE FIVE RATIONAL QUESTIONS

1. Is that thought based on obvious fact?
2. Will acting on that thought best help me protect my life and health?
3. Will acting on that thought best help me achieve my short-term and long-term goals?
4. Will acting on that thought best help me avoid my most undesirable conflict with other people?
5. Will acting on that thought best help me feel the emotions I want to feel?

It takes at least three honest "yes" answers for a thought to be rational. Now let's see what happened when I tried to get at least three honest "yes" answers to the Five Rational Questions from Professor Nelson about his mislabeled thoughts.

Me: Okay, your thoughts were, "My God, we can't afford to live right now, how can I possibly pay for an uninsured repair?" Incidentally, did you answer the question?

P-C: No.

Me: Why not?

P-C: Well, I spoke too fast. I said to myself, one possibility would be to go to my mother and ask if she could help us. But that is not a good possibility because I don't want to burden her. That's the only answer I had for the question.

Me: Okay, you asked, "My God, how can we pay for uninsured repairs?" And then you thought of asking your mother for help, but you decided against that. Okay, did you think any further than that about it?

P-C: No, I didn't see any other option.

Author's Note

You saw there one of the most common barriers to rational emotional control. People misinterpret: "I don't want to . . . ," or "I'm afraid to . . . " to mean "I can't . . . "; then they don't act. But they irrationally believe the fact that they don't *act proves that they* can't *act.*

I hope that by now you see why Professor Nelson didn't see any other options. His misleading rhetorical question blinded him. His refusal to think any further than his unacceptable alternative of borrowing from his mother revealed the rhetorical nature of his question. "My God! How can we pay for uninsured repairs?"

My insight was that the professor's question hid these beliefs: "My God! We can't pay for uninsured repairs and that's awful. I can't stand it." Here's how I made use of that insight.

Me: You didn't see any other options because you didn't ask yourself a real question. You posed a misleading, rhetorical question, which hid your belief about the matter behind a question mark. Now, what personal belief was hidden in the question "My God, how can we pay for uninsured repairs?"

P-C: My belief is that I can't afford to pay for them.

Me: Right, not only that you can't afford to pay for them, but there is no way you can ever afford to pay for them. And in your mind, what kind of situation is that?

P-C: That's something that just scares me; it just frightens me to death.

Me: Therefore, it's perfectly logical and correct to feel frightened to death. Now do you see how your thinking, and not your roof, is making you miserable? That's a very important insight because no amount of pills can safely stop you from doing that. But rational thinking can easily stop you. Which brings me to the next important fact. For your thinking to be rational, it has to have at least three of these five characteristics. First, it has to be based on obvious facts; second, it has to best help you protect yourself; third, it has to best help you achieve your short- and long-term goals; fourth, it has to best help you avoid your most unwanted conflict with other people; and fifth, it has to best help you to feel the way you want to feel emotionally. Now let's see how rational your thinking was. In the first place, you said, "My God, we can't afford to live right now." But is that an obvious fact? Are you affording to live now, or are you not affording to live?

P-C: Right now, yes. But I see a pattern developing. Up until this year, we have always lived within my university salary. On top of that, I do a fair amount of consulting and I have a very modest income from royalties. But according to my best estimates, we are spending everything I am making. And the thing that's frightening me is, I think that I may not be able to pay the income-tax liability on the additional money I've made and have already spent just to keep bread and butter on the table without going significantly into what little savings we have left.

Author's Note

Examining that monologue we can make two important insights. First, it was clear that the professor's beliefs, and not his roof, were the cause of his panic. Second, the professor was mentally converting a possible undesirable situation into an imaginary ongoing catastrophe.

That's the typical routine of irrational worriers. As soon as they imagine their feared event, they immediately start reacting as if that mere possibility were already happening. Next, the professor gives you a clear picture of that process.

P-C: And I've gotten myself in this pattern where the worst part of the month for me is when I have to sit down to try to pay the bills and balance the checkbook. Anything financial, and all my anxiety symptoms come up.

Me: No, your anxiety symptoms don't come up; you create them with your anxiety-eliciting thoughts. But let's get back to my question, "Are you not affording to live now?" The first rational rule is obvious fact. Is it a fact that you are *not* affording to live now? Is it a fact that you are *not* paying your bills, etc.?

P-C: It is not a fact.

Me: All right then, your thought "We can't afford to live now" is an obvious lie. Right?

P-C: (*He just sat, in deep reflective thought.*)

Me: Is it a lie, or isn't it a lie?

P-C: Yes, it's a lie.

Author's Note

The next bit of dialogue demonstrates the clinical use of a basic assumption that RBT therapists routinely make: Solving emotional problems rationally is just as logical and straightforward as solving any other problems in life.

Notice also how, as the therapist, I stayed in relaxed but firm control of both the direction and the pace of the therapeutic interactions.

Me: Now, you are a business consultant. So tell me, would you write on a company report "No assets" just because the company doesn't have as many assets as it had the last year, or because the president of the company didn't like the idea of possibly spending some of the company's cash reserves?

P-C: No, I would not.

Me: Why wouldn't you do that?

P-C: Well, it wouldn't represent the facts, so I couldn't do it.

Me: All right, I'll give you an important insight. You are not going to help yourself emotionally until you're willing to be as logical about your emotional control as you are willing to be about a year-end financial statement for one of your clients. You see what I mean?

P-C: I think I do.

Author's Note

To repeat: Solving emotional problems is just as logical and straightforward as solving any other problems in daily living. *To make clinical use of that assumption, pick an area of your P-Cs' lives that they handle well. Then point out that all they need to do for therapeutic success is to apply their already proven problem-solving skills in that area to solving their emotional problems.*

Me: Now you said, "My God, we can't afford to live right now." But that's a lie, right?

P-C: Right, it's a lie.

Me: But it's what we call an emotional white lie. An emotional white lie is an obviously incorrect statement that makes you feel as if it's an obvious fact. And it makes you feel as if it is an obvious fact because at that moment, you believe that lie. But that's a very irrational trick to play on yourself. It makes you act psychotically; that is, you act as if what is, really isn't and what isn't, really is.

P-C: Say that again. I didn't quite follow you.

Author's Note

Ignoring that request for clarification was a matter of clinical judgment, based on this reasoning:

1.   The insight about emotional white lies was interesting, but not crucial to the therapeutic point I wanted to make there.
2.   The insight was the result of simple, straightforward reasoning.
3.   I was tape recording the session and I would later advise the professor to listen to the recording.
4.   If the professor then followed my advice, he would discover the insight for himself.
5.   P-Cs usually remember best those insights they have discovered for themselves.

So, rather than restating the insight, I chose to describe the obvious facts that had led me to it. This decision was also based on two other important clinical facts: The only person who can convince a P-C (or anyone else) of any idea is the person himself or herself. All that psychotherapists can do is give P-Cs personally meaningful reasons why it seems to be in the P-Cs best interest to convince themselves of the idea being described.

Me: Look at it like this, you feel now the way you think you would feel if in fact you were unable to afford to live. Is that a fair statement?
P-C: Yes, that's right.
Me: All right, but are you in fact affording to live?
P-C: Yes, I am.
Me: Then how much sense does it make, to make yourself feel as if what you believe would be an utter catastrophe is happening to you, when it's not happening to you?
P-C: It doesn't make any sense.
Me: Right! It doesn't make any rational sense. But it makes a lot of the irrational sense of nonsense, and that's why I advise you to stop doing it.

THE THERAPETUIC CHALLENGE SANE PEOPLE RARELY REFUSE

Next, you will see in use the most effective technique I know for getting worried P-Cs quickly past their involuntary resistance to these three initially mind-boggling facts about emotional feelings: (1) IT (that is, their situation) does not upset P-Cs; instead, P-Cs irrationally upset themselves about IT. (2) P-Cs can stop upsetting themselves immediately without drugs. (3) By giving themselves a brief time-out from their irrational worry, P-Cs can't get any worse.

Me: All right, now suppose that I could guarantee you that eight months from now, you would be absolutely broke, and you would have to go on welfare. Let's assume that is absolutely an unavoidable fact. Would you have anything to lose by refusing to worry one iota about that fact now?
P-C: No.
Me: Would you have anything to gain by refusing to worry about it now?
P-C: No.
Me: Yes you would, you would have eight months of worry-free living. Now, are you telling me that eight months of worry-free living doesn't mean anything to you?
P-C: I would love to have eight months of worry-free living.
Me: But your current thinking makes worry-free living impossible; that's why you are not getting it. Now, how likely is it that you will be unavoidably destitute eight months from now?
P-C: Not very likely at all.
Me: Yet, you are reacting as if it were not only guaranteed, but as if it has already happened. If you were absolutely destitute, could you imagine yourself feeling any worse than you are feeling now?
P-C: No.

Me: Okay, that's why I'm going to give you the therapeutic challenge sane peo-
       ple rarely refuse. All you have to do is assume for just twenty-four hours at a
       time that I'm right and you are wrong about what is upsetting you. You say
       IT, your situation, is upsetting you; and I say it's you upsetting you about IT,
       your situation. I also say that you are going to continue upsetting yourself
       until you stop doing it. But the good news is, all you have to do to stop
       upsetting yourself is refuse to worry about what is not likely to happen. And
       I'm saying that even if it turns out tomorrow that you were right all along—
       that you really should have been just as miserably worried as you are now—
       you are still going to be better off in the meantime than you would have been
       if you hadn't believed in what I'm saying.

P-C: How's that?

Me: You would have had twenty-four hours of worry-free living by just refusing
       to worry about what's not likely to happen to you.

P-C: But that's not easy to do.

Author's Note

*In that one statement, the professor revealed two of the most irrational attitudes that emotion-
ally distressed people distress themselves with: (1) If a voluntary action is simple or easy to
understand, it should be easy to do; and (2) If people have tried to do a presumably simple or
easy act (such as controlling their emotions better) and they have failed, that proves the act
can not be easy but in fact, it's impossibly hard for them to do.*

*Here is an effective maneuver for helping P-Cs get rid of that first irrational attitude.
Say, "Imagine that you have decided to deliver a refrigerator to a second story walk-up apartment. That's a very simple, voluntary action. All you have to do is lift the refrigerator off the
truck and carry it up the stairs—very simple, but not very easy, right?"*

*Normally, people who have the first irrational attitude also have the second, and vice
versa. In addition, effectively dealing with either one often gets rid of the other at the same
time. The professor's statement seemed to reveal more of the second than the first irrational
attitude. Next is an effective maneuver for handling that second irrational attitude. Get your
P-Cs to discover the obvious—namely, that they can't stop doing something while they are
forcing themselves to do it. Here's exactly how I got the professor to make a "profound"
insight.*

Me: Just the contrary, it's very easy to do. Just stop accusing IT of doing to you
       what only you can do to yourself. What could be easier than that? Not very
       much! But you've never done that. Still, as soon as you do it (that is, stop
       doing it) you'll immediately start stopping your miserable feelings. I'm sure
       of that because I know you are a sane, intelligent person, who hates having
       miserable feelings. Now, you won't stop having them altogether immedi-
       ately. Complete behavior change just can't happen that fast without drugs or
       brain damage. But you can immediately start decreasing your misery, right
       this minute.

P-C: But the same thing applies to everything. It just ties me up.

Me: No, IT never does anything. *You* tie you up about IT. That's the important
       insight that you haven't made yet. Just like you were sitting there pulling
       your hair out, you also tie you up. And the reason you haven't stopped tying

you up is that you haven't admitted to tying yourself up in the first place. No sane person tries to stop doing what they don't see they are doing in the first place.

Author's Note

That's an important therapeutic insight. Normally, people don't try effectively to stop doing things they don't believe they are doing in the first place. That's why getting P-Cs to see and to say "I upset me about it" is such a powerful therapeutic maneuver.

But notice the strong resistance that even a highly educated P-C has against giving up the irrational belief in the magical IT. (Junior high school dropouts rarely have any more resistance on this point. They usually haven't learned as much skill as the professor showed in ignoring obvious facts.) Even more important, notice how a simple as well as easy focus on obvious fact—the first rule in RBT and for rational self control—enabled me to help the professor quickly help himself.

P-C: But it is happening to me.

Me: Yes, but it's happening to you in the same sense that sitting in that chair is happening to you. But who is making it happen? Who's making your sitting in that chair happen?

P-C: Well, I am by deciding to sit here.

Me: Beautiful! Now, if you really wanted to be standing up, would it help to sit there complaining about how frightening it is because sitting in the chair is happening to you? Or would it be more useful just to think, "I am sitting in the chair, but I don't want to sit anymore. So I'll just get up"?

P-C: The latter, because it's the active versus the passive. And I have control over the active, so I can change it.

Me: Right, anytime you get tired of sitting in that chair you can get up. And anytime you decide to stop making yourself miserable, you can stop doing that, too. But you've been practicing your worrying habits for years, and you can't get rid of a habit instantly. But you can instantly start getting rid of it by getting rid of the irrational belief you are now reacting to as if it were obvious fact. That belief is "My God, we can't afford to live now, and it's scaring me to death." But that belief doesn't obey Rational Rule 1. And it certainly doesn't help you protect yourself, because you've got all this churning inside your gut, which could very easily lead to an ulcer, surgery, and possibly even death. So that belief is not helping you protect your life or health. And that belief certainly isn't helping you achieve your short-term goal of feeling better and getting more sleep at night, right?

P-C: Right.

Me: Unless all your catastrophizing is resulting in your wife getting irritated with you, we can say your belief is irrelevant to Rational Rule 4. But your belief certainly is not letting you feel the emotional calm you want to feel, right? So we have here a belief that is at best, 80 percent irrational and, at worst, is 100 percent irrational. And yet you are sincerely clinging to it as tenaciously as you would cling to an obvious fact.

P-C: What is the belief?

Author's Note

After my long, detailed explanation of the Emotional ABCs and the Five Rational Questions, I was a bit surprised by the professor's last question. My surprise made me aware that I had been ignoring this obvious fact. Before learning their Emotional ABCs, university professors and junior high school dropouts usually are equally ignorant emotionally and equally unskilled at analyzing their emotions correctly.

Normally, I keep that fact in mind. That's why I don't usually cover the Emotional ABCs and the Five Rules for Rational Thinking in one session. That's usually too much for emotionally distressed people to integrate at one time. So, here are the three reasons I broke that rule with Professor Nelson.

First, I was leaving town the following day.

Second, I was recording the session and he seemed to be cooperative; so I thought he would follow my advice to listen to the recording every day until I could see him again the following week.

Third, if he listened to the tapes even half as often as I suggested, even with a chemically tranquilized brain he could still help himself.

So what did I do? I calmly suppressed my surprise and immediately told the professor again what his irrational belief was. To do so was to make use of this important clinical fact: Simple repetition really is the royal road to rapid therapeutic learning.

Me: Actually, you have two irrational beliefs. One is "My God, we can't afford to live now." And the other one is hidden in your emotion-charged rhetorical question, "How can we afford to pay for uninsured repairs?" That is not really a question at all. If it were, you would have answered it logically. But you refused to accept the obvious answer—namely, that you could borrow the money from your mother. You dismissed that idea because you didn't like it. In effect, therefore, you are demanding that you be miserable, if you can't get everything you want, exactly the way you want it. Now, I don't believe that you, a 33-year old associate professor, go around consciously thinking, "I demand to be miserable if I can't get what I want." But that seems to be your attitude. Do you follow what I'm saying?

P-C: Yes, I'm following you.

Me: Now, do you have to get everything you want financially, the way you want it, and when you want it, in order to stop being miserable? Is that a fact?

P-C: Yes.

Author's Note

Remember now, this a graduate school professor. I repeatedly mention that information to emphasize the importance of this fact: It doesn't matter what academic degrees P-Cs have; they still don't know their Emotional ABCs until they learn them. And until they learn their Emotional ABCs, even graduate school professors believe incorrectly, just as strongly as junior high school dropouts believe incorrectly, that they have no choice about feeling the miserable emotions they habitually feel. Professor Nelson's "yes" answer clearly demonstrated this fact.

Me: No, it is not a fact that you have to have what you want, when and how you want it, in order to stop feeling miserable. They're just the conditions you are demanding. But you don't have to have them.

P-C: But I just can't let go of it. I just keep thinking about it.

Me: No, it's not that you can't let go; it's just that you refuse to let go. But, you're not going to improve your emotional control until you do let go. And that means improving your thinking. But you can't improve your thinking without improving your choice of words. So, let's go through your Emotional ABCs again.

Author's Note

At this point, I had gotten the professor to see how he was upsetting himself with his irrational thoughts. But insight or knowledge alone does not solve emotional problems. That's just the first step. To solve emotional problems rationally, people must replace their self-defeating thoughts with rational thoughts.

Remember, though, rational thoughts don't slip up on P-Cs and grab them when they are not looking. P-Cs have to discover their rational thoughts. That's really what RBT is all about, helping emotionally distressed people discover rational ways to think, feel, and act. The Five Rational Questions are essential therapeutic aids for pursuing that therapeutic goal efficiently.

Chapter 12 "Helping P-Cs Discover What's Rational For Them" will show you how the Emotional ABCs and the Five Rational Questions were used to help the professor immediately discover a more rational way to think about the snow cap on his house.

The Memory Aids for this chapter are on page 225.

CHAPTER **12**

Helping P-Cs Discover What's Rational for Them

By the end of the last chapter, the professor had begun to see that his thinking at B was clearly irrational. Beginning therapists often think that this solves the immediate therapeutic problem; but it doesn't, and it's best to avoid that mistake. Getting P-Cs to see their irrational thinking is only half of the solution. The other half is helping P-Cs get rid of their irrational thinking.

Section I of this chapter shows you how to decide whether or not you have probably dealt adequately with a therapeutic concept, what to do if you haven't, why you need to be especially concerned about that question with worried P-Cs and how best to help P-Cs quickly overcome their initial difficulty in giving up the use of self-defeating irrational rhetoric.

Nature abhors a vacuum as much in the mind as it does in the rest of the body. So people can't just get rid of their irrational thoughts; they have to replace their irrational thoughts with other thoughts; otherwise, people just fall asleep. So to get improved emotional control, P-Cs must replace their irrational thoughts at B with more rational thoughts.

That necessity brings me to an important clinical fact: *Recognizing that a thought is irrational does not mean the person has or knows of a rational replacement for that thought.*

You will see the professor demonstrate that fact well in the early part of this chapter. Then after you see how I helped Professor Nelson discover the most rational thoughts for him in that situation, the chapter skips ahead to Professor Nelson's second RBT session, two weeks later. There Professor Nelson described his success in rationally controlling his worry during the two weeks between this first and that second session.

Section II of the chapter shows you how to recognize and deal with cognitive-emotive dissonance in a session, and how rapidly effective therapy-tape listening and bibliotherapy can be in a worry crisis. Then it summarizes Professor Nelson's course of RBT and ends with his one-year follow-up.

SPECIAL VOCABULARY—SECTION I

Irrational rhetoric: incorrect ways of describing events that create and maintain emotional problems. Probably the most common example of irrational rhetoric is "IT, HE, SHE, or THEY upsets, frightens, angers, depresses, or worries me." (See also Chapter 13.)

Rational rhetoric: correct ways of describing events that help create and maintain optimal emotional health. A good therapeutic example of rational rhetoric is: "I upset myself about it, him, her or them; but I can and will stop doing it any time I decide to control myself rationally." (See also Chapter 13.)

FOCUS ITEMS —SECTION I

1.   What does a new emotion consist of?
2.   What incorrect interpretation did Professor Nelson put on the ABCs of his panic, and what did it mean?
3.   Do you think I talked too much or just enough in this part of the session?
4.   Were Professor Nelson's emotional feelings really "screwed up" as he said they were?
5.   Do people really believe what they perceive, or do they perceive what they already believe?

CHAPTER 12

Helping P-Cs Discover What's Rational for Them

We rejoin Professor Nelson's first RBT session at the point where I checked to see if I had talked enough.

Me: Now let me hear you go over the ABCs of your panic.

P-C: A is what, the fact?

Me: Yes, the fact that you have a snow cap on your house and it's causing damage to your roof which is not covered by insurance.

P-C: And my B is?

Me: B_1 is your thought, "My God, we can't afford to live now." And B_2 is, "We can't possibly afford to pay for uninsured repairs." And B_3 is, "It's awful and terrible for this to be happening to me."

P-C: Okay, and C?

Me: C is the real, logical, and correct emotional feelings that you, and anyone with a normally functioning brain, would have in response to those sincerely frightening thoughts.

P-C: Which is my anxiety, right?

Me: Yes, and the whole, A, B, C complex is your emotion of panic; but the C is just one part of it; it's the emotive or emotional-feeling part. Once the A, B,

C model of emotions shows you how you are upsetting yourself, you immediately see why you don't need a tranquilizer to feel better. All you need is to
start thinking better at B about what you are aware of at A, and you will have
to feel better at C. If you don't, it will mean your brain isn't working right.
But we know your brain is working right, so you don't have to worry about
that.

P-C: I think I understand what you are saying. But let me just walk through the
       illustration once more. I started with that snow cap up there on my roof; and
       you're saying that I made the mistake of thinking the worst of all possible
       circumstances is going to occur, and something is screwed up with my emo-
       tional reaction to my thoughts.

Author's Note

*Professor Nelson's last statement showed that he still had the incorrect idea that it was his
emotional feelings, instead of his thoughts, that were "screwed up." That meant he still had
not seen, or was ignoring the most obvious fact that the A, B, C model of emotions clearly
shows—namely, that it was his Bs, his sincere, but "screwed up" thoughts, that were triggering his real, logical, and correct, but miserable emotional feelings at C. That is, his emotional feelings were real, logical, and correct for his "screwed up" thoughts, beliefs, and
attitudes; but his emotional feelings were neither logical nor correct for the real world.*

*Obviously I needed to talk some more. But before we go to that, I'd like to discuss my
insights about why Professor Nelson was still confused. It was mainly because of this important fact of human neuropsychology: People habitually perceive what they already believe
exists (Luria 1973, pp. 229–244). In addition, people often don't perceive what they don't
have a label for (Luria 1976, pp. 7–48). That's why it's therapeutic to get P-Cs to give up
subjective labels and names (such as human mouse, S.O.B., fascistic or chauvinistic pig) that
don't match objective human things.*

*Like most emotionally distressed people, Professor Nelson had the incorrect belief that
his healthy brains guaranteed that all his sincere thoughts would be realistic and valid and,
therefore, the best thoughts he could have. In reality though, nothing was further from the
facts about healthy brains. But remember, people don't control themselves with facts; people
control themselves with their beliefs about facts, as well as with their beliefs about the things
they imagine.*

*I don't think I can repeat this point too much. Healthy brains do not prevent people
from having sincere but irrationally self-defeating beliefs; neither do healthy brains protect
people from the real, logical, and correct emotional pain that irrationally self-defeating beliefs often cause. All healthy brains guarantee is that people will have every bit of the emotional pleasure or pain that their rational or irrational beliefs trigger. Next, I talk more to the
professor about those facts.*

Me: No, your emotions are not screwed up. You are having perfectly logical and
      correct emotional reactions to your irrational thoughts. But it's obvious to
      me that you, at least, have average intelligence and a fine mind. It's just that
      you have the mistaken idea most normal people have. You think that because
      you have a normal brain, anything that goes on in it, is worth happening. But
      that's a big mistake. A normally functioning brain does not protect you
      against idiotic beliefs. All a normally functioning brain guarantees is that it

will process most efficiently any idiotic or sensible beliefs you happen to have. And because of the way normal brains and bodies interact, you will always get real, logical, and correct emotional feelings that are most appropriate for your beliefs, however idiotic, stupid, irrational, or sane, logical, and rational your beliefs may be. Do you see what I mean?

P-C: I think I do.

Author's Note

Worriers usually listen less attentively than most P-Cs . So with worriers, I check myself more often than normally to see if I have talked enough. Such frequent checking has the added value of breaking up the antitherapeutic debates most P-Cs, and especially worriers, carry on with themselves in their heads about what the therapist is saying.

Me: All right, explain your emotional understanding to me.

P-C: Okay, in my situation, what I can't understand is how you evaluate what is a rational thought and what is an irrational thought in relation to the facts.

Author's Note

Obviously I had not talked enough. But I wasn't surprised. Thinking rationally about his emotions was a new behavior for Professor Nelson. To learn any new behavior takes time, repeated thought, and effort.

So how did I react? I calmly repeated the Five Rules for Rational Thinking that I had just covered a few minutes before (see Chapter 11). Calm repetition really is the unmistakable path to rapid therapeutic teaching and learning.

Me: Just check your thoughts with the Five Rules for Rational Thinking we went over a few minutes ago. You have the idea "My God, we can't afford to pay for uninsured repairs." All right, ask yourself this rational question: Is that an obvious fact? Of course it isn't; you can find a way to afford your repairs. But even if you couldn't, you don't have to feel panic-stricken about that fact. Also, your belief that you can't pay for uninsured repairs causes you excessive worry, which does not help you preserve your health, nor help you achieve your goal of restful sleep; and it keeps you from feeling the way you want to feel. So, that thought disobeys rational rules 1, 2, 3, and 5. See what I mean?

P-C: Yes.

Me: All right, so more rational thinking for you would be, "I can find a way to pay for those repairs. But even if I couldn't pay for them I still don't have to feel panic-stricken about that fact. In reality though, I don't know yet how much damage has to be repaired. So I am just creating catastrophes in my head, and then reacting to them as if they were in the real world." Now let's talk about why you and all other normal people sometimes upset themselves about things that don't exist. It's because you either don't know, or you ignore this important fact about your brain. Human brains work like cameras. So you can't—and therefore don't—perceive obvious facts directly. All you can do is perceive the pictures your brain takes of obvious facts. But unlike real cameras, human brains are not limited to taking pictures of the outside world of obvious facts. And your brain is not taking pictures of obvious facts now. Instead, your brain is taking pictures of what you think the facts might be eight to twelve months from now. And because those ideas are the only ones you are focusing on, their images are all your brain can use to control your emotional reactions now. That's why your brain is making you react as if your imaginary catastrophes were already happening to you, even though you are reasonably sure they won't ever happen to you. See what I mean?

P-C: Yeah, I've gotten myself into this business of finding everything that's wrong with that house, everything. I have a master list of forty items that deep down I know there is just no way I'm ever going to get them fixed up. But I keep worrying about them and feeling sorry for myself with a why-is-this-happening-to-me? kind of reaction.

Me: But the most logical question to ask is, "Why am I doing this idiotic thing to myself? That's the question you need to answer.

P-C: It's out of ignorance, right?

Me: Yes, out of ignorance of your Emotional ABCs and the Five Rules of Rational Thinking. That's why I took the extra time to teach you those facts today. I could have easily written you a prescription in two minutes, an hour ago; I didn't, because I know pills would only create the illusion of helping you, without really helping you. But your Emotional ABCs and the Five Rational Questions can really help you.

Author's Note

In the next exchange, notice how difficult it was to get Professor Nelson to change his irrational rhetoric—" Another thing [meaning the magical IT] that frightens me is . . . —to "Another thing I am frightening myself about is . . . "

P-C: I'll tell you another thing that frightens me.

Me: No, another thing that you frighten yourself about.

P-C: Another thing that is frightening me.

Me: No, another thing that you are frightening yourself about. Repeat after me, "Another thing that I'm frightening myself about is."

Author's Note

Inexperienced therapists might incorrectly accuse the professor of being uncooperative or re-sistant there; or they might accuse me of being overbearing and authoritarian. I disagree with both points for these reasons: My clinical experience told me the professor was most likely just revealing the tremendous power that a longstanding belief in some all-powerful, magical IT has on people's self-perceptions. Remember, people perceive what they already believe much more readily than they believe what they newly perceive.

In my experience, the best way to get P-Cs to make correct perceptions about IT, is to get them in the habit of saying "I frighten, or upset, myself about IT." Those accurate thoughts trigger accurate self-images of themselves as potent, but self-made, victims of poor emotional control, instead of the P-Cs' usual inaccurate self-images of being helpless victims of the external world, without any emotional control. This new, accurate self-image maximally frees P-Cs to quickly replace their irrational habits of emotional control with ra-tional habits of emotional control.

So my conclusion was that the professor was not resistant and neither was I overbear-ing or authoritarian. I was merely authoritatively insistent enough to get the professor to make the therapeutic switch from his old self-defeating irrational rhetoric to emotionally healthy rational rhetoric. That switch opened the door for me to prepare him for the realities of thera-peutic change.

Me: That thought, "Another thing that I'm frightening myself about," feels a little bit odd, right? It doesn't feel as natural, normal, and right as the thought, "Another thing that's frightening me," does it?

P-C: That's right, it doesn't. It feels strange, almost unreal.

That ends Section I of this chapter. Next are the Special Vocabulary and Focus Items for Section II.

SECTION II

SPECIAL VOCABULARY—SECTION II
None.

FOCUS ITEMS —SECTION II
1. What is cognitive-emotive dissonance?
2. Why do some otherwise intelligent, sane people opt to be miserable?
3. What is a simple but highly effective way to handle such people?
4. How would you have handled Professor Nelson's worry about his sanity?
5. Give a two-minute talk on magical worry.

At the end of Section I, the professor had just said that his thought, "Another thing I frighten myself about is . . . " felt strange and unreal. That strange feeling was the normal, natural cognitive-emotive dissonance that all people feel when new ideas conflict with their old beliefs. Most people naively describe cognitive-emotive dissonance by saying, "That feels wrong" or "It doesn't feel right."

Even obvious facts that conflict with old beliefs still feel wrong at first. And unfortunately, *emotionally naive people believe that ideas (even facts) that feel wrong must be wrong* and should be rejected. So almost as a reflex, emotionally naive people initially reject all such new ideas.

AN IMPORTANT CLINICAL INSIGHT

Usually, when emotionally naive people act on ideas that feel wrong, they think, "I feel phony" or "I feel I'm being a phony" or "This is not the real me." Unfortunately, rather than feel (or seem to be what they call) phony, most such people will opt to feel or be what they call "the real me," even though that means feeling or being really miserable.

You can easily protect your P-Cs from that antitherapeutic trap. Simply teach them the facts about cognitive-emotive dissonance and the other four stages of emotional reeducation (Those facts are described in the next chapter). Normally, though, it's a waste of therapy time to teach P-Cs about cognitive-emotive dissonance before they commit themselves to learning rational self-control. Usually P-Cs commit themselves by the third session. Clearly Professor Nelson hadn't reached that point yet. And his emotional naivete was a potential therapeutic barrier. My technique for handling such situations is simple. It is to focus on a well-known example of the disadvantage of arbitrarily ignoring new facts that feel wrong. One good example is the idea that the world is flat.

Me: It's an obvious fact that you frighten yourself; but it doesn't feel right when you think that idea, because it's a new fact for you; and it's in conflict with your old lifelong belief that some external, magical IT frightens you. So your odd feeling is perfectly natural and normal; all new facts feel wrong when they conflict with old beliefs. For example, the idea that the world is round felt so wrong when the first people said it that most other people just laughed and ignored this scientific fact for hundreds of years. But their irrational laughter did not change the shape of the world, did it?

P-C: No, it didn't.

Me: But the irrational ideas—that the world was flat and that if people sailed out of sight of land they would fall off into hell—did keep the people in the old world ignorant of the new world for hundreds of years. Right? Well, that's a classic example of the danger of what I call "trying to think with your gut instead of with your brain."

P-C: I see what you mean.

Me: That's why two of the most emotionally helpful insights you can make and act out are, Just because an idea feels wrong, that does not mean the idea is incorrect. And when there is conflict between your rational thoughts and your gut, it's usually best to go with your rational thoughts. Not only are your rational thoughts the most objectively correct way to think, they are the healthiest way to think. That's why the sooner you start thinking that way, the better it will be for you. So, another thing that you are frightening yourself about is what?

P-C: Is this illness thing, or whatever you want to call it. This episode of depression and anxiety and all the rest of that. What's frightening me is, or what I'm making myself afraid of, is that I am going to end up being emotionally incapacitated.

Me: You mean lose your mind?

P-C: Yes, that I'm going to be a wacko. More than everything else, that's the thing I'm hitting myself the hardest with. I had a physician who said, "Don't depend on those damned pills. You shouldn't have to use them." So I want to get this straight in my mind. You said this is not an illness that's happening to me, but that I am doing this to myself. That makes me feel a little better; and if there is something I can do to avoid this in the future, I want to do it, because it's hobbling me; I can't work effectively.

Author's Note

Please note that Professor Nelson corrected his irrational description of his fear, "What's frightening me," to the rational "What I'm making myself afraid of is . . . " This showed he was cooperative and that he was learning. The excerpt also gives you objective evidence that well-educated P-Cs have the same fears about their sanity that uneducated P-Cs have. But only rarely will new P-Cs describe their fears about their sanity, even in their third or fourth session, as freely as Professor Nelson did in his first. So let's consider for a moment why he did it.

I think he did it mainly because he was pleasantly surprised and reassured by the logical way RBT theory enabled me to help him understand himself in a scientifically valid, yet immediately useful way. Remember, in the minds of lay people, immediately logical, understandable and controllable behavior means normal behavior and sanity. And that's why most new P-Cs are intensely, though secretly, concerned about what their illogical behaviors may mean about their sanity.

But what about Professor Nelson's seeming reluctance to accept my easily understandable, ABC explanation of his panic? I think that was just his way of getting extra reassurance that he had heard me correctly. Up until then, all he had heard and believed about his emotions was the popular nonsense about some magical IT. Like most otherwise intelligent people, he was initially surprised and a bit incredulous to learn that the magical IT was really him.

The professor's response was the most common response at that stage of therapy. I would have been concerned about the appropriateness of his therapeutic involvement, had he responded more gullibly. I believe, therefore, it was the professor's willingness to learn new facts plus my ability to explain his problems in scientifically valid, yet easily understandable and immediately useful terms, that gave him the courage to mention his intense fear about his sanity.

And how did I deal with the sanity issue? With the first rule for rational thinking—I simply stated the obvious facts. In addition, I continued to demonstrate to Professor Nelson that I understood his worry problem better than he did.

Me: Based on what I have learned about you today, and what I saw in your medical record, the worst thing I can say about you is that you have several well-learned, irrational habits of emotional control, which you are diligently, but unwittingly, practicing every day. But the solution to the problem is not pills. The solution is to give yourself a therapeutic emotional reeducation. Now all I can do today is write the prescriptions you want, and let you carry the tape of this session home with you to listen to at least once a day, every day until I see you again. I also suggest that before you leave today, you get a copy of my book *You and Your Emotions* and read Chapters 1 and 2. They cover the Emotional ABCs and the Five Rules for Rational Thinking. You can read the whole book if you want to. But all I want you to read are Chapters 1 and 2, once a day, every day, until I see you again. If you start applying the Emotional ABCs and the Five Rational Questions to yourself every day as directed, when I see you again you will be feeling significantly better. But you are not going to get rid of your lifelong habit of magical worry in a week. So don't expect that. I'm fresh out of miracles.

P-C: Magical worry? Why do you say it's magical worry?

Me: Because that seems to best describe the kind of worrying you do. You see, magical worry is worrying in an unnoticed attempt to keep the thing being worried about from happening. That's what you seem to be doing. For example, I'll bet that when you catch yourself not worrying, you immediately get worried about the possibility of having overlooked something to worry about.

P-C: That's right; I do. You sure hit the nail on the head.

Me: That's because the things you worry about the most have only rarely, if ever, happened to you. And like most magical worriers, you misinterpret that fact to mean that your worry somehow has been protecting you. So you end up being afraid not to be afraid. But the obvious fact is, all worry does is make you miserable. Still, because the things you worry about have only rarely happened, or they've never happened to you, you keep yourself afraid not to worry. In RBT, we call such fear-motivated worry *magical worry*.

P-C: I see; but that's what I do, and it's silly once you think about it, right?

Me: Right, once you think about it rationally.

Author's Note

The session ended there. And because of conflicts in our schedules, I didn't see the professor for two weeks. Next are excerpts from that second session:

Me: Well, it has been exactly two weeks since I first saw you. So bring me up to date.

P-C: Okay, over the past two weeks, there has been a tremendous amount of improvement in my feelings. I'm back to sleeping eight hours a night and feeling a lot more comfortable. I read the whole book; I'm listening to that tape of the first session twice a day and I'm writing my ideas down for rational checks, the way you said. So I'm at a stage right now where I've seen the enemy and I know the enemy is me. I don't have the darn thing licked yet, by any means, but I'm sleeping well at night and I'm functioning a lot better, and I'm on top of my work.

Me: Great! Are you taking any medication?

P-C: No, I got the prescriptions filled and I took one tablet the first night. Then after that, I didn't take any more.

Me: Well, it seems that you have now discovered the obvious, that your undrugged brain is by far your best tranquilizer, as well as the best solution to personal problems.

Author's Note

That type of immediate positive feedback is the rule after P-Cs get as appropriately involved in self-help as the professor had gotten. But did you wonder why I ignored, rather than reinforced, the professor's report of having read the whole book? Such reports indicate that P-Cs have read the book as if it were a novel, once over lightly, then to be forgotten, or only haphazardly remembered. That's okay for novels. Novels are not usually meant to be learned and remembered; novels usually are meant only to be read as fast as possible so that they can be enjoyed as intensely as possible, but remembered only well enough to lead to buying another, as quickly as possible, preferably by the same author.

The rational bibliotherapeutic material I assign is easy, pleasant reading (see Appendix B). But it's meant to be learned, remembered, and used to improve one's emotional and behavioral control. That goal requires that the material be repeatedly read, repeatedly thought through, repeatedly remembered, and deliberately used, preferably every day. That's why I usually limit my comments about unassigned readings to "That's great! But I still want you to read the chapters I assign once a day every day, according to the printed instructions, until we have covered the first five chapters. Still, the more extra reading you do the better."

Both the professor and I knew he had not yet solved his worry problem. And when I asked, "Where do you want to start today?" he said: "With my magical worry." That topic necessitated an in-depth discussion of attitudes and attitude formation, as they are described in Chapter 4. During the discussion, we pinpointed the core irrational attitude that had maintained his longstanding habit of chronic, magical worry; that attitude was, "The world is a thoroughly threatening place that's just waiting to pounce on me at any second."

Professor Nelson believed it had only been through his constant vigilance (that is, intense magical worry) and "good luck" that he had graduated from high school and Yale University with high honors and had achieved his above average professional successes. But none of that really counted any more because "one never knows when one's good luck is going to run out."

During the next four months Professor Nelson became quite skilled in using Rational Self-Analysis (RSA) and Rational Emotive Imagery (REI), the two main emotional self-help techniques used in RBT (Chapters 14 and 15 in this book).

THE REMAINDER OF PROFESSOR NELSON'S RBT

After Professor Nelson's twenty-second RBT session, I went away on sabbatical leave for six months. But Professor Nelson chose not to consult my colleague who was covering my clinical practice in my absence. Next are excerpts from the follow-up session with Professor Nelson eleven months after his last session with me.

Me: All right, it's been exactly eleven months since the last time I saw you.

P-C: That's right.

Me: So, has the roof fallen in on you?

P-C: (*We both laughed.*) No; not many big things have occurred. And the ones that have, I have handled very rationally.

Me: Very good; now, as I recall, you came to me requesting medication.

P-C: That's right, I came in wanting the only mode of help I'd ever had before, which was medicine. And as you know from my file, I have a long clinical history of those pills. I guess in a sense, I'm a classic case history of the medical treatment of anxiety because in my teenage years, I was treated for it and a later psychiatrist put me on a regimen for it that went from Compazine to Thorazine and some others I don't even remember. And then the next round was when they put me on those last pills when I first sought help here. But I see now that this is not a medical illness that happens to me externally that needs a magic pill.

Me: Right.

P-C: That was an important insight for me to make. I know you probably have many patients tell you this, but it's an amazing insight and a wonderful feeling to have a set of tools that give me some control over my emotional reactions. As the accountants say, "That's the bottom line, right there." I think I have a significant degree of control over things now, that I didn't have eleven months ago.

Author's Note

Space limitations do not permit a more detailed presentation of that follow-up session here. But Professor Nelson described the many ways he was applying rational thinking in his work and in his family relations. He could advantageously do that because the rational way really is the most emotionally healthy way to deal with any situation in life. That's why increased coping skills in all life's areas, similar to those Professor Nelson and Mrs. Morrsey demonstrated, is the expected rule with cooperative P-Cs in RBT.

Written Rational Self-Analysis (RSA) is probably the single most important self-help maneuver that increases P-Cs' general coping skills. Chapter 14 gives you a detailed discussion of written RSA. But I recommend explaining cognitive-emotive dissonance to P-Cs before introducing them to written RSAs. That's why the next chapter is about cognitive-emotive dissonance.

PART FOUR

More Theory and the Technology of Therapeutic Self-Help

The success of any psychotherapeutic technique depends on appropriate P-C cooperation. In RBT, we call appropriate P-C cooperation *therapeutic self-help.* RBT is relatively unique in its neuropsychophysiological justification of (and its consistent, systematic use of) research-tested concepts and techniques of therapeutic self-help.

This section describes in detail the main self-help concepts and techniques routinely used in RBT—it also tells you exactly how to use them.

1. Cognitive-Emotive Dissonance (Chapter 13)
2. Written Rational Self-Analysis (RSA) (Chapter 14)
3. Rational Emotive Imagery (Chapter 15)

The therapeutic self-help concepts and techniques routinely used in RBT are equally effective in group RBT and individual RBT. In my opinion, individual RBT supplemented by group RBT is the ideal therapeutic formula for P-Cs who are able to have both experiences at the same time. And for certain types of P-Cs group RBT seems to be better than individual RBT.

So why hasn't group RBT been mentioned before now? There are two reasons. First, without a special training experience, it is difficult to become an effective RBT group therapist before you become an effective individual RBT therapist.

Second, the *Professional's Self-Training Kit for Group RBT* (Maultsby 1982), with its narrated audio-tape recordings of actual RBT groups, gives interested therapists and counselors detailed instructions in how to do group RBT.

CHAPTER 13
Cognitive-Emotive Dissonance

Cognitive-emotive dissonance is the strange or unusual emotional feeling people get when they have new thoughts or actions that conflict with their old attitudes and beliefs or habitual actions. Usually people describe that experience as "feeling wrong." So you can expect many therapeutic insights and ideas to "feel wrong" to P-Cs at first. That's because those insights and ideas will be in conflict with many of the P-Cs' pretherapy problem-related attitudes and beliefs. Understandably, therefore, cognitive-emotive dissonance is an unavoidable stage in therapeutic change.

Cognitive-emotive dissonance is the main reason people who don't know their Emotional ABCs refuse to make what they admit would be desirable behavioral changes. Those new behaviors (and their supporting ideas) initially "feel wrong." And typical "gut" logic is, "If an idea or action feels wrong, it can't be correct, so I should ignore it." Understandably, therefore, emotionally naive people automatically reject ideas or actions that "feel wrong," even when the ideas are objectively correct and the actions they justify are both healthy and highly desirable.

These insights make it easy to see why most people fail when they try to help themselves emotionally without outside help. The new ideas that they must believe and act out to improve their emotional control initially "feel wrong"; so the people reject those new ideas and actions, either without acting them out at all, or long before they act them out enough times to make them "feel right."

Dan, the college student with pre-exam anxiety in Chapter 1, was a good example of this type of person. Dan asked me to tell him what to think about exams. I naively told him: "Think the obvious facts about exams. Exams are neutral events, so they can't frighten you. It's you who frighten you about exams; however, you could keep yourself calm about exams. And you can stand to flunk them; you already have flunked two and you didn't die; so that proves you can stand it. Granted, you stood it miserably, rather than calmly, but you still stood it."

Why was it naive of me to tell Dan what to think? Because P-Cs rarely benefit from being directly told: "Think this." P-Cs benefit most reliably from thinking new ideas they first give themselves personally meaningful reasons to think.

As if to prove my point, what did Dan do? He did the same thing most emotionally distressed people do when they follow advice they don't believe: Dan followed my advice in a way that proved to him that my advice was "wrong." So he started his next session with: "I tried what you said, but it didn't work. Every time I thought that exams don't frighten me, and that I can stand to flunk them, my gut told me I was lying. The whole idea *felt totally wrong*. Exams do frighten me and I don't see any point in trying to pretend they don't. That would be phony and I hate phonies. I'm sorry, but good or bad, anxious or not, I've just got to be me, the real me."

That is the classic response of P-Cs whose therapists have not adequately prepared them for cognitive-emotive dissonance. Like most normal people, Dan had the strong human tendency to fear and hold in sacred, magical awe his emotions and other things that he didn't understand, but that caused him intense pleasure and pain. That's why, also like most normal people before they fully accept their Emotional ABCs, Dan held his negative emotions in the most sacred, magical awe of all. That magical awe blinded him to this obvious fact: Human emotions are merely neuropsychophysiological states that people create and eliminate at will with their beliefs and attitudes.

In his emotional blindness, Dan saw his negative emotions as essential components of his existential self. Understandably therefore, he had the incorrect belief that his habitually miserable feelings were the essence of being his real self. And people like Dan insist on being their real selves, even if it means being really miserable.

In short, Dan had the neurotic fear that I call "the phony fear." Briefly, people with "the phony fear" want to feel better without thinking better.[1] But the Emotional ABCs show you clearly why people can't do that without addictive drugs, electric shock, or some type of brain damage. From the first therapy session, therefore, RBT therapists focus on helping emotionally distressed people to accept that fact rationally, and then use it to justify improving their thinking. RBT therapists also repeatedly show resistant P-Cs that, other than improving their thinking, these are their emotional choices: They can go on accepting (either happily, stoically, or with whining) the irrational idea that their miserable feelings are the essence of their real selves; they can use drugs to make themselves less aware of how miserable they usually are; or they can get brain damage and become incapable of being aware of their misery.

I hope that by now you clearly see the importance of adequately preparing your P-Cs to handle cognitive-emotive dissonance rationally. If you don't adequately prepare them, they will experience needless, though temporary, frustration and disappointments. This chapter shows you how RBT helped Dan quickly get past those therapeutic barriers. You will also see how you can routinely help your P-Cs avoid having Dan's type of antitherapeutic experience.

---

[1]For a detailed clinical discussion of the cause and cure of "the phony fear," see *Help Yourself to Happiness* (Maultsby 1976).

SPECIAL VOCABULARY

Metaphor: In RBT, thinking that doesn't say what people mean, nor mean what they say. Metaphors are irrational when they trigger different (usually more negative) emotional feelings than the ones people usually have when they say what they mean and mean what they say. For example, "I'm a gutless mouse," is an irrational metaphor. That's why the Mouse Lady (see page 5) immediately felt less miserable when I got her to say what she meant and mean what she said.

FOCUS ITEMS

1. What are the three essential steps for eliminating an emotional habit without brain damage?
2. What can learning to drive in England teach an American driver about emotional reeducation?
3. What is the most accurate answer to this question: How long will it take me to solve my problem with RBT?
4. Why didn't Mrs. Morrsey have as much cognitive-emotive dissonance as Dan had?
5. How would you explain cognitive-emotive dissonance to P-Cs?

CHAPTER 13

Cognitive-Emotive Dissonance

In my experience, the simple straightforward way is the best way to handle people like Dan. I start with these basic facts. There are three simple yet essential steps in rapidly eliminating emotional habits.

1. People must completely reject the beliefs and attitudes that support the undesirable habits.
2. Because nature abhors mental vacuums just as much as it abhors physical vacuums, people must replace their old beliefs and attitudes with new ideas they are willing to make their new beliefs and attitudes.
3. People must practice acting out their new ideas until those ideas become their new beliefs and attitudes.[2] Then, and only then, will people have created the semipermanent, behavioral unit called a new behavioral habit.

I pointed out to Dan that he had not even bothered to question his old self-defeating beliefs, much less reject them. Instead his attitude was, "I really don't believe this A, B, C stuff. But because I have an open mind, I'll try it and see if it works."

In reality, though, IT (a new idea) never works emotionally by itself. To benefit from a new idea, people always have to work it; that is, they have to act out the new idea as if it were already their personal belief. That means taking the three steps (described earlier) at least as diligently as people take them to learn any behavioral habit.

[2]In RBT we teach P-Cs a special mental-practice technique called Rational Emotive Imagery (or REI). I explain that technique in Chapter 15.

After telling Dan the three steps in eliminating habits, I helped him compare the stages of emotional and behavioral *education* to the stages of emotional and behavioral *reeducation*. That comparison makes two important facts immediately clear. (1) Eliminating an old habit is a slightly different process from the process used to learn the habit. (2) The one big difference between education and reeducation is cognitive-emotive dissonance, the third stage of reeducation.[3]

STAGES OF BEHAVIORAL EDUCATION VERSUS REEDUCATION

Education	Reeducation
1. Intellectual insight	1. Intellectual insight
2. Practice	2. Practice
a. mental	a. mental
b. real-life	b. real-life
3. Emotional insight	3. COGNITIVE-EMOTIVE DISSONANCE
4. New personality-trait formation	4. Emotional insight
	5. New personality-trait formation

Finally, to get Dan to personalize that comparison, I carried him through a realistic example of driver's reeducation. As it does for most people, this example quickly got Dan to see clearly that he already knew all he needed to know to be able to overcome his antitherapeutic cognitive-emotive dissonance; he just didn't realize he knew it.

DRIVER'S REEDUCATION

"Imagine," I said to Dan, "that after this session, you go to the airport and fly to England. At the London International Airport you will have an English car waiting for your personal use.

"I assume you already know how to drive. If I'm right, then you already have a driver's education.[4]

"For some strange reason, the English people drive on the left side of the road and, therefore, have their auto-driving mechanisms on the right side of their cars. For Americans to drive safely in England, therefore, they have to give themselves a driver's reeducation.

"You now see clearly and understand the driving situation in England, right? Therefore, you have intellectual insight into your driving-reeducational problem.

[3]Remember, according to RBT theory, *therapeutic changes are really instances of emotional and physical reeducation,* provided the changes didn't result from drugs, brain damage, electric shock, or similar organic treatments.

[4]Even people who don't know how to drive know the physical reeducational process so well that they still benefit from this analogy.

13-1   Cognitive-Emotive Dissonance

But would you expect your intellectual insight alone to eliminate your American driving habits instantly and enable you to feel as normal driving in England as you now feel driving in America?

"Of course not! You know too much about learning and replacing physical habits to be that naive about driver's reeducation. But like most people, before they see that their emotions are just learned habits, you were just that naive about your emotional reeducation; otherwise, you would not have been disappointed about the results of your first attempt to decrease your preexam anxiety.

"Now, imagine yourself seated behind the wheel on the right side of your English car, driving off in the busy traffic at London International Airport. How do you think you would feel? Strange? Odd? Like you were driving wrong, right? Of course, and that would be *cognitive-emotive dissonance*.

"Your conscious, verbal mind[5] would be telling you the correct way to drive; but your wordless, superconscious mind of American driving attitudes would still be triggering your old auto driving feelings; so, your 'gut' would make you feel as if the objectively correct way to drive were really incorrect. That's why, at any point on your way to your hotel, if you suddenly found yourself 'feeling right,' that is, feeling like your old normal, natural, American-driving self, what would you hear immediately? You would hear police whistles, auto horns, and English obscenities. Why? Because you'd be feeling right, but driving wrong, dangerously wrong.

"That's a clear-cut example of the hazard of following 'gut logic' and 'gut thinking' instead of brain logic and brain thinking.

"In RBT, we teach people to think with their brains and to let their 'gut' digest their food, as Mother Nature seemed to have intended it to do. When we mere FHBs (fallible human beings) try to reverse the wisdom of Mother Nature, we get ulcers, ulcerative colitis, hypertension, and a host of other psychosomatic disorders. But if we stay in step with Mother Nature, we stay healthy."

At that point, Dan was ideally ready to achieve:

_____

[5]Whether or not to talk to your P-Cs about their right and left brains is a matter of clinical judgment. I usually base this decision on the education and clinical resistance of each P-C.

TWO IMPORTANT CLINICAL INSIGHTS

"What would you have to do to drive safely to your London hotel? You'd have to ignore your 'gut feelings' and consciously think exclusively rational, English-driving thoughts with your brain, right?

"Now let's assume you did ignore your 'gut feelings,' and you drove safely to your hotel. Would that mean you had then replaced your American driving habits completely with the correct English driving habit? Of course not. You wouldn't be so unrealistically demanding as to expect that. You know that doing something just one time does not mean you have learned it. But you were just that unrealistically demanding in your expectations for instant emotional change with your preexam anxiety."

Before you explain the five stages of emotional reeducation to your P-Cs, they will be just as unrealistically demanding in their expectations as Dan was. So expect and rationally challenge their irrational demands, as I did Dan's. After that rational challenge, Dan was ideally prepared to give himself:

THE ANSWER TO A COMMON CLINICAL QUESTION

"How long would you have to practice in English traffic before you would have replaced your American driving habits completely with English driving habits? The most accurate and honest answer you can give yourself is, It would take as long as it takes. And that's the most accurate and honest answer you can give yourself to the question: How long will it take you to get over your preexam anxiety? As long as it takes.

"But if you were to practice your English driving two or three times a day, every day, you would achieve your driver reeducational goals much faster than you would if you just practiced once every week or so. Right? Well, the same facts apply to learning how to replace your preexam anxiety with self-confidence of success."

AN OUNCE OF THERAPEUTIC PREVENTION

Helping P-Cs understand cognitive-emotive dissonance before they experience it is the best first step in helping them get through it most quickly without confusion. The next and final step in getting P-Cs smoothly through cognitive-emotive dissonance is encouraging them to do diligent, daily emotional practice.

The idea of practicing emotions is foreign to most people. But RBT not only emphasizes the importance of daily emotional practice, RBT teaches P-Cs an efficiently effective emotional practice technique; it's called Rational Emotive Imagery (see Chapter 15).

Now let's compare Mrs. Morrsey's case to Dan's case. In contrast to Dan's many years of emotional practice, Mrs. Morrsey had only been practicing her emotional problem about six months. So when she started RBT, she had just entered the stage of emotional insight for her depressive habit. Her right brain's super-conscious, attitudinal control of her depression was still relatively weak. To stay depressed, she had to give her depression frequent, conscious self-talk support from her left brain. Consequently, immediately accepting the following insights did *not* cause her significant cognitive-emotive dissonance.

MORE EXCERPTS FROM MRS. MORRSEY'S FIRST RBT SESSION

Me: You have the mistaken idea that because you are in an objectively miserable marriage, you have to feel emotionally miserable about it. But that's just a mistaken idea. Also, I'll bet you have also been calling yourself miserable names like "stupid" and "idiot" for being in your situation.

P-C: Yes, I have done that, too.

Me: Well, those are the things you will have to stop doing, if you are going to get over this depression. The reality is you don't have to feel miserable about a miserable mistake. The reality is you are not those miserable names you call yourself. Therefore, it's silly to make yourself feel as if you were those things. Now you alone are doing that, and only you can stop doing it. On the other hand, if you go on believing those irrational ideas about yourself, how are you going to feel?

P-C: I guess you feel the way you believe.

Me: That's right. And that's why you can quickly solve your problems by replacing your depressive beliefs with more rational beliefs.

USEFUL CLINICAL INSIGHTS

Normally, people seek psychotherapy because they want to feel and behave better; but they almost never expect to have to *think* better to achieve that goal. That's because they rarely think about their thinking, and they don't know their Emotional ABCs. So they don't see that their own beliefs and attitudes prevent them from feeling and behaving better. Out of emotional ignorance, therefore, these people accuse their external perceptions at A of causing their emotional feelings at C.

This obvious but consistently ignored example of magical thinking seems almost universal, and it is usually independent of formal education. I wonder, therefore, if magical thinking might mean that the human fear of the unknown is so strong that any explanation of puzzling events is preferable to no explanation. Since the human fear of the unknown is so universal, this idea is an attractive theory for why highly educated people still commonly engage in some form of magical thinking when they try to understand their emotions.

Theoretical speculations aside, to fully understand cognitive-emotive dissonance and how to resolve it, you must accept Pavlov's important insight: "For people, the word is an entirely real stimulus; it signals and substitutes for every other stimulus and elicits every kind of reaction elicited by other stimuli'' (Pavlov as quoted in Volgyesi 1954 and slightly paraphrased). People's left-brain verbiage, therefore, can and does trigger a-B belief-triggered emotions. Getting P-Cs to understand their emotions on that basis is a major early goal in RBT. And the best way I know to pursue that goal is to emphasize continually the hazards of:

IRRATIONAL RHETORIC IN EMOTIONAL PROBLEMS[6]

Probably the most common examples of irrational rhetoric are the irrational IT beliefs. The almost universal, but irrational, beliefs that IT, HE, SHE, or THEY upset me can cause up to 50 percent of people's emotional distress. That's why just getting people to accept responsibility for their undesirable emotions immediately causes a noticeable drop in their emotional distress. Sane people willingly tolerate their undesirable emotional pain largely because they believe they have no other choice about it. The habitual use of rational rhetoric shows such people they can refuse to have undesirably miserable emotions about anything.

Probably the most confusing type of irrational rhetoric is the irrational metaphor. To understand why irrational metaphors are unhealthy, you must first remember the RBT concept of a metaphor. In RBT, a metaphor refers to thinking that doesn't say what people mean nor mean what they say. Metaphors are irrational when they trigger different (usually more negative) emotional feelings than the ones the people would have if they were to say what they mean and mean what they say in a specific situation.

For example, let's look at criticized employees who have these sincere thoughts: ''My boss really stated his negative opinions of my work.'' They probably would have less intense anger than those who thought: ''My boss really chewed me out.'' Therefore, unless the Camera Check of Perceptions would have shown the boss actually biting those upset employees, their RBT therapists would reject the metaphorical accusation: ''My boss really chewed me out'' and insist on the more accurate statement: ''My boss really stated his negative opinions of my work.''

At this point many new P-Cs will ask, ''Isn't that just semantics?'' But I always insist, ''No, *it's not just semantics; in emotional and behavioral self-control, it's never just semantics; it's always all semantics.''*

Hardly a day passes without most people spending at least a few minutes in active self-debate about the most or least appropriate words to say to someone else. Clearly, people know that what they say to others directly influences how those other people feel and act toward them.

The A, B, C model of emotions makes this fact clear: *The words people use to talk to themselves directly influence their feelings and actions toward themselves.* Much research on semantic conditioning firmly supports the A, B, C model of emo-

[6]Chapter 12 defines irrational rhetoric.

tions (Grant 1939; Hall and Prior 1969; Lacey and Smith 1954; Lacey et al. 1955; Menzies 1937; Mowrer 1966; Razran 1935, 1949, 1949a, 1961; Skinner 1957; Staats and Staats 1957, 1958) as do many other research reports these authors cite. Understandably, therefore, RBT teaches P-Cs to be as rational in choosing words for their own self-talk as they are for their talks with other people.

FOUR IMPORTANT CLINICAL FACTS TO REMEMBER

1. The Emotional ABCs and the Five Rational Questions give P-Cs relatively objective, easy-to-use ways to check their thoughts and the mental picture-maps they trigger. Once P-Cs begin questioning the rationality of their thoughts and the objective accuracy of their mental picture-maps, they begin replacing their irrational ones with more rational ones.

2. Making such replacements once or twice will not solve emotional and/or behavioral problems. To solve those problems, P-Cs must form the habit of consistently supporting their new, rational, right-brain mental picture-maps with sincere, new, rational, left-brain thoughts. Then, rational emotions and physical behaviors will have to follow.

3. To replace old emotional or physical habits with new ones, people must practice; that is, they must think and act out the new ideas that are logical for their new behavioral habits. But just one or two instances of practice are not nearly enough to complete the reeducational process; people must practice enough times to move themselves from cognitive-emotive dissonance through emotional insight (the fourth stage in reeducation) and into a new personality trait; that's the fifth and final stage in this process. Only then will the old habit disappear and the new behavior occur as naturally, normally, and automatically as the old behavior formerly occurred.

4. Improved thinking is essential for improved emotional and behavioral control. And the only way to improve one's thinking is to improve one's use of words to the level of rational rhetoric.

The Memory Aids for this chapter are on page 228.

CHAPTER **14**
Written Rational Self-Analysis (RSA)

Most people have the incorrect idea that self-analysis is difficult; fortunately, it isn't. In fact, self-analysis is so easy that most people do it every day without even realizing they are doing it. Common examples of self-analysis are "I work because I have to; I have no choice about it." "My urge to eat just overwhelms me; I can't resist it." "I'm just lazy; that's my only trouble." "If I just had more self-confidence, I would ask for a date." "I'm just naturally good at math." "My strong point is, I always look at the bright side of everything." "I'm not masculine enough; that's all there is to it."

Every belief people have about themselves is a self-analysis. In addition, people's self-analyses direct both their emotional and physical control. Unfortunately, the self-analyses that emotionally distressed people make most often are irrationally negative and more harmful than helpful. But Rational Self-Analysis (RSA) is one of the two healthiest self-help maneuvers that people can learn to do (Rational Emotive Imagery, discussed in Chapter 15, is the other one.)

Rational Self-Analysis is a structured self-help technique used in RBT to help P-Cs discover the cause-effect relationships between the cognitive, emotive, and physical components in their behavioral problems. RSA enables P-Cs to:

1. Identify and separate their thoughts, emotional feelings and actions.
2. Check whether their thoughts, emotional feelings and actions are rational for them.
3. Where needed, learn more rational habits of thinking, emotionally feeling, and physically acting.

Section I of this chapter gives you the standard format and specific steps for doing written Rational Self-Analysis. I hope you, the reader, will do an RSA as you read the instructions. That's why I wrote the instructions the way I give them to my P-Cs and the way I recommend you give them to yours. So, as you read, imagine that you are a P-C and I'm the therapist.

Remember, you can do an RSA of desirable as well as undesirable behavior. The topic is irrelevant. It's the technique of RSA that I want you to learn. And as you know, you never really learn something well until you actually do it. That's why participatory training is an important feature of the intensive training program for psychotherapists and counselors held at the Rational Behavior Therapy and Training Center at the University of Kentucky College of Medicine. Having psychotherapists experience what they put their P-Cs through enhances both their professional skill and personal growth.

Section I of this chapter clearly describes the standard format and sequence for doing written Rational Self-Analysis (RSA) and gives you an example of a well-done RSA. Section II of the chapter gives you detailed, clinical discussions of the four self-defeating cognitive habits involved in the TGIF (Thank Goodness It's Friday) syndrome and chronic irrational anger, at the same time it shows you how RSAs help people eliminate those problems. Section III of the chapter gives you a step-by-step discussion of how to structure your therapy session around a P-C's RSA.

SPECIAL VOCABULARY—SECTION I
None.

FOCUS ITEMS —SECTION I
1. What are the parts of the standard RSA form?
2. What is the standard sequence in writing an RSA?
3. Recite the Five Rational Questions.
4. Can you do the Camera Check of an emotional feeling?
5. What are the only two things that RSAs do?

CHAPTER 14

Written Rational Self-Analysis

SECTION I

For the best results, use the standard RSA format and your everyday language. Write down your experiences as soon as possible after they occur. That way you will get the fastest, most lasting results possible. And remember, *You are never too upset to do an RSA; an RSA is a faster and safer way to calm yourself down than tranquilizers.*

THE CORRECT RSA SEQUENCE

Stop here and copy the standard RSA format (see the top of page 176) on a separate piece of paper. Then refer to it as you read about the individual sections below.

First Step: Describe A, the activating event, on the left side of an imaginary line down the center of your paper. In your usual language, simply state the facts as you saw and experienced them. For example: "For a month now, I have had three letters of recommendation hanging over my head and it's driving me crazy." That was the A section of a real RSA, done by Dr. F., an English professor whose RSA will be used in this chapter as a teaching example.

THE STANDARD RSA FORMAT

A. ACTIVATING EVENT: What you perceived happened.

Da. CAMERA CHECK: If you perceived anything a video camera would *not* show, correct that to what a video camera *would* have shown.

B. YOUR BELIEFS: Your sincere thoughts about A, plus your attitudes about each B sentence.

Db. RATIONAL DEBATE OF B: Answer "yes" or "no" for each rational question about each B sentence or write DNA ("does not apply"). Then write *rational alternative self-talk* for each irrational B idea, and "That's rational" for each rational B idea.

B_1.

B_2.

ETC.

Db_1.

Db_2.

ETC.

C. CONSEQUENCES OF B
  1. Emotional feelings
  2. Actions

E. EXPECTED NEW BEHAVIORS
  1. New emotional feelings
  2. New Actions

Five Rational Questions

1. Is my thinking here based on obvious fact?
2. Will my thinking here best help me protect my life and health?
3. Will my thinking here best help me achieve my short- and long-term goals?
4. Will my thinking here best help me avoid my most unwanted conflicts with others?
5. Will my thinking here best help me habitually feel the emotions I want to feel?

Second Step: Immediately under your A section, write B, your beliefs. As best you remember, state word for word your sincere thoughts, self-talk, or inner speech about the A event.

Number each B-section idea. Then show whether you had a positive, negative, or neutral attitude about it by writing "(positive or good)," "(negative or bad)," or "(neutral)" in parentheses following each B-section idea. Dr. F.'s first two B-section ideas were: B_1 "What can I say?" (negative) and B_2 "Why should I have to write letters I don't want to write?" (negative).

Both of those B items were unanswered questions. In the B section, P-Cs are to label all unanswered questions, rhetorical questions. Next, P-Cs are to state the personal beliefs that are hidden in those questions; then in the Db section, P-Cs are to debate rationally each of those stated beliefs (see Dr. F.'s B_1 on page 181).

Normally, it takes about six times as much space to correct irrational thinking as it does to write it. So leave six times as many blank lines under each B-section idea. That way, you will probably have enough space on the opposite side of the page to debate that idea rationally in the Db section. Of course, you can always use the back of the page if you need more space for your rational debate.

After you complete your B section, count up your positives, negatives, and neutrals. Your totals will show you the main types of attitudes that helped trigger your emotional feelings and the other reactions you had in your C section about A, the activating event. This maneuver makes clear how and why your superconscious, wordless attitudes can be more important than your conscious, verbal thoughts in some of your reactions.

Third Step: In the C section, write the behavioral consequences of your B ideas. The C section has two parts: Emotional feelings and Actions. In the appropriate section, simply state how you felt emotionally and what you did physically. In Dr. F.'s RSA (given later in this chapter) the C section lists these consequences: Emotional feelings: anger, anxiety, and shame. Action: procrastination.

Fourth Step: Immediately under the C section, write the Five Rational Questions. In reality, questions are neither rational nor irrational. The label *The Five Rational Questions* is just a shorthand way of saying, "the five questions that help ensure that your cognitions, emotional feelings, and physical actions will be rational."

The Five Rational Questions

1. Is my thinking here based on obvious fact?
2. Will my thinking here help me protect my life and health?
3. Will my thinking here best help me achieve my short-term and long-term goals?
4. Will my thinking here best help me avoid my most unwanted conflict with others?
5. Will my thinking here best help me habitually feel the emotions I want to feel?

Fifth Step: Opposite the C section, write the E section; it contains the new emotional feelings and actions you want to have in similar future A-type events.

Don't put wishes of the "oh, if I only had . . . " type in your E section. The E section is for wishes or wants that you have already decided to make your habits. So list only the actions for which you can honestly say: "The next time I shall . . . " Remember, the E section describes only *your choices* of new emotional and physical actions for similar future A events. So ignore completely behaviors that others (including your therapist) may want you to learn, but which you are not yet convinced are right for you.

Initially, in RSAs of negative emotions, the most rational new emotions to try to create will be to feel less negative or more calm in similar future A events. "But what," you may wonder, "if I want to enjoy an event I now hate or fear?" That's okay; you have that emotional choice, too. But the most rational emotional goals usually will be those you are most likely to achieve most quickly. That brings me to this important insight: *To replace a strong negative emotion with a positive emotion people always have to pass through the calm or neutral emotional state first.* Re-, member, neutral emotions are real emotions too. And the opposite of negative emotions is not positive emotions; it's neutral emotions.

If, for example, you want to stop reacting hatefully toward an A event, you must first get rid of the hateful attitude that maintains your hateful responses. If at the same time you are doing that, you require yourself to learn loving responses toward that A event, you'll probably fail; you will be demanding more immediate emotional change and new emotional learning than most people can handle efficiently. That's why the most rational first emotional goal would probably be to hate the event less and less until you can react to it calmly or indifferently. Then, if you still want to, you can learn to love it.

Common examples of hated behaviors people often want to learn to like are studying; doing certain types of work; having sex or certain types of sex; writing; speaking in public; and refusing to overeat, drink, or smoke. Usually, though, your P-Cs won't want to like the events they hate; they will just want to get rid of their self-defeating hate.

Sometimes you may not be quite sure what emotions or actions you want to have in future A events. In those cases, leave the E section blank. Just make sure you put your most sincerely rational thoughts in your Db section. Your sincere rational thoughts will point you directly to the most rational emotional and behavioral goals for you to want to learn. When you discover them, write them in your E section.

Remember, rational E sections will be logical for your rationally chosen Db section ideas. So it's a waste of time to write "to feel calm" at E if you have Db ideas like these: "It really is awful. No one in their right mind would stand for it. I'll just die if it happens again."

A Common Question

Isn't it unhealthy for people to stop having emotions? Yes, to stop having all emotions completely would be most unhealthy. Fortunately, though, doing RSAs can't stop people from having any emotion completely. The minds of physically healthy people force their brains to trigger and maintain some type of emotional state every second they are awake. So if you are conscious and have a healthy, undrugged brain, you will always have some type of emotion. It may not be the emotion you prefer; it may even be the one you hate the most. But you will definitely have an emotion.

THE ONLY TWO THINGS RSAs DO

First, without alcohol or other drugs, RSAs help people have fewer undesirable emotions and physical reactions.

Second, RSAs help people have more desirable emotions and physical reactions, also without alcohol or other drugs.

So, avoid or reject meaningless E section statements such as "I want to have no feelings at all." No one can achieve that emotional goal and remain healthy and awake.

Sixth Step: The sixth step in doing an RSA is Da, the Camera Check of A. Ask yourself, "Would a video camera have recorded the A events as I described them?"[1] If your answer is "yes" for each A section sentence, simply write "factual" or "all facts" in the Da section and go on to the Db section. But if you have "no" answers, that means you have mistaken one or more personal opinions for a statement of fact. In the Da section, correct any such statements to what a video camera would have recorded. For example, you would correct "I cried my heart out all the way home" to "I cried intensely until I got home, but my heart didn't leave my body, not even for a second."

Do camera images always accurately describe facts? No, just like the human brain, cameras can misrepresent obvious facts. But the value of the Camera Check is not based on what a video camera might have recorded. The value of the Camera Check is based on what a video camera *could not* have recorded. For example, take the self-perception "I cried my heart out." No video camera could have recorded a person's heart leaving, or being out of his or her body. So that A section statement would not pass the Camera Check of A, because it would not fit the obvious facts of that person's situation. But to have the most emotionally healthy self-control, people's perceptions must accurately fit the obvious facts of their situation.

What About An A Section About Feelings?

You cannot do a Camera Check of an emotional feeling. But emotional feelings are neuropsychophysiological facts. You either have them and describe them accurately, or you don't. In addition, you are the only one who can do either. So you *can* put simple statements of emotional facts, such as "I was sad" or "I felt depressed" in the A section. But you would still write "sad" or "depressed" in the emotion part of your C section. Then in your Da section, you'd simply write "factual" for your Camera Check of an A section about feelings.

Remember, though, that in RBT, feelings are almost always one-word nouns (see Chapter 11). If at A you said, "I just died from embarrassment," in the Da section you would correct that to "I didn't die, but I did feel more embarrassed than I wanted to feel." Then in your C section you would also write "embarrassed."

Seventh Step: The seventh step in doing an RSA is Db, the check of each B section idea using the Five Rational Questions. Then as needed, you replace irrational B ideas with rational ideas in the Db section. First, read over your B_1 idea; next, see if you can give three or more honest "yes" answers to the Five Rational Questions about it; if you can, write "That's rational" at Db_1 and go on to B_2.

But if you cannot give at least three honest "yes" answers to the Five Rational Questions, at Db_1 write "That idea is irrational." Then think of different ideas about the situation that have these two features:

---

[1] I say video camera, because it usually records both sound and sight.

1. You can give at least three honest "yes" answers to the Five Rational Questions about the new ideas.

2. You are willing to make the new ideas your personal beliefs by acting them out in future A situations.

Then, write those ideas in your Db section. But remember, it doesn't matter how rational an idea may be. If you are not willing to make that idea your personal belief by habitually acting it out, that won't help you.

14-1   An Activating Event

Dr. F., a widowed English professor, and her teenage daughter had received RBT to learn how to interact more rationally with each other. About a year after therapy Dr. F. decided to use her skill in doing RSAs to solve her problem with procrastination. When Dr. F. later told me of her success, I asked her to let me present her RSA here as a teaching example. Let's now examine each section of her complete RSA. It demonstrates well how and why having P-Cs learn to do Rational Self-Analysis helps make RBT a comprehensive, short-term psychotherapy that produces long-term results.

DR. F'S RSA

A.   ACTIVATING EVENT
For a month now, I have had three letters of recommendation hanging over my head and it's driving me crazy.

Da.   THE CAMERA CHECK OF A
Nothing is hanging over my head and I am the only IT that can drive me crazy. But since I don't like the idea of being crazy, I refuse to drive myself there. A month ago, I promised three students I would write letters of recommendation for

them. But instead of writing the letters, I'm making myself miserable while I put off doing it.

B.	BELIEFS	Db.	RATIONAL DEBATE OF B

B_1. What can I say? (negative) That's a rhetorical question hiding the belief that I don't know what to say.

Db_1. My belief gets a "No" for RQs[2] 1, 3, 4, and 5. Rational thinking is, I can say anything I want to say. I don't have to be effusive or dishonest. I can simply say I believe the students have whatever potential I believe they have to do graduate work in English. Then I can describe what they have done in my classes.

B_2. Why should I have to write letters when I don't want to? (negative) That's another rhetorical question hiding the belief that it's unfair that they should expect me to write letters I don't want to write.

Db_2. That belief gets "No" for RQs 1, 3, 4, and 5. Rational thinking is: Writing letters of recommendation is part of my job. Therefore, I am obliged to write letters within reason for students, if they request them. Three letters is a reasonable number. So to say that I shouldn't be expected to write them is absurd. And it's even more absurd for me to feel angry about it. I'm just trying to justify avoiding my responsibilities. I agreed to work for the university; writing these letters is part of my job. So I calmly choose to write them.

B_3. I hardly know these students. (negative)

Db_3. That idea gets "No" for RQs 1, 3, 4, and 5. Rational thinking is, If I want to know these students better than I do, I can easily schedule conferences with them and get better aquainted.

B_4. I'll be forced to say things about these students that I don't believe. (negative)

Db_4. My thinking here gets "No" for RQs 1, 3, 4, and 5. Rational thinking is, I won't be forced to say anything I don't believe. I alone will write the letters. I alone will decide what I say in them, and I alone will mail them. My belief just doesn't make rational sense, so I'll give it up and write the letters.

[2]RQ stands for Rational Question

B_5. I don't want to write letters when I don't know the facts. (negative)

Db_5. That idea gets "No" for RQs 3, 4, and 5. My thought is a fact, but it's irrelevant. If I want more facts than I already have about my students, all I have to do is study their files.

B_6. I don't like being forced to do anything I don't want to do. (negative)

Db_6. That idea gets "No" for RQs 3, 4, and 5. My thought is a fact, but it's irrelevant to this situation. No one is going to overpower me and force me to write the letters. So I don't and won't have to write them. But I choose to write them because it is part of my job and I choose to do my job well.

B_7. I know I shouldn't be procrastinating like this. (negative)

Db_7. That idea gets "No" for RQs 1, 3, and 5. I should be procrastinating, exactly as I am doing.[3] But since I don't like this experience, I'll change it immediately.

C.   CONSEQENCES OF B
  1. *Emotional feelings*
      a. anger

      b. anxiety
      c. shame
  2. *Actions*
      a. procrastination

E.   EXPECTED NEW BEHAVIORS
  1. *New emotional feelings*
      a. calm, if not positive feelings

  2. *New actions*
      a. Immediately write these and future letters of recommendation

HOW P-Cs RECOGNIZE WELL-DONE RSAs

Well-done RSAs immediately decrease negative emotions and immediately reinforce rationally positive emotions. Analyzing positive emotions helps people because it makes them aware of their essential contribution to their happiness. That awareness makes people less irrationally dependent upon other people and "fate" for their happiness.

Dr. F.'s well-done RSA is typical of the type of RSAs that cooperative P-Cs start doing after eight to ten RBT sessions. Skill in doing RSAs makes P-Cs rapidly and happily independent of their therapists. That's why therapy termination in RBT is usually both smooth and mutually pleasant.

---

[3]Yes, you read it correctly. This will become clear in Section II of this chapter when you read about *rational* versus *irrational shoulds*.

```
┌─────────────────────┐
│                     │
│   SECTION II        │
│                     │
└─────────────────────┘
```

SPECIAL VOCABULARY—SECTION II
None.

FOCUS ITEMS —SECTION II
1. Name the four self-defeating cognitive habits usually found among people who have the TGIF syndrome?
2. What three facts make it important to explain the difference between force and choice to people who have the TGIF syndrome?
3. What belief is the single most common cognitive cue for self-defeating anger?
4. Why is the belief in Item 3 usually irrational?
5. State the three basic assumptions that are the bases of all empirical sciences.

Most P-Cs have at least one of the following four self-defeating cognitive habits:

1. confusing irrelevant facts with rational thoughts
2. wanting guaranteed success before being willing to act
3. calling personal, though undesirable choices of actions, "being forced" to act
4. failing to separate *rational shoulds* from *irrational shoulds*.

People who have the TGIF (Thank Goodness It's Friday) syndrome, people who have chronic irrational anger, and procrastinators usually have all four of those self-defeating cognitive habits. Predictably, therefore, Dr. F. had all four of those self-defeating habits when she consulted me about her parent-child problems. In fact, those self-defeating habits were the main causes of her parent-child problems and became the main focus of her RBT.

The following discussion will explain those four self-defeating cognitive habits and show the rational thinking that enabled Dr. F. to solve her parent-child problem. You will find continual therapeutic use for these concepts when you discuss RSAs in therapy, especially those RSAs that deal with irrational anger or guilt. Either or both of these emotions are almost always involved in learned depressions.

CONFUSING IRRELEVANT FACTS WITH RATIONAL THOUGHTS

A fact is irrelevant when it has no *necessary* influence on your doing a specific thing. For example, Dr. F. stated: "I don't want to write letters when I don't know the facts" (B_5), and "I don't like being forced to do anything I don't want to do"

(B_6). In her rational debates of those facts, Dr. F. pointed out that those facts had no necessary influence on her goal of writing the promised letters.

When emotionally distressed people fill their minds with irrelevant facts they naively believe they are thinking rationally. In terms of rational emotional control, however, neither are irrelevant facts helpful, nor do they make rational sense. That's why Dr. F. rationally dismissed her irrelevant B-section facts.

WANTING GUARANTEED SUCCESS

Procrastinators usually have the irrational fear that making their best effort but still not achieving optimum success would prove they are incompetent. They know they can't have the guaranteed success they want, so they put off doing things until the last minute. That way they are rushed and have only one chance to perform. If they fail to get optimum success, they always have the "cop out" that they didn't have enough time to do their best; so they don't have to feel too bad about their below-par results.

CONFUSING CHOICE WITH FORCE

One of the core components in procrastination and the TGIF syndrome is calling personal, though undesirable, choices of action "being forced" to act. The obvious facts are: People choose to do their personally undesirable tasks. But if they believe they are being forced to act, they have the angry feelings they would have if they really were forced to act. That's why the first step in the rational solution to procrastination is to get procrastinators to focus on the following four facts:

1. Objectively, *choice* means having two or more ways of voluntarily responding to a given situation, whether these ways are desirable, undesirable, or mixed.
2. Objectively, being *forced* to act means being physically overpowered and, therefore, having no voluntary way of responding.
3. The normal emotional responses to being forced are anger and self-dislike.
4. The normal emotional responses to choosing, even between undesirable options, is at worst mild irritation, and at best, self-satisfaction about having chosen the "lesser of two or more evils."

To make the rational view of force versus choice perfectly clear, imagine that a robber points a loaded gun at a woman and says: "Give me your money or I'll shoot you." Now, if she gives the robber her money, would she have been forced to give up her money, or would she have chosen to give up her money? The rational answer is, she would have chosen to give up her money.

The concept of force would be inappropriate in that situation because being forced means *no choice* of action. The woman could have (as many people would have) chosen to keep her money and risk being shot. So the concept of force in that example would be inappropriate as well as irrational.

Now, imagine a purse-snatcher having snatched a woman's purse and escaped. Then she would have been forced to part with her money.

At this point, many trainees ask, "She would have lost her money in either case, right? So why is the distinction between force and choice so important here?" To understand fully the neuropsychoemotional significance of seeing oneself as being forced versus choosing to do things, you must remember this: Objectively being forced means that the forced people have no self-control; their desires are irrelevant. Forced people are therefore like impotent, mindless objects of benevolent or malevolent manipulations at the whim of overpowering people or events. That's why it's hard to imagine a self-image that people normally hate more than the self-image of being forced.

Remember, though, as a stimulus for emotional responses, *the illusion of being forced is as neuropsychoemotionally powerful as the reality of being forced.* Therefore, the incorrect belief that one is being forced triggers the same intense anger and self-dislike that the reality of being forced triggers. Next are the three emotionally healthy reasons why RBT therapists insist that P-Cs call choice *choice* and being forced *being forced*.

1. Rationally choosing to do undesirable things to avoid experiencing even more undesirable consequences is what intelligent people habitually do. It's the healthiest basis for the self-image of having sane, mature, self-control. That's why people deserve to feel good about themselves for making such choices.

2. Admittingly having chosen to do even foolish things rarely triggers as much prolonged, intense anger and self-dislike as the belief that one was forced to do even sensible, or personally desirable things, such as study, practice, or go to work each day.

3. When people inaccurately perceive themselves as being forced to do things that in fact they choose to do, they deny themselves the emotionally healthy reinforcement that is logical for having rationally acted in their own best interests.

Now we are ready to look at the final two steps in the rational solution to procrastination as well as the TGIF syndrome. Get the P-Cs to list in writing all the positive benefits they hope to get by choosing to do their hated tasks. Then have them read over that list every time they are tempted to delay doing their hated tasks.

By delaying tasks and finally doing them angrily, procrastinators self-defeatingly prove (and at the same time deny) the next obvious facts: They have the choice of when and how (that is, angrily, instead of happily or calmly) they do the task; they are therefore in complete control of themselves. But, by denying that fact, they "force" themselves to have the hated self-image that people usually have when they really are physically overpowered and forced to do things.

In summary, here are the main three reasons it's rational and healthy for people to admit they choose to do what they do: (1) It's impossible for people to become or stay as undesirably upset (even about choosing to do the most personally undesirable tasks) as they would become if they were forced to do those tasks. (2) People who admit to choosing to do what they do have the healthiest possible basis for a positive self-image of themselves as being in healthy self-control. (3) These people prevent or quickly get rid of the TGIF syndrome. That's because the TGIF syndrome is the direct result of incorrectly perceiving oneself as *having* to go to work, rather than *choosing* to go to work.

RATIONAL AND IRRATIONAL CONCEPTS OF *SHOULD*

In her Db_7 rational debate, Dr. F. wrote "I should be procrastinating exactly as I am doing." That statement indicated that Dr. F. had replaced the widely popular but magical, and therefore *irrational concept of should* with the scientific, and therefore *rational, concept of should.*

To prepare yourself for the important clinical difference between using the scientific, and therefore rational, concept of *should* and the magical concept, answer this question. Have you ever seen anyone (including yourself) who felt undesirably angry or guilty and, at the same time, was convinced that everything was exactly as it then should have been? Of course not. In fact, what would happen if you were to discover that an instance of your anger or guilt is based on your mistaken idea that something isn't the way you believe it should be? If you are like most people, once you see that what you believed should be really is, your anger or guilt would immediately vanish.

Keep in mind that RBT is an empirically scientific approach to human behavior. The following three assumptions are the bases of all empirical sciences:

First, *events occur only if what's necessary for them to occur has been done.*

Second, *when what's necessary for events to occur has been done, those events have to and therefore should occur and vice versa.*

Third, *when events don't occur, the most objectively valid explanation is: what was necessary to make those events occur was not done.*

If those assumptions were not valid, empirical scientific research would be a waste of time. Scientists, as empirical researchers, could never be reasonably sure whether or not whatever they found at a specific time should have, or should not have, been found. That's why the scientific, and therefore rational, concept of *should* is this:

Everything is always exactly as it now should and has to be, even though this situation is not what I wanted for me. But I am not God; therefore, there is no objective reason why I should have what I want, just because I will it or want it.

Where people's emotional control is concerned, the majority of them believe in the common magical, irrational concept of *should* which is "If I want something sincerely enough, and/or I sincerely try to get it, and/or if that thing is the right (that is, the generally accepted, or most desirable) thing, then it should be, or it should come into being, and I should be undesirably upset if it doesn't.''

For clear-cut examples of common magical *shoulds* in everyday life, just visit the locker rooms of most athletic teams after a one-point loss in a hard-fought game. More often than not, you will hear angry protests such as these: *"We really should have won that game. Nobody should have to lose a game like that."* But the objective reality will always be that *they should have lost,* because they didn't do what was necessary to win. Only through magic can teams win without doing what's necessary to win, or can any reality be a way it should not be.

At this point, many P-Cs protest, ''Oh, those teams don't really mean that they should have won. That's just semantics.'' But I firmly disagree. Where healthy emotional and other self-control is concerned, it's never *just* semantics; it's always *all* semantics. People's current beliefs and attitudes trigger their emotional feelings as well as their physical actions. That's why, when people fail and *really believe* that they should have failed, they don't get angry about their failure. That's also why, when people who are rationally interested in succeeding fail, they calmly accept the fact that everything was exactly as it should have been for them to fail. Then they rationally analyze their failing behavior so that they can identify the things that made their failure unavoidable, and begin to replace them with things that favor future success.

Now, compare that behavior with the behavior of people who fail but who sincerely believe they should have succeeded. They are least likely to rationally analyze their failing behavior. Even if they do analyze it, they rarely recognize any failing behavior to correct. Their anger about having failed is the evidence they use to convince themselves they should have succeeded. Their irrational ''gut'' logic is: ''I'm not crazy. It would be crazy to be angry about failing if I really should have failed. I'm angry; therefore, I really should have succeeded.''

Only through magic can a reality exist without the prerequisites for its existing having first been met. That's why people's anger about their failures *never proves they should not have failed. Their anger only proves they believe in the common magical, and therefore irrational, concept of should.*

Now let's talk about the best way I know to get P-Cs to replace their common, *magical shoulds* with *rational shoulds*. First, tell them about the rational and irrational *shoulds*. Emphasize that the *rational should* accurately describes the objective cause-effect relationships in the real world. But the *irrational should* merely describes what the speaker wants or demands at the moment, even though the objective cause-effect relationships needed to produce it do not yet exist.

At this point, some of my P-Cs ask, ''But don't I have a right to my wants?'' My answer is: ''Of course you have a right to your wants. But that fact is irrelevant for your healthy emotional control. In addition, it doesn't matter at all that what you want may be the best possible thing for you to have; if it is, that fact merely explains why it's rational to want it. But there is no objective reason why you should get even what you rationally want without doing what's necessary to get it.''

Those facts seem to cause a few P-Cs to develop a hearing defect. So they say,

14-2   Rational Use of Should

"I hear you saying that people should never get angry, or feel guilty, or be depressed about anything, but I don't agree with that." My answer always is, "No, I'm not saying that at all; and as a physician who's interested only in healthy behaviors, I would not say that. I know that to get angry, or otherwise upset, sometimes is just as normal and healthy as it is to eat. But I also know that if you eat, or get upset too much, you will make yourself sick, sometimes even sick enough to die.

"On the other hand, even though you consistently use the rational and therefore scientific concept of *should,* you will still get rationally upset and rationally act in your own best interest. But you won't get self-defeatingly upset. Consequently, your being upset won't make you sick. That's because *even though everything is always exactly as it now should be, you don't have to let anything that you can change stay the way it now is.*

Obviously, helping your P-Cs keep clear in their minds the big difference between irrational and rational *shoulds* is very important for their therapeutic success. It's recommended, therefore, that you get your P-Cs to learn the following five major differences between the two types of shoulds.

Irrational *Shoulds*	versus	**Rational *Shoulds***
1. refer to what is *not* reality now		1. refer to what *is* reality now
2. are merely the speakers' opinion that what's right for them should be right for everyone else		2. are factual; they recognize that what's right for the speaker is often wrong for other people
3. are magical and are based on the belief that things should happen just because the speaker sincerely wants or demands them to happen		3. are based on the objective fact that things happen only when what is necessary to make them happen has been done

4. lead to inappropriate anger about the fact that the speakers, or someone else, either could not, or just did not, do what was necessary to give the speakers what they wanted

5. creates personal confusion that can prevent people from doing the things needed to get what they want most quickly[4]

4. leads to calm, corrective action after the speakers or someone else either could not, or just did not, do what was necessary to give the speakers what they wanted

5. create a problem-solving attitude that helps people do the things needed to get what they want most quickly

SECTION III

SPECIAL VOCABULARY—SECTION III
None.

FOCUS ITEMS —SECTION III
1. In RBT therapy sessions, what is the standard sequence for RSA presentation?
2. Why isn't that sequence the same as the sequence in writing an RSA?
3. What is the most common error new P-Cs make when they begin doing RSAs?
4. Why was it clinically useful for Dr. F. to correct her perceptions at A?
5. What if the session ends before you finish discussing the RSA?
6. What are two advantages of focusing therapy on RSAs?

Written Rational Self-Analysis is one of the two main emotional self-help maneuvers P-Cs learn in RBT. Repeatedly remind your P-Cs that there is no undesirable emotion that's too trivial to be handled rationally. This fact makes written Rational Self-Analyses the ideal basis for conducting RBT sessions. Ideally, therefore, each P-C brings at least one written RSA to each RBT session.

Remember though, that a small percentage of learners who are mainly spoken-word oriented (as opposed to written-word oriented) will not do bibliotherapy or RSAs diligently. Still, they can benefit from RBT as much as the

---

[4]If you send an addressed, stamped envelope to me at the RBT Center, College of Medicine, University of Kentucky, Lexington, KY 40536, I'll send you a free, printed summary of rational uses of *should* that we use at the RBT Center. You have my permission to reproduce that summary at will for your P-Cs to use in therapy.

other P-Cs, particularly if their therapists discuss their problems using the A, B, C sequence and RSA format.

This part of the chapter uses a hypothetical therapy session with Dr. F. as an example of how to conduct your sessions when a P-C brings a written RSA.

WHEN A P-C BRINGS AN RSA TO THERAPY

To get the most from this discussion, imagine that Dr. F.'s RSA was her first attempt at writing one and presenting it in therapy. The routine for focusing therapy on RSAs is the same for the first RSA as it is for the fiftieth one. So, I would have started with, "Okay, let me hear your A section." After she had read her A section, I would have asked to hear her C section and her E section. Those sections would have told me how Dr. F. had perceived and experienced her A event and how she hoped to react to similar, future A events. (Always ask your P-Cs to read their RSAs to you. That way you will prevent possible embarrassment P-Cs may have about poor grammar, spelling, or illegible writing.)

Next, I would have asked her to read the Da section, her Camera Check of A. Since this would have been her first attempt at RSAs, this probably would have been her third or fourth session. At that early stage of therapy, most P-Cs usually still believe that what is real to them is obvious fact. Understandably, therefore, these P-Cs tend to be negligent about the Camera Check of A; so expect this and be prepared to handle it rationally.

Remember, we are now pretending that Dr. F. is presenting in a therapy session her first attempt at writing an RSA. Although this dialogue never actually took place, it's typical for such therapy sessions. Therefore, expect this little fantasy to clearly show you the therapeutic technique that later enabled Dr. F. to write her excellent RSA, even after being out of therapy for almost a year.

Me: Let's hear your Camera Check of A.
P-C: My A section was, "For a month now, I've had these three letters of recommendation hanging over my head and it's driving me crazy;" and since that's the way I feel, I wrote, "That's all fact," for my Camera Check.
Me: Do you mean to say that a videotape recording of your situation would show three letters hanging down over your head driving you crazy?

Author's Note

Or, I might have first asked, "What is this IT that's driving you crazy?" She probably would have responded, "The fact that I have these three letters to write." Then I would have pointed out, "Facts don't drive people crazy. People who have healthy, undrugged brains and still go crazy have to drive themselves crazy; there's just no other way they can get there. But is it a fact that you are going crazy? And where are those letters that are hanging over your head? I don't see them."

It doesn't matter which objection I would have made to her incorrect Camera Check.

As a typical beginner at rational thinking, Dr. F. probably would have made some form of this most common protest, which new P-Cs often make about the Camera Check, namely, "Oh, that's just semantics. You know what I mean."

My response, then, would have been something like "No, I don't know what you mean; I only know what you said. But if what you said is not what you meant, then why not say what you meant? In trying to solve emotional problems it's very important to say what you mean and mean what you say."

Then I probably would have used the "Mouse Lady" example (see Introduction) to emphasize this next fact: One of the main causes of emotional distress is people thinking what they don't mean, and meaning what they don't think, but believing every word of it.

The only goal of my responses there would have been to teach Dr. F. how to do an objectively correct Camera Check. That's why I would have made sure that we arrived at a Camera Check that was similar to the one she wrote in her real RSA. Then we would have moved on to her B and Db sections.

Me: All right, what was your B_1 idea?
P-C: My B_1 was, "What can I say?" And I put "negative" in parentheses. But I also put, "What can I say?" in my Db_1 section, too, because I just didn't know how to answer that.
Me: What do you mean? Of course you know how to answer that. You know what you think about your students' potential for success in graduate school, don't you?
P-C: Yes, but, what if I don't say enough to get them accepted? I don't want to feel responsible for that.

Author's Note

Dr. F's response would have revealed that her question was really a rhetorical question, hiding her attitude or belief that she didn't know what to say that would guarantee her students' successful entry into graduate school. And she was probably correct. But that fact was irrelevant. Her letters were never meant nor expected to guarantee anything.

That insight would have led me directly to a discussion of both the rhetorical question as a cause of irrational emotional distress, and the irrational demands she wanted to make her letters fulfill. After that discussion, I would have helped her discover a Rational Debate similar to the one she wrote in her real RSA.

Me: Now let's hear your B_2.
P-C: My B_2 was "Why should I have to write letters when I don't want to? (Negative)." I didn't quite know how to debate that because I don't feel I should have to do it. That's why I'm so angry.

Author's Note

That response would have led to a brief analysis of that rhetorical question and its hidden attitudes and beliefs. Then I would have pointed out that her "I don't feel I should . . . " was not a real feeling. Then I would have discussed in detail the concepts of rational and irrational shoulds, after which I would have given her a copy of the printed summary of the rational use of should.

Me: Okay let me hear your B_3.
P-C: My B_3 was "I hardly know these students (Negative)."
Me: And when you checked that idea with the Five Rational Questions, what did you decide?
P-C: My rational debate was "That's true; that's why I hesitate to write the strongest possible recommendations."
Me: Tell me, did you write the Five Rational Questions under your C section?
P-C: No, because I didn't think I had to.
Me: It's not a matter of having to or not having to write the Five Rational Questions; it's simply a matter of following the correct format for writing an RSA. Can you tell me what the Five Questions are?

Author's Note

To fully understand what my therapeutic goals would have been here, you need to know these facts:

1. Neglecting to write the Five Rational Questions is probably the most common error new P-Cs make when writing RSAs.
2. When new P-Cs write in their Db section, "That's true . . . " or "That's the way I felt, so it must be rational" or "I didn't know what to say about that" those P-Cs almost always will have neglected to write the Five Rational Questions. Or, they will have written them but will not have used them to check the rationality of their B section ideas.

For those reasons, any time you get some form of the responses given in item 2 above, ask about the Five Rational Questions. More often than not, you will have a golden opportunity to review the correct RSA format. At those times I also point out that actually writing the Five Rational Questions ensures that people learn and remember them. That's important because people cannot use self-help aids they neither know nor remember.

Most new P-Cs mistake their quick understanding and ready agreement with the Five Rules for Rational Thinking to mean they already know them well. That's the main reason they neglect to learn them; people don't try to learn what they believe they already know. But when you ask these P-Cs to tell you the Five Rational Questions, they have to face up to not having learned them yet, if that's the case.

Of course if your P-Cs know the Five Rational Questions, you will have a golden opportunity to reinforce them for having learned them. Afterward, ask them to answer each question for the B section idea being discussed. Now let's get back to the assumption that Dr. F. had neither written nor learned the Five Rational Questions.

After stressing the importance of writing and using the Five Rational Questions, I would have had Dr. F. use them to check the rationality of her B_3 idea "I hardly know these students." The cognitive stimulus of actually answering the questions would probably have been enough to get her to make this insight: her B_3 idea was a good example of the intelligent-sounding noise with which emotionally distressed P-Cs unwittingly confuse themselves. After rationally checking Dr. F.

probably would have seen that she knew those students as well as she thought was appropriate. But if this were not well enough for her to write the letters, she would have seen that she could easily get better acquainted.

You may now be wondering why I wouldn't have asked Dr. F. about the Five Rational Questions when we discussed her B_1 and B_2 questions. Only the answers to questions (and not the questions themselves) can be checked for rationality. That's another reason to get your P-Cs to answer all of their self-generated questions; even if their answer is "I don't know," get them to say it. If they answer their questions, they'll protect themselves from the hazard of unwittingly hiding irrational attitudes behind question marks.

What if the Session Ends Before the RSA?

If a therapy session ends before you have completely discussed the RSA, just put a check mark at the point where the session ended. Then pick up there in the next session. If P-Cs have begun to develop significant skill in doing RSAs, you may tell them to review the undiscussed parts alone. If they have any questions, ask them to write them down for discussion in their next session.

What about therapeutic closure when the session ends in the middle of an RSA? Every completely discussed part of an RSA is a therapeutic closure. That's why you can stop at any point, and your P-Cs will still have valuable therapeutic insights they can immediately use to help themselves. This is one of the two main reasons why RSAs are such valuable therapeutic aids. The other reason is that RSAs keep therapy focused on P-Cs' most immediate concerns and interests.

SUGGESTED ORDER FOR WRITING AN RSA

1. Begin with the A section.
2. Next write the B section.
   a. Write all the thoughts you can remember.
   b. Identify the attitudes.
3. Write the C section.
4. Write the Five Rational Questions.
5. Write the E section.
6. Apply the Camera Check; correct the A section as needed and write the Da section.
7. Apply the Five Rational Questions to each B idea and write the Db Rational Debate for each B idea.

SUGGESTED ORDER FOR DISCUSSING COMPLETED RSAs WITH P-Cs

1. Ask for the A section.
2. Ask for the C section.
3. Ask for the E section.

4. Ask if they wrote the Five Rational Questions.
5. Ask for the Camera Check.
6. Ask for B_1.
7. Ask for the rational check of B_1.
8. Ask for the Rational Debate of B_1.
9. Ask for B_2 and repeat instructions 7 and 8 for all Bs.

The Memory Aids for this chapter are on page 229.

CHAPTER 15
Rational Emotive
Imagery (REI)

An essential part of learning a habit is constant, split-second-to-split-second, brain–body feedback. Visual stimuli and the constant stream of emotive feelings that accompany every thought and physical action are the feedback people usually rely on most. Without that feedback, the left brain would not know if its second-to-second verbal instructions were triggering the correct right-brain mental pictures. In addition, the right brain would not have the second-to-second knowledge needed to ensure that the body is responding with the correct response sequence for the desired behavior.

Typically, when people thoroughly learn physical actions, they form three sets of conditioned reciprocal connections: (1) the connections between the physical actions with their associated right-brain and left-brain thoughts; (2) the connections between the physical actions with their associated emotive feelings; and (3) the connections between the right-brain and left-brain thoughts with their associated emotive feelings. When behavior becomes habitual, therefore, *either* the vocal, propositional left-brain thoughts or the silent appositional right-brain thoughts can trigger the complete, correct response. The only exceptions to that basic neuropsychophysiological principle seem to be caused by brain damage such as Hohmann (1962) and Luria (1973, pp. 43–101 and 162–168) have described.

Progressive efficiency of correct-response potential with minimal conscious thought is probably the most reliable evidence of habit formation. That's because for correct habitual behaviors, a split second of the right brain's mental pictures is a more efficient trigger than the left brain's cumbersome verbal directions. For example, both the speed and the quality of typing decrease as soon as skilled typists start trying to think the printed material they are typing. Fortunately, therefore, after people form habits, their silent right brains automatically take over primary control of those habitual responses. And their silent right brains keep those habits in force until people do enough of the practice that's essential for reeducation—whether emotional, behavioral, or both.

That's an important fact to remember; it explains why sincere left-brain wishes, hopes, and resolutions by themselves are never enough to enable people to get rid of undesirable emotional habits; that fact also explains why emotionally distressed people usually fail in their unaided attempts at emotional improvement, and why most traditional psychotherapy and counseling are so inefficient. The emotionally distressed people don't do enough neuropsychophysiologically valid emotional practice. And, without such practice, the silent right brains do not rapidly deprogram and reprogram themselves.

The most rapid and reliable right-brain deprogramming and reprogramming seem to require the same initial, continuous, directive influence from the left brain (that is, conscious practice) that were required for undesirable emotional responses to become habits. Otherwise, behavioral extinction and reeducation may not occur at all.

Rational Emotive Imagery (REI) is a form of intense mental practice for learning new emotional and physical habits (Maultsby 1971a, 1976, 1978, 1980; Maultsby and Hendricks 1974a). To do REI people intensely imagine themselves thinking, emotionally feeling and physically behaving exactly the way they want to think, feel and act in real life. When people combine REI with physical practice, they learn new emotional as well as physical habits in the shortest possible time.

Part I of this chapter tells you the therapeutic value, use, and neuropsychophysiology of REI. Section II of this chapter gives you the instructions for REI that I give to my P-Cs.

As you read this chapter, keep these three facts in mind:

1. Words, or people's verbal thoughts, are inextricably involved in their mental pictures or images (Luria 1968; 1973, pp. 229–244; 1976, pp. 8–47).
2. People's verbal thoughts, mental pictures and accompanying superconscious, wordless attitudes all trigger emotive feelings that are both logical and correct for those conscious thoughts, mental pictures, and accompanying superconscious, wordless attitudes.
3. Emotional feelings do *not* prove that the verbal thoughts, mental pictures, and accompanying superconscious, wordless attitudes that triggered those feelings are rational for the current situation. Only by applying the Five Rules for Rational Behavior can people decide whether or not their emotional feelings or the cognitions that triggered those feelings are rational for the current situation.

SPECIAL VOCABULARY—SECTION I

Emotive Imagery: having thoughts, and the mental pictures they trigger, plus the emotive feelings they both elicit. *Synonym:* mental practice.

Irrational Emotive Imagery: having irrational thoughts, and the mental pictures they trigger, plus the irrational emotive feelings they both elicit.

Physical Practice: as used in RBT, physically acting out in the external world the thoughts and mental images or picture-maps of the new behaviors people want to make their habits.

Rational Emotive Imagery (REI):   a form of intense mental practice for learning rational emotional and physical habits. When people combine REI with physical practice, they learn new emotional as well as physical habits in the shortest possible time.

FOCUS ITEMS —SECTION I

1. According to RBT theory, how do people get into the habit of validating their thoughts with their emotive feelings?
2. In cognitive-emotive dissonance, how do naive people confuse themselves, rather than help themselves emotionally?
3. What does REI do for such people?
4. Why is just promising oneself not to have a habitual emotional response usually ineffective?
5. How is driver reeducation a useful analogy for understanding the process of emotional reeducation?

CHAPTER 15

Rational Emotive Imagery

People do not sincerely think or mentally picture events they believe are objectively incorrect. In addition, all sincere thoughts and mental pictures trigger emotive feelings that are real, logical, and correct for those thoughts and mental pictures. Understandably, therefore, people normally get into the habit of evaluating new ideas and mental pictures on the basis of how they feel. If a new idea triggers the emotive feelings old beliefs trigger, people tend to assume that new idea or mental image is correct; it feels right. People probably form that habit because of the unnoticed influence of these operational assumptions: "It would be crazy to feel as if my thoughts and mental pictures were facts, if they really weren't. I'm not crazy; therefore, my feelings prove my thoughts and mental pictures are facts."

A REVIEW OF EMOTIONAL FEELINGS IN SELF-CONTROL

The only thing that emotive feelings prove is that, at the moment they occur, the people believe in the validity of the thoughts and mental pictures that triggered those feelings—however inaccurate and self-defeating those thoughts and mental pictures objectively are. Cognitive-emotive dissonance is the main exception to that rule. But that exception is more apparent than real.

A REVIEW OF FEELING RIGHT AND FEELING WRONG

In cognitive-emotive dissonance, people have new ideas and mental pictures about an old event; but those people still have their old unextinguished, superconscious attitudes about that event; those old attitudes still trigger their old habitual emotive feelings in response to the event itself, to the old beliefs about it, or both.

Those old habitual emotive feelings, however, are illogical for these people's new ideas and mental pictures. That fact creates cognitive-emotive dissonance. And cognitive-emotive dissonance makes people feel emotionally the way they would feel if their new ideas and associated mental pictures really were objectively incorrect. That's why emotionally naive people almost always react to cognitive-emotive dissonance by thinking: "Those new ideas feel wrong and I should ignore them." Then they ignore them.

But what does it really mean when an idea "feels wrong"? All "feeling wrong" really means is that the people have not yet thought and acted on the new ideas (that is, practiced them) long enough to extinguish and replace the old, competing emotive feelings and to allow emotional reeducation to occur.

Only by thinking and acting out new ideas and their associated mental pictures long enough can people make those ideas and mental pictures "feel right." When people don't know or they ignore that fact, they don't do enough practice to succeed in their attempts to improve their emotional control. Naturally, therefore, these people's stronger, old, competing, superconscious attitudes continue to trigger their familiar, stronger, habitual emotional feelings.

Emotionally distressed people then decide: "My old way of looking at this situation must be right. It (the old A situation) really does upset me, and I'd be lying if I say it doesn't. But people have to be true to themselves; otherwise, there's no point in anything." Understandably, therefore, those sincere, intelligent-sounding beliefs cause emotionally naive people to go on thinking, emotionally feeling, and physically acting in their old "right-feeling" but miserably self-defeating ways.

THE ESSENTIALS FOR REPLACING HABITS

To replace undesirable emotional or physical habits with desirable ones, people must practice. There are two kinds of practice: (1) emotive imagery or mental practice and (2) physical practice. Both types of practice require the same active left-brain and right-brain cooperative interactions; but the left brain has to initiate and direct the beginning phases of practice. That's why the first step in RBT (or any efficiently effective psychotherapy and counseling) is to get P-Cs started consciously thinking rationally about their thinking.

Then the second step is getting P-Cs to do daily Rational Emotive Imagery. Rational Emotive Imagery (REI) is an excellent therapeutic technique for making rational ideas and mental pictures that initially "feel wrong" begin quickly to start "feeling right." That's why REI is the safest and most efficiently effective aid to learning any new habit. After a week of daily REI, most P-Cs are ready for the last step in efficiently effective therapeutic learning—physical practice of the desired new behaviors.

RATIONAL INSIGHTS ABOUT PRACTICE

Physical practice means physically acting out in the external world the thoughts and mental images or picture-maps of the new behaviors people want to make their habits. During REI, physical practice, and real life events, every sincere cognitive and physical behavior triggers a corresponding, logical emotive response. But, as the learned fear of snakes demonstrates (see Chapter 4), people don't have to do physical practice in order to learn emotional habits. Mental practice (that is, emotive imagery) alone is enough. In fact, for irrational fears, the safest and most rapid therapeutic emotional learning often comes from rational mental practice (REI) alone.

Take the irrational fear of speaking in public, for example. To do the physical practice needed to replace that irrational fear with self-confidence about success, people have to speak in public. But if their fear of public speaking is strong enough, people won't practice public speaking; therefore they won't get rid of their fear of speaking in public.

Fortunately, human brains process in the same way both the cognitive events triggered by the external world and those triggered by people's imaginations (Eccles 1958; Luria 1968; Pavlov, as quoted in Volygesi 1954; Razran 1934; 1949; 1949a; 1961). That's why, with frequent REI alone, people can quickly replace much of their incapacitating fear of public speaking with self-confidence about success. Then they can start speaking in public with ever-increasing, personally satisfying success.

Doing REIs on public speaking simply means that people mentally picture themselves speaking in public, while at the same time they think and feel exactly the way they want to think and feel in the real speaking situation. Frequent, daily REIs will keep the left and right brains ideally working together to extinguish their irrational fears; and at the same time, these people will autocondition ever-increasing self-confidence about success in public speaking.

Unfortunately, most people rarely think of their emotions as being autoconditioned, self-controlled events. Understandably, therefore, rarely do uninstructed people knowingly learn a specific technique of emotional practice. Consequently, they only rarely or unwittingly practice their desired new emotions. That's why, without professional help, most emotionally distressed people don't do enough emotional practice to learn desirable new emotions, or even to decrease significantly their tendency to have undesirable emotions.

BRIEF REVIEW OF THE RATIONAL NEUROPSYCHOLOGY OF PRACTICE

To practice, people's left brains must verbally tell them what to do. Their words trigger right-brain picture-maps of both the individual steps and the developing behavioral gestalt to be acted out.[1] Next, people's left brains direct (that is, self-talk) them through the individual steps of their right brain's mental picture-maps.

With enough physical practice, their right brains quickly tie the individual actions together into a vivid, semipermanent, holistic mental picture-map of the complete behavioral gestalt. People's self-talk and their behavioral picture-maps, plus their physical actions, all trigger emotive feelings that function like behavioral cement, which holds the psychophysiologic gestalts together in computerlike cognitive maps or programs. When that happens, people begin to say: "I *feel* I've got it," or "Now I've got the whole picture."

From that point, the second-to-second, minimally conscious, automatic control of those behavioral acts will come from the right brain instead of the left brain. But throughout the period of behavioral education and habitual reactions, people's right and left limbic systems trigger the same type of emotional responses for any specific behavioral gestalt. That's why people's habitual reactions always "feel right," regardless how self-defeating they are.

In cognitive-emotive dissonance, people's right brain's old A-b attitudes are in conflict with their left brain's new B self-talk. When that conflict is mild, people experience it as the vague, negative feeling usually associated with something being wrong. So they say, "That feels wrong," or "That doesn't feel right." But when that conflict is intense, sudden, or both, people can have an immediate, right brain-triggered flight/fight reaction that completely cancels the new idea and destroys the desired, new behavioral response. For example, imagine that you are calmly seated discussing with your friends their harmless pet snake. Now, what if that snake suddenly fell into your lap? You might well feel instant panic, even though you know the snake is harmless.

Fortunately, people's conscious thoughts really do have ultimate direct control over both their emotional and their physical behaviors. Therefore, after P-Cs understand the left- and right-brain conflict called cognitive-emotive dissonance, they can quickly resolve it in favor of rational thinking and new therapeutic learning.

Even new P-Cs usually know how to deal rationally with the cognitive-emotive dissonance involved in physical behavioral reeducation. But almost never do they automatically see that success in therapeutic emotional reeducation requires them to deal with cognitive-emotive dissonance in the same rational way they already know how to deal with it during physical behavioral reeducation. That's why the example of English driver's reeducation in Chapter 13 is an effective tool for getting P-Cs to make that valuable therapeutic insight.

---

[1]The left brain probably also forms pictures of the individual parts or steps in the behavioral act. But the right brain seems primarily responsible for producing the semipermanent gestalt.

Almost without exception, your new P-Cs will readily understand the example of English driver's reeducation. Why? Because they will have already learned from their daily lives the cause and cure for cognitive-emotive dissonance in physical reeducation. So your only therapeutic task is to get your P-Cs to make these two important insights:

1. *The same basic principles of learning and practice apply to both emotional and physical reeducation.*
2. *For the safest and most rapid emotional reeducation,* people must do frequent (preferably daily) emotional practice using rational emotive imagery.

If your P-Cs are appropriate for RBT, you won't have much trouble getting them to make those insights about emotional change.

SECTION II

SPECIAL VOCABULARY–SECTION II

None.

FOCUS ITEMS —SECTION II

1. What is the Instant Better Feeling Maneuver?
2. What's the second step in REI?
3. What's the most important step in REI?
4. What's the only way people can get rid of habits without practice?
5. What are the three potential problems with REI and their solutions?

As you read the instructions and comments about REI, imagine that you are one of my P-Cs. Then carry out the instructions. (To help make that little experiential learning exercise as easy as possible, where it's appropriate, the instructions have been written as instructions to you the reader, in doing REI.)

HOW TO DO RATIONAL EMOTIVE IMAGERY

First, do an effective Rational Self-Analysis of the event you want to handle rationally. The rational rule is, *Always do an RSA before doing REI.* Otherwise you may unwittingly end up practicing your old irrational habits and incorrectly accusing REI of not working.

Second, memorize your camera checked Da section, the main points of your Db section, and your E section. Many P-Cs prefer to record the second step on audio tape and listen to it as they take steps four through seven.

Third, do the Instant Better Feeling Maneuver for one to three minutes, or until you are noticeably relaxed.

The Instant Better Feeling Maneuver is a slow, diaphragmatic breathing technique. When you use this technique correctly, it will calm you faster, more safely, and more reliably than tranquilizers. That's because to maintain a drug-free state of significant emotional arousal, people must increase their respirations. But if healthy people continually breathe at the slow rate advised below, they almost always calm down in much less time than it takes a tranquilizer to start getting out of the stomach.

To begin the Instant Better Feeling Maneuver, first get physically comfortable while standing, sitting, or (preferably) lying down. Close your eyes, put a warm, soft smile on your face and slow your breathing rate to between four and six complete intake-output cycles per minute. Remember, this is "belly" breathing; so your abdomen should bulge outwardly as you breathe in.

Begin by calmly breathing in for three to four seconds while simultaneously thinking: "A, I'm breathing in." Then immediately breathe out for three to four seconds while you slowly think: "B, I'm breathing out." At the end of breathing out, pause for three to four seconds, while thinking: "C, I'm relaxing." Then, just repeat that slow breathing routine over and over until you get noticeably calm.

For the first three or four times you practice the Instant Better Feeling Maneuver, keep your eyes open and time your breathing cycles. Pace yourself so that each third of a complete cycle takes you three to four seconds. Then you will be breathing between four and six cycles per minute.

A few people prefer a three-cycle-per-minute rate; if you do, too, that's all right; just lengthen each third of your breathing cycle to five to six seconds. The majority of people, however, will relax most quickly with a rate between four and six cycles per minute. So most probably, you too will relax if you maintain that slow, rhythmic, breathing rate.

Fourth, after you are noticeably calm (usually, within one to three minutes), begin mentally picturing yourself as vividly as possible back in the situation described in the Da section of your well-done Rational Self-Analysis.

Fifth, keep your eyes closed and maintain both your warm soft smile and your slow breathing rate as you create your Da images and think *only* the main points of your rational thoughts in the Db section of your Rational Self-Analysis.

If old B-section thoughts pop into your mind, calmly replace them with your rational Db thoughts. Illustration 15-1 (on p. 204) will show you how Dr. F., the English professor, did her REIs.

Sixth, and most important of all, as you vividly picture yourself in your Da situation thinking your rational Db thoughts, vividly imagine yourself having your E-section emotional feelings and physical behavior. Use the full power of your imagination to imagine exactly how you would feel emotionally and act physically if

15-1   Starting the Day with REI

you had already achieved the new emotional and behavioral goals you desire. Be sure to maintain your slow breathing rate throughout your REI session.

Seventh, repeat your imagery again and again for five to ten minutes. If you have two RSAs for practice, spend five minutes on each. But don't do REI on more than two RSAs in any ten-minute REI session.

OLD HABITS DON'T JUST DISAPPEAR BECAUSE YOU DON'T WANT THEM ANY MORE

Tell your P-Cs not to expect an emotional miracle after just one or even a few REI sessions. Instead, advise them to do REIs on the same RSA for five to ten minutes every day until they are consistently getting the behavioral results they want in real life.

Continually remind P-Cs that replacing old emotional habits takes time and repeated practice; without enough time or practice, no new learning occurs. Experiencing brain damage is the only way people can get rid of old habits instantly, without practice.

RECOMMENDED REI ROUTINE

Put yourself to sleep every night with REI. It's cheaper, safer, and quicker than sleeping pills. And do ten minutes of REI just before you get out of bed each morning. Morning REIs let you start your day with the pleasantly powerful emotional feelings associated with confidence of success.

Do ten minutes of REI just before lunch, and instead of cigarette breaks, take REI breaks. Then you will be improving your emotional control and fighting lung cancer, heart disease, and bad breath at the same time.

Do ten minutes of REI before your first afternoon cocktail. That way, you probably will drink only one or two cocktails, enjoy your dinner, and remember

15-2   Using REI to Reinforce Rational Behavior

having enjoyed it. You can also do REI with your eyes open, for example, while riding to work. (See Figure 15-2.)

Doing the Instant Better Feeling Maneuver alone with your eyes open, without REI is a helpful way to pass the time as you wait in lines, wait in traffic, or wait for someone who's late. The Instant Better Feeling Maneuver at those times will help keep your blood pressure down, prevent tension headaches, and improve your disposition.

By following that daily schedule, you will be reprogramming your brain for your new, more rational behavior in the shortest time possible for you. Soon, you and your family and friends will begin to notice positive emotional changes in you.

Verbally outlining the REI routine just once, or even twice, with P-Cs often is not enough for them to learn it. For that reason, I wrote a special REI instruction article for P-Cs. Routinely giving a copy of those instructions to all of my P-Cs has decreased almost to zero the times I need to explain the correct REI routine to them a second or third time.[2]

REI ON RELATED EVENTS

After you have practiced REI on one RSA for four or five minutes, switch to related scenes or situations that are logical for your Db section's rational thinking and your E section's goals. With that type of daily comprehensive emotional practice, Dr. F. quickly eliminated her irrational procrastination about writing articles and preparing her lecture outlines. She also started planning and doing household shopping more rationally.

[2]For a free reproduction-ready copy of these REI instructions send an addressed, stamped envelope to me at the RBT Center, College of Medicine, University of Kentucky, Lexington, KY 40536. You have my permission to reproduce the instructions in whatever quantity you need for your practice. Please include any questions or comments you may have about this book or RBT.

POTENTIAL PROBLEMS WITH REI AND THEIR SOLUTIONS

In my experience, REI has only three potential problems. First, some P-Cs initially feel mildly odd or strange doing REIs. Second, sometimes P-Cs have a problem with distracting thoughts while doing REIs. Third, often P-Cs have vague, unclear images in doing their REIs. Let's discuss each problem in that order.

Having Strange Emotions During REI

This is almost never a significant problem if therapists have already explained cognitive-emotive dissonance to their P-Cs and if P-Cs do REI correctly. That's why, for the rare P-Cs who have a significant problem with strange feelings, the problem will usually have one or a combination of these three causes. First, some P-Cs will be using a poorly done Rational Self-Analysis for their REI. Usually, they will have just labeled their old B section's irrational beliefs as "rational" in their Db sections. Consequently, these P-Cs will be consciously (instead of unwittingly) practicing their undesirable emotional habits.

Such incorrectly done RSAs usually tell you two important things about these P-Cs. First, they usually will have omitted checking their B-section thoughts with the Five Rational Questions. Second and even more important, these P-Cs still will not have accepted their Emotional ABCs. They still will be clinging to their beliefs that magical HEs, SHEs, or ITs in the outside world really do upset them emotionally. But because these P-Cs are then in therapy, they will incorrectly accuse their REI of upsetting them. Understandably, therefore, they will want to stop doing REI and try something else, usually drugs.

You can easily prevent as well as solve that problem. Just make sure your P-Cs check each of their B-section thoughts with the Five Rational Questions. And initially, have your P-Cs restrict their REIs to well-done Rational Self-Analyses that the two of you will have already gone over together in therapy. I routinely caution my new P-Cs, "Do *not* attempt to do REI before the two of us have completely discussed the RSA that is to be the focus of your REI."

Here's the second cause of strange emotions during REI. It's doing REI using ideas that the P-Cs intellectually know are rational, but that they have not yet accepted as being the best way for them to think about their emotional problem. If you question these P-Cs directly about that possibility, they readily admit to that fact.

Here is the easiest way I know to solve that problem. First, resist the urge to try to persuade these P-Cs to accept the still rejected, though admittedly rational ideas. Instead, ask those P-Cs to take the Five Rational Questions and show you how and why it seems rational to them to cling to their contrary beliefs. Second, advise these P-Cs to stop attempting REI on that event, until they come up with new ideas that are both rational and personally acceptable to them.

The third and most common cause of strange emotions during REI is simply cognitive-emotive dissonance. To solve that problem easily, just make sure your P-Cs thoroughly understand what cognitive-emotive dissonance is before they attempt REI. Then, simply refresh their memory as often as they need it, and get them to do more intense, rather than less intense, REIs. That's the fastest and safest way to convert cognitive-emotive dissonance into therapeutic emotional insight.

Here's the best way I've found to prevent complaints about strange emotions during REI. Predict the possibility of your P-Cs having strange emotions before they ever attempt REI. Say, "You may start to get a little upset; if so, immediately stop your imagery and calm yourself down with the Instant Better Feeling Maneuver; then restart your imagery. If you start getting upset again, immediately stop your imagery, calm yourself down again, and this time reread the Da, Db, and E sections of your Rational Self-Analysis.

"As you reread your RSA, look for errors in answering the Five Rational Questions. If you find any errors, correct them. If you do not find errors to correct, ask yourself if you sincerely believe your Da, Db, and E sections are both rational for you and acceptable to you as new beliefs and attitudes about your A section event.

"If your answer is yes, simply resume your REI and be patient with yourself. More frequent and more intense REIs will soon replace your strange feelings with pleasantly familiar ones. But if your answer to that question is 'no,' or 'I don't know' then rewrite your Da, Db, and E sections to your rational satisfaction; then resume daily REI.

"If you ever find it necessary to stop any REI session three times because of strange or otherwise undesirable emotions, *do not* restart that REI session, and *do not* do any more REI on that event until we have discussed that REI experience and your Rational Self-Analysis in your next therapy session."

Having Distracting Thoughts During REI

This is a common but minor problem. You can usually solve it by advising your P-Cs to keep their external environment as quiet as possible, simply ignore any extraneous thoughts, and be patient with themselves.

In some rare cases, P-Cs will have the same distracting thoughts over and over. That usually indicates magical worry (see Chapter 11). These P-Cs are afraid to stop worrying about their problems. They have the irrational belief that worrying about their problems somehow helps them cope with those problems. Therefore, they are afraid that if they stop worrying, their problems suddenly will overwhelm them completely.

Treat such cases of magical worry the same way you would treat any case of magical worry. Have the P-Cs do a well-done RSA on their worry; then have them do frequent REIs on replacing their worry with calm emotional control.

Having Vague Unclear Images During REI

People vary greatly in their ability to evoke vivid mental images. Some people evoke images so effortlessly that I call them image thinkers. Their minds work like televisions. They see a vivid mental picture of virtually everything they think or talk about.

At the other extreme of normal human variation, there are P-Cs whose minds work like radios. Without diligent effort, they rarely see a mental image of anything they think or talk about. I call these people concept-thinkers, or word-thinkers. But with all P-Cs, I emphasize the following facts:

"With enough mental practice, the brains of concept thinkers process concepts with the same ultimate, thorough learning that results when the brains of image-thinkers process images. On the average, though, it may take concept-thinkers a bit longer than image-thinkers to achieve the same level of therapeutic results. But that fact does not mean that image-thinkers are necessarily more fortunate than concept-thinkers.

"As a rule, concept-thinkers tend to have fewer irrational emotional experiences and changeable moods, and are less phobic than image thinkers. Consequently, concept-thinkers usually have fewer intense emotional hang-ups to eliminate than do image-thinkers. So, the extra effort concept-thinkers usually must put forth to get optimal therapeutic results tends to be balanced off by their having fewer problems to solve in the first place. Therefore, concept-thinkers and image-thinkers usually end up requiring about the same total time to achieve relatively comprehensive emotional reeducation.

"So, if you don't evoke clear-cut, vivid images when you are doing REI, *don't worry about it.* Just concentrate on the Da, Db, and E sections of your RSA as intensely as you can according to the daily routine I have given you.

"Of course, if you do REI more often than I suggested for your daily routine, you will progress faster. But REI just four times a day, every day, gives most people a satisfactory rate of therapeutic change."

By the time your P-Cs are ready to do REI, you will have become quite familiar with their cognitive habits. That familiarity will usually give you a feel for the common problems your P-Cs may experience while doing REIs. So point out those possibilities and give your P-Cs the solutions to those problems before they experience them.

If you have done REIs yourself and have personally dealt with any of those potential problems, share that experience with your P-Cs.[3] That maneuver increases your P-Cs' faith in you and their confidence in REI and in their ability to do it correctly.

MY PARTING WORDS

You have just completed all the chapters in this book. I appreciate very much your demonstrated interest in RBT. In the next page the normal sequence for doing RBT is summarized. Most readers say: "That brief summary pulls the whole book together into a tidy gestalt of RBT." I hope that will be your experience, too.

[3]As a rule, RBT therapists keep their self-disclosures in therapy to an absolute minimum. The rare self-disclosures I make all have a specific, instructive function for my P-Cs. And I describe only experiences wherein I had obvious clear-cut success.

THE NORMAL THERAPEUTIC SEQUENCE IN RBT

First in RBT is the intake. Almost always the intake can be completed in an hour. However, in rare instances, an unusually distressed P-C with an unusually compli- cated situation will require as many as three hours of intake ventilating before being willing to get involved in therapy. But, when I have heard all I want to hear about a new P-C's problem and the P-C seems ready to start looking for therapeutic solu- tions, that ends my intake.

Normally, the next step in RBT is to introduce P-Cs to their Emotional ABCs. If you are using the recommended Rational Bibliotherapy,[4] you would assign your P-Cs Chapter 1 in *You and Your Emotions* (Maultsby and Hendricks, 1974a); or for alcoholics or other drug abusers, you would assign Booklet One in the Rational Bibliotherapeutic series *Freedom From Alcohol and Tranquilizers* (Maultsby, 1979). Depending on how diligent your P-Cs are, you might spend one to two ses- sions on the Emotional ABCs.

Next you would cover the five rules for optimal emotional health—the Five Rules for Rational Thinking. The bibliotherapy assignments would be Chapter 2 in *You and Your Emotions* or Booklet Two in the bibliotherapeutic series.

Again, depending on your P-C's diligence, you might spend one, two or maybe even three sessions on getting your P-Cs used to thinking of and applying the Five Rational Rules to their problem-related thinking and behavior.

Next, you would explain to your P-Cs cognitive-emotive dissonance and the five stages of therapeutic change (Chapter 13). Then you would introduce your P-Cs to the idea of doing regular, written Rational Self-Analysis, or RSA (Chapter 14 of this book, Chapter 3 in *You and Your Emotions,* and Booklet Three in the bibliotherapeutic series). For the 80 percent to 85 percent of P-Cs who will bring at least one written RSA per week to therapy, you would structure the therapy sessions around discussing those RSAs.[5]

After your P-Cs discuss with you a well-done RSA, they are then ready to learn Rational Emotive Imagery, or REI (Chapter 15 in this book, Chapter 4 in *You and Your Emotions,* and booklet four in the bibliotherapeutic series).

After P-Cs begin doing REIs, they are still given weekly bibliotherapy assign- ments until they complete the six chapters in *You and Your Emotions* or the five booklets in the bibliotherapeutic series. Then, only if P-Cs request further reading materials (about 25 percent do), I refer them to one of my more advanced self-help books: *Help Yourself to Happiness* (Maultsby 1976), *Your Guide to Emotional Well Being* (Maultsby 1980), or *A Million Dollars for Your Hangover* (Maultsby 1978).

---

[4]Bibliotherapy (see Appendix B) is merely a therapeutic aid; it's not essential for therapeutic success.

[5]Up to 20 percent of your educated P-Cs will not diligently do either bibliotherapy or written Rational Self-Analysis; but they will still benefit from RBT if they keep regular appointments and if you discuss their problems using the A, B, C format and the Five Rules for Rational Thinking. In my opinion, these P-Cs learn most comfortably from vocal as opposed to written communications. They especially like and benefit from listening to recordings of their RBT sessions.

PART FIVE

The Appendices

This book has two appendices. Appendix A consists of the Memory Aids and answers for each chapter.

Appendix B consists of examples of the Rational Bibliotherapy materials routinely used at the RBT Center. Also in Appendix B are two short articles, "The Professional's Guide for Rational Bibliotherapy" and "How to Get the Most Benefit from Your Rational Readings" (the daily bibliotherapeutic reading instructions P-Cs receive at the RBT Center).

For information about the narrated audio and video tapes of the case histories presented here, or information about RBT training programs, write to the RBT Center, College of Medicine, University of Kentucky, Lexington, KY, 40536.

Memory Aids

MEMORY AIDS FOR BOOK INTRODUCTION

1. The behavioral concepts in this book describe _____ human behavior.

2. You don't have to have an emotional problem to apply _____ concepts to yourself.

3. The Mouse Lady's case history was a good example of the problems people create by thinking what they _____ mean and meaning what they don't _____, but _____ every word of it.

4. One of the oldest, but still most useful, insights into human self-control is: "Every way of people is _____ in their own _____."

5. This book was designed to change the way you do _____ and maybe even your _____.

6. Expect some of the ideas in this book to feel _____ when you first read them.

7. As was proven by the example of people initially laughing at the idea that the world is round, if an idea _____ wrong, that _____ mean it is wrong.

Answers for Introduction

1. normal
2. RBT
3. don't; think; believing
4. right; eyes

5. psychotherapy; life
6. wrong
7. feels; doesn't

MEMORY AIDS FOR CHAPTER 1

1. RBT has the _____ characteristics that identify all _____ psychotherapies.

2. RBT is cross-cultural psychotherapy because it's acceptable to and _____ for people who are different from their psychotherapists in race, culture, and life style.

3. Medical science has not yet been able to improve on nature at its best. True or false?

4. An undrugged, undiseased brain is an example of _____ at its _____.

5. I'ACT stands for The _____ Association For Clear _____.

6. RBT is the result of a combination of _____ research-supported approaches to human _____.

7. In RBT, *Rational* means any reasonable and credible idea. True or false?

8. In RBT, the meaning of *rational* has _____ characteristics. Name them.

9. What's rational for you as a therapist has to be rational for your P-Cs. True or false?

10. What's real to you is the only reality you need to know about. True or false?

Answers for Chapter One

1. six, ideal
2. effective
3. true
4. nature; best
5. International; Thinking

6. nine; behavior
7. false
8. five; p. 16
9. false
10. false

MEMORY AIDS FOR CHAPTER 2

1. The first functional brain unit keeps people alert enough to react. True or false?

2. The human brain is the main organ of _____ and _____.

3. Unlike many other books on psychotherapy, this book discusses the human _____.

4. The limbic systems of the _____ are primarily responsible for the _____ parts of _____.

5. The emotional feelings are the _____ important part of emotions.

6. Every sensory stimulus gets immediately typed in the brain for its behavioral _____ potential.

7. Through the corpus callosum, the right and left brains _____ informed about each other's current _____.

8. The experiential memory of the brain is in the _____ functional brain unit.

9. The third functional brain unit is the most important of the three units for independent, adult living. True or false?

10. What is holography?

11. Why is holography important to understanding how the brain works?

12. The first rule for healthy living is: behavior must be based on _____. _____.

Answers for Chapter 2

1.	true	7.	keep or stay; activities
2.	survival; comfort	8.	second
3.	brain	9.	true
4.	brains; feeling or emotive; emotions	10.	See page 29
5.	least	11.	See pages 29–31
6.	motivating	12.	obvious or objective; fact

MEMORY AIDS FOR CHAPTER 3—SECTION I

1. A paralyzed right hand usually means there has been damage to which brain?

2. Would you be surprised if that person also had trouble talking?

3. How can people use their brains to generate neuropsychosomatic stimuli that have little to do with reality?

4. The world-of-not-words is the left brain's creation. True or false?

5. If you have trouble naming things, that would interfere with your ability to recreate events from memory. True or false?

6. Dr. Wigan was the first physician to make the insight that people have one head, but two brains. True or false?

7. The left brain controls the _____ side of the body.

8. With the onset of language, the _____ brain begins to specialize in wordless mental activities.

9. Split-brain patients have had their corpus callosum surgically cut completely through, so that the right and left brains no longer communicate. True or false?

10. Therapeutic behavioral reeducation is another name for _____.

Answers for Chapter 3—Section I

1.	left	6.	false
2.	no	7.	right
3.	imagination	8.	right
4.	false	9.	true
5.	true	10.	psychotherapy

MEMORY AIDS FOR CHAPTER 3—SECTION II

1. The right brain usually enables people to react instantly, without preceeding thought. True or false?

2. Ravel's musical disability indicates that the right brain maintains people's habitual reactions, but the right brain cannot _____ habitual reactions.

3. Either cues from the _____ world or the left _____ must initiate habitual acts.

4. A person with a right-brain injury may have trouble using his right hand to zip up his zipper. True or false?

5. Bogen, the famous American neurosurgeon, suggested the term appositional _____ to describe _____-brain thought.

6. For overeaters to keep themselves from overeating, all they need to do is sincerely make up their mind not to overeat. True or false?

7. Which brain processes negations easily? _____

8. The _____ brain seems to maintain old habits.

9. The right brain shows people the _____, whereas the left brain shows people the individual _____.

10. A right-handed person whose right brain has been surgically removed can still write but cannot copy simple geometric figures. True or false?

11. Neither the human brain nor a camera can form an image of a state of _____ being.

12. Item 11 explains why most people _____ to keep behavioral resolutions not to _____ things.

13. A sincere promise not to repeat an undesirable act is much more effective for your self-control than choosing a new behavior with which to replace the old one. True or False?

Answers for Chapter 3—Section II

1. true
2. initiate
3. outside or external; brain
4. true
5. thought; right
6. false
7. left

8. right
9. forest; trees
10. true
11. not or non
12. fail; do
13. false

MEMORY AIDS FOR CHAPTER 4—SECTION I

1. The backbone of RBT and its emotional self-help concepts and techniques is the assumption that the same _____ processes of learning and practice produce people's _____ habits and their _____ habits.

2. Emotional education has _____ stages.

3. People can make purely objective perceptions. True or false?

4. Learning to type follows the same _____ sequence as learning to feel depressed.

5. Attitudes and beliefs are simply different forms of the results of repeatedly pairing the same _____ s with the same _____ s and _____ s.

6. Beliefs free _____ from subhuman _____ like dependence on the external world for appropriate _____ and physical behavioral cues.

Answers for Chapter 4—Section I

1. mental; physical; emotional
2. four
3. False

4. A, B, C
5. A; B; C
6. people; animal; emotional

MEMORY AIDS FOR CHAPTER 4—SECTION II

1. Much research supports the RBT theory of attitudes and beliefs. True or false?
2. Most new P-Cs believe they didn't learn their emotions. True or false?
3. List two useful functions attitudes serve.

_____

_____

4. At the same time that the _____ brain forms beliefs, the right brain forms _____.

5. Prosody and dysprosody deal with the nonverbal aspects of speech and _____ language.

6. People's _____ create the illusion that some external HE, SHE, or IT magically causes those people's emotional feelings.

7. You can easily convert wordless attitudes to spoken beliefs. True or false?

8. If an idea feels right, this only means that (1) the idea is wrong, (2) the idea is correct, (3) you believe the idea.

9. The _____ brain initiates new learning.

10. You can easily demonstrate to most people that simply by changing their minds, they can and do change their emotions. True or false?

11. P-Cs usually don't understand and are most likely to get confused in the state of _____ emotive _____.

12. The five stages of emotional reeducation are intellectual insight, _____-_____ dissonance, _____ insight, and new _____ formation.

Answers for Chapter 4—Section II

1. true
2. true
3. See page 62
4. left; attitudes
5. body
6. attitudes

7. true
8. you believe the idea
9. left
10. true
11. cognitive; dissonance
12. practice; cognitive-emotive; emotional; personality-trait

MEMORY AIDS FOR CHAPTER 5

1. Intake Principle 1 is: _____ a standard _____ form.

2. Pre-intake forms help the therapist but not the P-C. True or false?

3. A good pre-intake form is a short-cut to P-C evaluation. True or false?

4. Two ways pre-intake forms help P-Cs are: (a) They can indicate problem areas P-Cs are too _____ to talk about and (b) Pre-intake forms are often _____ distractions.

5. It doesn't matter why people decide to live, if they get involved in RBT, they will soon start living for emotionally _____ reasons.

6. Intake Principle 2 is: Focus primarily on the _____ and _____.

7. RBT is primarily a here-and-now psychotherapy. Why?_____

_____.

8. In formulating behavioral dynamics, it's best to view P-Cs' hopes, fears, and anger as too superficial for concern, and focus on their deep, mysterious, and forgotten past memories. True or false?

9. What are the three human motivations for repeated behaviors?

    a._____

    b._____

    c._____

10. Intake Principle 3 is: Get the best possible view of your P-Cs' world as they ought to see it. True or false?

11. Teaching people their _____ ABCs is one of the fastest ways to help them

    get _____ hope and create drug-free _____.

12. In RBT, the behavioral grouping is the main factor determining if P-Cs are appropriate for RBT and where to treat these people. True or false?

13. People's pasts affect them in the present largely through their _____ of them.

14. People choose how their past affects them. True or false?

15. Emotional _____ is one of the main reasons people with miserable pasts suffer in the present.

16. In RBT, people learn to focus on this important fact: Today is every body's _____ of tomorrow.

17. RBT therapists completely ignore P-Cs' pasts. True or false?

Answers for Chapter 5

1. Have; pre-intake
2. false
3. false
4. ashamed; therapeutic
5. healthy
6. here; now
7. See p. 76
8. false
9. hope; fear; anger
10. false

11. emotional; realistic or rational or healthy; relief or happiness, or life or living.
12. true
13. memory
14. true
15. ignorance
16. past
17. false

MEMORY AIDS FOR CHAPTER 6

1. The acts of alcoholics in DTs are learned behaviors. True or false?

2. The fears of people with flying phobias are not-learned emotions. True or false?

3. Smythies (1966) describes numerous well-done studies that support the behavioral groupings used in RBT. True or false?

4. Delusions usually indicate _____.

5. Hallucinations usually indicate neurosis. True or false?

6. Practice means repeatedly pairing the same _____ or As with the same sincere evaluative thoughts or _____ s with the same _____ and/or _____ reactions or Cs.

7. What's the first question RBT therapists want to answer after intake?

8. Why is it important to separate learned from not-learned behavioral problems?

9. Name five of the eight major signs of not-learned behaviors.

10. Name the four major signs of learned behavioral problems.

11. Can you apply the signs of learned behavioral problems to flying phobia? Do it.

12. It's only when people knowingly practice their emotional problems that they cause themselves clinical difficulties. True or false?

13. The minds and brains of flying phobics are usually diseased. True or false?

14. People learn flying phobias and all other emotions using the same _____ s of _____ involved in practicing _____ and physical _____.

15. Psychosomatic behavioral problems are partly _____ and partly _____.

16. One of the main mechanisms of psychosomatic disorders is usually _____ cognitions.

17. Research indicates that _____ would be an ideal therapeutic addition to the medical treatment of psychosomatic disorders.

18. Give a half-minute summary of the case history of incorrect behavioral grouping described in this chapter.

Answers for Chapter 6

1. False
2. False
3. True
4. psychosis
5. False
6. perceptions or activating or external events; B; emotional; physical
7. See page 80
8. See page 80
9. See pp. 80–81
10. See page 81
11. yes
12. False
13. False
14. A, B, C; learning or (practice); emotional; habits
15. learned; not-learned
16. faulty, or inaccurate or false
17. RBT
18. See page 84

MEMORY AIDS FOR CHAPTER 7

1. _____ is the single most important thing people do.

2. Emotionally naive people want to _____ better without thinking _____.

3. New P-Cs naively expect the miracle of feeling better without _____ better.

4. _____ damage and drug use are about the only ways to feel better without _____ better.

5. List two reasons Mrs. Morrsey was an ideal candidate for RBT.

_____

_____

6. The main reason nonpsychotic people make themselves undesirably miserable emotionally is, that they _____ believe they have _____ other _____ choices.

7. Even well-educated people are _____ to consult psychotherapists.

8. Teaching P-Cs their emotional ABCs shows them that they _____ their own _____.

9. The admission of emotional _____ is the first step in rapid therapeutic learning.

10. Emotional feelings are just one third of, and the _____ important factor in, useful emotional understanding.

11. People have to support their emotional _____ with logical _____; otherwise the feelings _____.

12. The Emotional ABCs show people that emotional distress is a matter of personal _____.

13. Just knowing one's Emotional ABCs causes up to a _____ percent drop in people's emotional _____.

14. Give a three minute lecture on neutral emotions now.

Answers for Chapter 7

1. Thinking
2. feel; better
3. thinking
4. Brain; thinking
5. See page 88

6. don't; any; emotional or personal
7. afraid, or reluctant
8. control; emotions
9. ignorance
10. least

11. feelings; thoughts; disappear or stop 13. 25; distress
12. choice   14. See pp. 95–96

MEMORY AIDS FOR CHAPTER 8—SECTION I

1. If you routinely carry P-Cs through a transfer of their Emotional _____ to a personal event, you can easily get P-Cs to see that the Emotional ABCs do _____ to them.

2. There are no objectively trivial emotional problems. True or false?

3. Every time people get more upset than they want to be, that's a significant problem. True or false?

4. It's not important to spend time showing P-Cs that their emotions work like everyone else's emotions. True or false?

5. Attitudinal control of a response indicates _____ formation.

6. Name the Five Rational Questions.

7. What is Rational Bibliotherapy?

8. _____ is probably the simplest, yet most effective way to get P-Cs actively involved in psychotherapy immediately.

9. What are three essentials for consistently successful bibliotherapy?

10. Why is it useful to ask P-Cs to look for things they disagree with in their bibliotherapeutic readings?

11. Making stupid mistakes means the person is _____ like everyone else.

Answers for Chapter 8—Section I

1. ABCs; apply
2. True
3. True
4. False
5. habit
6. See page 104

7. See page 105
8. Rational Bibliotheraphy
9. See page 105
10. See page 106
11. fallible

MEMORY AIDS FOR CHAPTER 8—SECTION II

1. After P-Cs thoroughly understand the rest of the human emotional story, they almost always _____ any lingering resistance to applying the Emotional ABCs to themselves.

2. People learn their emotional beliefs, attitudes, and habits by using the same A,B,Cs of _____ that they use when they acquire their behavioral beliefs, attitudes, and habits.

3. It's correct to think there's more to human emotions than just A, B, C. True or false?

4. Normally,   Dr.   Maultsby   starts   RBT   sessions   by   _____ what _____ have done to _____ themselves since the last session.

5. Can you now describe the hypothetical example Dr. Maultsby used to teach Mrs. Morrsey about attitudes? Do it.

6. Converting A-b attitudes to their_____forms helps take the magical _____,   _____,   _____ and   _____   out of emotional understanding.

7. P-Cs automatically transfer their insights about their responses to snakes to their personal problems. True or false?

8. How did Dr. Maultsby avoid eliciting a crying response from Mrs. Morrsey when he discussed suicide?

9. Why was Mrs. Morrsey reluctant to talk insightfully about the hypothetical suicide attempt?

10. Give a short explanation of the RBT concept of the rhetorical question.

Answers for Chapter 8—Section II

1. lose
2. learning
3. true
4. reviewing; P-Cs; help
5. See page 109

6. belief; HEs; SHEs; ITs; THEYs
7. false
8. See pp. 110–111
9. See page 111
10. See pp. 111–112

MEMORY AIDS FOR CHAPTER 9

1. The   two   basic   ways   people   can   try   to   do   things   are   _____ _____ and _____ .

2. It's inappropriate for people to try to control their emotions. True or false?

3. The words people use are irrelevant to their sincere feelings. True or false?

4. Self-distraction from a conflict situation is always bad. True or false?

5. You can switch therapists without stopping therapeutic progress, if you are using _____ .

6. The two most common types of self-distractions are those due to insufficient personal _____ and those motivated by _____ .

7. Standard RBT routine includes introducing P-Cs to the Five Rules for Rational Thinking between the _____ and _____ sessions.

8. New   P-Cs   often   confuse   _____   thinking   with   irrational _____ thinking.

9. In RBT, therapeutic progress usually continues even when the P-C gets a different therapist. True or false?

Answers for Chapter 9

1. rationally or effectively; irrationally
    or ineffectively
2. false
3. false
4. false

5. RBT
6. interest; fear
7. third; sixth
8. rational; positive
9. true

MEMORY AIDS FOR CHAPTER 10

1. RBT therapists are concerned about possibly talking too much in therapy. True or false?
2. You can check on whether you have talked enough by asking the P-C to _____ what you have just covered.
3. Self-analysis is too difficult to let lay people do. True or false?
4. What are three things it's well to tell P-Cs *not* to worry about when you introduce the RSA technique?
5. If you neglect the maneuver in item 4, some P-Cs will _____ doing _____.
6. RBT therapists are being objective when they reassure P-Cs that they probably have all the brain power they need to solve their emotional problems. True or false?
7. What are the three possible conclusions one could have easily drawn at the beginning of Mrs. Morrsey's fifth session?

    _____

    _____

    _____

8. All things rational start with obvious _____ .
9. Chapter 10 lists three reliable ways to identify adequately treated P-Cs. What are they?

    _____

    _____

    _____

10. The main reason normal people willingly suffer undesirable emotions is they don't believe they have any other emotional _____.

11. What are the six other emotional choices emotionally distressed people have?____

    _____

    _____

12. RBT helps people have helpful _____ on other people.

13. Talking about superficial versus deep therapeutic change is _____ and therefore _____.

14. According to the criteria for optimal mental and emotional health, at her nine-month and three-year follow-ups Mrs. Morrsey had evidence of _____ mental and emotional _____ .

15. With RBT Mrs. Morrsey got over her depression in less time than it often takes to establish the traditional so-called therapeutic relationship. True or false?

Answers for Chapter 10

1. true
2. explain, or describe
3. false
4. See page 123
5. resist; RSAs
6. true
7. See page 124
8. facts
9. See page 125
10. choices
11. See page 125
12. influences
13. nonoperational; meaningless
14. optimal; health
15. true

MEMORY AIDS FOR CHAPTER 11—SECTION I

1. Depressed people are usually reacting to _____ events.

2. Worried people are usually upset about events that have not yet _____.

3. What can calm people down much faster and safer than tranquilizers?

4. Normally, in RBT psychoactive drugs are not prescribed for _____ people.

5. Worriers tend to be _____ thinkers.

6. Name two remotely possible medical disorders that could have been factors in the professor's emotional distress. _____

_____

7. In RBT, who finally decides if a P-C's ideas are irrational, the therapist or the P-C? _____

8. People often will ask: "But where's the supporting evidence?" in response to another's surprising thought or belief. True or false?

9. But if the surprising thought or belief in item 8 is expressed as "It's my very strong feeling that . . . , " even the most surprised people rarely ask: "But where's the supporting evidence?" They just say: "Well, I'm sorry you feel that way." True or false?

10. Saying I feel, when I think or believe is more accurate, is often just a socially approved excuse for refusing to think rationally. True or false?

Answers for Chapter 11—Section I

1. past
2. happened
3. undrugged brains
4. nonpsychotic
5. magical

6. See page 134
7. P-C
8. true
9. true
10. true

MEMORY AIDS FOR CHAPTER 11—SECTION II

1. "I feel that . . . " describes a legitimate emotional feeling. True or false?

2. It takes only one yes for the Five Rational Questions to check an idea. True or false?

3. When emotionally distressed people say "I can't," they usually mean "_____ _____ ."

4. Professor Nelson's panic was perfectly logical for his _____ and_____ .

5. The professor was reacting to a possible future _____ as if it were an on going _____ .

6. Part of the professor's problem was that he was _____ himself with _____ _____ lies.

7. In RBT, solving emotional problems rationally is just as logical and straightforward as solving business _____ .

8. The professor was reacting to an _____ white _____ .

9. An emotional white lie feels as if it were a fact because the person _____ that obvious lie at the moment.

10. To get the professor's quick cooperation, I gave him the _____ challenge _____ P-Cs rarely refuse.

11. Sane people do not try to _____ doing what they don't see they are doing in the first place.

12. There were _____ reasons for covering so much therapeutic material with the professor.

13. What were those reasons? (See Item 12)_____ _____ _____

14. The higher a person's academic degree is the faster that person will pick up the self-help concepts in RBT. True or false?

15. Insight and knowledge are all that P-Cs need to solve their emotional problems. True or false?

Answers for Chapter 11—Section II

1. false
2. false
3. I'm afraid, or I don't want, or I refuse
4. beliefs; fearful attitudes
5. undesirable event; catastrophe
6. deceiving; emotional; white
7. problems

8. emotional; lie
9. believes
10. therapeutic; sane
11. stop
12. good or three
13. See page 146
14. false
15. false

MEMORY AIDS FOR CHAPTER 12—SECTION I

1. Getting P-Cs to see that their thinking is irrational solves the immediate therapeutic problem. True or false?
2. What do therapists need to do next?
3. What common incorrect belief did Professor Nelson have?
4. What do healthy brains guarantee?
5. Worriers are so uncomfortable they usually listen most attentively to therapeutic advice. True or false?
6. _____ therapists might think Dr. Maultsby acted in an _____ way when Professor Nelson resisted using rational rhetoric.
7. What was Dr. Maultsby's view? Explain the logic of this view.

_____

_____

_____

Answers for Chapter 12—Section I

1. false
2. See page 148
3. See page 151
4. See page 151

5. false
6. Inexperienced; overbearing
7. See page 154

MEMORY AIDS FOR CHAPTER 12—SECTION II

1. Briefly explain the RBT explanation of "feeling wrong."
2. What antitherapeutic trap do P-Cs often fall into when they don't understand what "feeling wrong" really means?
3. What historical example was used to point out to Professor Nelson the hazard of ignoring ideas that "feel wrong"?
4. What fears do educated and uneducated P-Cs share about psychotherapy?
5. What explanation was given for Professor Nelson's readiness to talk about his fear of going insane?

6. Would it have been preferable for Professor Nelson to have agreed with Dr. Maultsby more readily than he did about the cause for his panic?

7. How was the insanity question dealt with?

8. Why wasn't reinforcement given for Professor Nelson's having read all of *You and Your Emotions?*

9. How did Professor Nelson explain his life of above average success?

10. Briefly describe Professor Nelson's one year follow-up session.

Answers for Chapter 12—Section II

1. See page 155
2. See page 155
3. See page 155
4. See page 156
5. See page 156

6. See page 156
7. See page 157
8. See page 158
9. worry and good luck
10. See page 159

MEMORY AIDS FOR CHAPTER 13

1. Cognitive-emotive _____ is the _____ emotional feeling people get when they entertain a _____ idea.

2. What's the main reason people refuse to make admittedly desirable personal changes?

3. Why do most unaided people fail to significantly improve their emotional control?

4. When inadequately prepared P-Cs experience cognitive-emotive dissonance, they are likely to say they are being _____ .

5. Such people often say, "I have to be _____ ."

6. Why is it often not helpful to tell P-Cs directly, "Think this . . . "?

7. Dan had the neurotic fear Dr. Maultsby calls the _____ fear.

8. Name the three steps in eliminating emotional habits.

9. Compare the number and names of the stages in emotional education and reeducation.

10. What were the two important clinical insights revealed by the driver's reeducation example?

11. How long does it take P-Cs to overcome their emotional problems completely?

12. Give a brief talk on how you would impress upon P-Cs the value of using rational rhetoric.

Answers for Chapter 13

1. dissonance; unusual or strange; new
2. Cognitive-emotive dissonance
3. See page 163
4. phony or unreal
5. real, or me, or the real me
6. See pp. 163–164

7. phony
8. See page 166
9. See page 167
10. See page 169
11. as long as it takes
12. See page 171

MEMORY AIDS FOR CHAPTER 14—SECTION I

1. For best results from RSAs encourage P-Cs to use the _____ RSA format and their _____ language.
2. It's best to delay writing an RSA of an event until you've had time to think it through and sort out your opposing ideas. True or false?
3. Can you write the standard RSA format? Do it.
4. Why put "positive or good," "negative or bad," or "neutral" in parentheses at the end of each B-section idea?
5. What does the relative number of positive, negative, or neutral B-section statements reveal?
6. What goes on in the E section?
7. If your C emotion was hate, a good initial E emotion would be love. True or false?
8. It's kind of crazy to want to love what you hate. True or false?
9. What if P-Cs don't know what new emotional habits they want to learn?
10. What's the rational response normally given to the question "Isn't it unhealthy for people to stop having emotions?"
11. Explain the only two things RSAs do.
12. Explain the value of the Camera Check.
13. What two features are essential for an idea to be rational and helpful?

Answers for Chapter 14—Section I

1.	standard; everyday	8.	false
2.	false	9.	See page 178
3.	See page 176	10.	See page 178
4.	See page 177	11.	See page 178
5.	See page 177	12.	See page 179
6.	See page 177	13.	See page 180
7.	false		

MEMORY AIDS FOR CHAPTER 14—SECTION II

1. Dr. F. made use of the "IT never does anything" concept in her Da section. True or false?
2. Why is it important to counsel P-Cs about relevant versus irrelevant facts?
3. How would you explain the important difference between force and choice to P-Cs?
4. Confusing _____ with _____ is the main core cause of procrastination.
5. The first simple step in overcoming procrastination is simply telling yourself the _____ you will get from doing the things you don't _____ to do.
6. When are people forced to do things?

7. If procrastinators didn't believe they were forced to do undesirable tasks, they'd rarely _____ them.

8. Most procrastinators call _____ or more undesirable _____ no choice.

9. What does it mean to be forced to do things?

10. Name four reasons why it's best for people's self-image to say that they choose to do X, Y, Z when that's the reality?

11. Explain the rational concept of *should*.

12. Rationally thinking ''I choose'' instead of irrationally thinking ''I'm forced'' or ''I have to'' is the best solution to the TGIF syndrome. True or false?

13. What three basic assumptions are basic to all empirical sciences?

14. Emotional self-control is one area where even empirical scientists are likely to use magical thinking. True or false?

15. What's the common, though irrational concept of *should?*

Answers for Chapter 14—Part II

1.	true	9.	See pp. 184–186
2.	See page 184	10.	See page 185
3.	See pp. 184–186	11.	See pp. 186–189
4.	force; choice	12.	True
5.	benefits; want	13.	See page 186
6.	See pp. 184–186	14.	True
7.	do	15.	See pp. 186–189
8.	two; choices		

MEMORY AIDS FOR CHAPTER 14—PART III

1. Written _____ _____ is one of the _____ main emotional self-help maneuvers P-Cs learn in RBT.

2. If P-Cs don't do RSAs, they can't benefit from RBT. True or false?

3. What is the most common error new P-Cs make when writing RSAs?

4. What is the standard sequence for RSA presentation in therapy?

5. Why is the Camera Check important in RSAs?

6. What is one of the main causes of emotional distress mentioned in Section III of Chapter 14?

7. What action is recommended when P-Cs have omitted writing Five Rational Questions?

8. It is a bad technique to end a therapy session before completely discussing an RSA. True or false?

9. What are the two main reasons RSAs are valuable therapeutic aids?

Answers for Chapter 14—Part III

1.	Rational Self-Analysis; two	3.	neglecting to write the Five Rational Questions
2.	false		

4. A, C, E, Da, Db.
5. See pp. 190-191
6. See p. 191

7. See pp. 192–193
8. false
9. See page 193

MEMORY AIDS FOR CHAPTER 15—SECTIONS I AND II

1. An essential part of learning is _____ brain- _____ feedback.

2. One of the most predictable aspects of habit learning is _____ efficiency of correct _____ probability.

3. For quick, correct responses a right brain's image is worth ten thousand left-brain words. True or false?

4. Typing speed and accuracy _____ when skilled typists try to think printed material as they type it.

5. Why do most lay people fail in their attempts to help themselves emotionally?

6. Briefly describe the neuropsychology of practice.

7. Describe how to do REI.

8. For best results, P-Cs must practice REIs for how many days, weeks, or months?

9. Name the three common problems P-Cs sometimes encounter doing REI.

10. What's the recommended way to handle each problem?

Answers for Chapter 15

1. split-second-to-split-second; body
2. increased; response
3. true
4. decrease
5. See page 199

6. See pp. 201–202
7. See pp. 202–204
8. See pp. 204–205
9. See pp. 206–208
10. See pp. 206–208

Rational
Bibliotherapy

THE PROFESSIONAL'S GUIDE FOR USING RATIONAL BIBLIOTHERAPY

Rational Bibliotherapy means the use of easy-to-understand self-help reading materials that are based on RBT theory. This is a simple yet highly effective way to get people quickly involved in analyzing and solving their emotional and behavioral problems rationally. But, as with any self-help maneuver, therapeutic results tend to vary directly with how structured and goal-oriented are the instructions people receive.

In my experience, the most effective instructions for bibliotherapy consist of daily reading goals. My standard routine is this:

Immediately after the intake evaluation I say, ''Once per day, every day, until you see me again I want you to read Chapter 1 in this illustrated booklet entitled *You and Your Emotions*. Even if you read slowly, you can probably read the chapter in twenty minutes. Surely you are willing to invest twenty minutes per day in learning how to solve your problems as quickly as possible, right? And remember, you can do the daily reading more than once, if you want to. The more times you read it the faster you will progress.''

RATIONALE FOR READING GOALS

The reading on the first day is merely for readers to get a clear understanding of the material.

The second day's reading is for readers to discover ideas with which they disagree. I tell them to write those ideas down and bring them to their next session for discussion.

When people first start psychotherapy, they often want to disagree with almost anything that will require them to change their beliefs and habitual behaviors. That's why showing interest immediately in their possible disagreements is an important treatment strategy. It quickly gets that potential therapeutic resistance out in the open where it can be eliminated quickly.

The third day's reading is for people to find and briefly write down the ideas with which they agree, and why they agree with them. That action will aid therapeutic progress in two ways. First, it increases the probability that they will put those insights to daily use. Second, it increases the probability that people will avoid the antitherapeutic game of "fool-the-therapist."

For the fourth day's reading, I ask readers to look for and write down notes about events described in the book that P-Cs have seen in the lives of relatives, friends, coworkers, and even enemies, if they have any. This exercise helps them quickly get over the self-defeating idea that their lives are uniquely complicated or difficult.

For the fifth day's reading, I ask the readers to look for and make written descriptions of events from their daily lives in which they applied the insights gained from their reading. This instruction shows them they already have some skill in rational self-control, even though they may not have realized it before.

For the sixth day's reading, I ask the readers to look for events in their daily lives in which they could have applied the self-help insights gained from their reading, but did not. Again, I remind them to write brief notes for therapeutic discussion.

Since repetition is the royal road to rapid learning, for the seventh day's reading, I tell the readers to review their notes as preparation for discussing them in their next therapy session.

After those instructions, 80 percent to 90 percent of new P-Cs will return to therapy having read their assignment at least once; of those, 40 percent to 60 percent will have read it twice; between 10 percent and 30 percent will have read the assignment three to five times; and about .1 percent will have read it six or more times. Many of this fourth group will have moderate to severe problems with obsessive-compulsive behavior. You can expect them to be the most worrisome and difficult people to treat. But calm persistence will usually yield good therapeutic results.

I consider regular therapy tape listening to be a special form of bibliotherapy. It is helpful to have P-Cs listen to the therapy tapes of teaching cases (such as Mrs. Morrsey) when the P-C has the same type of problem. P-Cs with irrational fears usually find it's therapeutic to listen to the case history tapes from "Overcoming Irrational Fears—Series A and B" (Maultsby, 1973). It's usually helpful for P-Cs who have problems with fear of failure, irrational anger, or chronic depression to listen to the tapes (Insights For Success, 20 Seconds To Drug-free Happiness, and How to Have a Happy Day Everyday) in the *"Create Your Own Happiness"* kit (Maultsby, 1982). Procrastinators usually get significant help from listening to the therapy tapes on procrastination that are in *The Professional's Self-Training Kit for Group RBT* (Maultsby 1982).

Next are the daily reading and tape listening instructions routinely given to P-Cs at the RBT Center.

YOUR DAILY READING INSTRUCTIONS

Following these directions will help you help yourself feel and act the way you want to in the shortest time possible.

Set aside 15 minutes a day for your self-improvement time. It's best if you set aside the same time each day; that helps make your self-improvement reading become a habit for you.

Your mind is most open to new learning when you first wake up in the morning and right before you go to sleep at night. So, why not get up 15 minutes earlier than usual and immediately do your rational self-help reading? Or you may do your 15 minutes of rational self-help reading right before you go to bed. Presleep rational self-help reading leads to restful and rational dreams. In any case, read your assignment at least once per day, *everyday,* until your next RBT session.

Day 1 -   Read your assignment once, just to see what it's about.
Day 2 -   Read your assignment again. While you're reading it, look for ideas that you disagree with. Then write them down so that you can discuss them in your next RBT session.
Day 3 -   Read the assignment again. As you read, pay attention to finding ideas you agree with. Write these ideas down and bring them with you to your next RBT session.
Day 4 -   Today as you do the recommended reading, look for events that are similar to events you've seen in the lives of relatives, friends, or even enemies, if you have any. Again, write down these events and bring them to your next RBT session.
Day 5 -   As you read today, look for events similar to events in your life in which you've already applied some of the self-help ideas discussed in the reading.
Day 6 -   While reading the assignment today, think about how you could have applied what you've learned to make your day happier or more productive or more satisfying. Write down why you didn't use your new knowledge. Common reasons include: ''I didn't know about it then'' and ''I didn't think about it.''
Day 7 -   Read your assignment again, and review your notes for discussion in your next RBT session.

YOUR DAILY TAPE LISTENING INSTRUCTIONS

We've found that people who schedule a specific 15-minute period each day for therapy-tape listening help themselves the most in the shortest time possible.

Remember, time is never lost or found—so don't waste your time looking for time to listen to your tape. Commit yourself to a daily listening time *now*.

When you listen to your tape, listen with the same goal you have when you do your daily self-help reading. Also, be sure to make notes for discussion in your next therapy session.

All P-Cs who come to the RBT Center receive a copy of *You and Your Emotions* (Maultsby and Hendricks 1974) at the end of their intake session. People working on alcohol and drug problems do bibliotherapeutic readings in *Freedom From Alcohol and Tranquilizers* (Maultsby 1979). Participants in the RBT Center's Intensive Therapeutic Self-Help Program have bibliotherapy assignments in the *"Create Your Own Happiness"* kit (Maultsby 1982).

The material on pages 236 and 237 provide two examples from the rational bibliotherapy which we routinely give to P-Cs at the RBT Center.

THE ABC'S OF WHERE EMOTIONAL FEELINGS COME FROM

When you have an emotional feeling, you first *perceive* (that is, see, hear, physically feel, smell, taste) something. Next you *think* and *believe* something about your perceptions. Then you have an *emotional feeling,* triggered by your thoughts.

The following illustrations were taken from *You and Your Emotions* (Maultsby and Hendricks 1974a).[1]

The ABCs of Positive Emotional Feelings

The ABCs of Negative Emotional Feelings

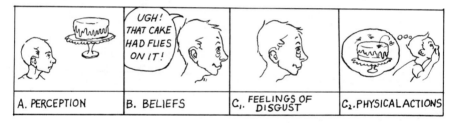

The ABCs of Neutral Emotional Feelings

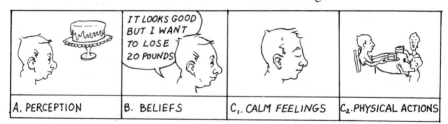

Facts don't cause your feelings.
By your thoughts, you choose how you feel.
and
Your actions usually follow your feelings.

[1]For a free printed copy of these illustrations in Appendix B that you can reproduce for your P-Cs to use, send a stamped, self-addressed envelope to the RBT Center, College of Medicine, University of Kentucky, Lexington, KY 40536.

Confusing _truth_ with _fact_ is a common cause of clinical emotional distress. But by using _truth_ and _fact_ in the operational ways described here, people can improve their self-control, emotional well-being, and relationships with others.

The concepts of _truth_ and _fact_ must refer to some perception. For example, Ralph saw the can of paint on the shelf:

Truth is any idea that someone believes. Believing an idea makes it true for the believer. Personal beliefs or truths trigger a person's hopes, fears, likes, dislikes, and expectations; but truths often have little or nothing to do with facts.

When making statements of _personal truth_, the appropriate words to use are "I believe . . ." and _not_ the popular, though semantically incorrect phrases "I feel that . . . " or "It's my feeling that . . . "

Facts are parts of the real world, independent of what people think or believe. _Facts_ exist whether or not people know about them, accept them, believe them, or like them. The illustration on the right shows what usually happens when people act on truth that's in conflict with fact.

YOU'LL FEEL BETTER EMOTIONALLY AND GET MORE OUT OF LIFE WHEN YOUR _PERSONAL TRUTHS_ ARE BASED ON _OBVIOUS FACTS_

APPENDIX C

References

Adams, R. D., and M. Victor. *Principles of Neurology*. New York: McGraw-Hill Book Company, 1977.

Alajouaine, T. H. "Aphasia and Artistic Realization." *Brain*, 71 (1948), pp. 229–241.

Beritoff, J. S. *Neural Mechanism of Higher Vertebrate Behavior*, trans. W. T. Liberson. Boston: Little, Brown & Company, 1965.

Bever, T. G., and R. J. Chiarello, "Cerebral Dominance in Musicians and Non-Musicians." *Science*, 185 (August 1974), pp. 537–539.

Blumstein, S., and W. E. Cooper. "Hemispheric Processing of Intonation Contours." *Cortex*, 10 (1974), pp. 146–158.

Bogen, J. F. "The Other Side of the Brain, I: Dysgraphia and Dyscopia Following Cerebral Commissurotomy." *Bulletin of the Los Angeles Neurological Society*, 34:2 (April 1969), pp. 73–105.

————. "The Other Side of the Brain, II: An Appositional Mind." *Bulletin of the Los Angeles Neurological Society*, 34:3 (July 1969a), pp. 135–162.

Bogen, J. F., and G. M. Bogen. "The Other Side of the Brain, III: The Corpus Callosum and Creativity." *Bulletin of the Los Angeles Neurological Society*, 34:4 (October 1969), pp. 191–203.

Bower, T. "The Object in the World of the Infant." *Scientific American*, 225 (October 1971), pp. 30–38.

————. "Competent Newborns." *New Scientist* (March 14, 1974), pp. 672–675.

Brandsma, J. M., M. C. Maultsby, and R. Welsh. *Outpatient Treatment of Alcoholism*. Baltimore, MD: University Park Press, 1979.

Carmon, A., and I. Nachson. "Effect of Unilateral Brain Damage on Perception of Temporal Order." *Cortex*, 7 (1971), pp. 410–418.

Cohen, G. "Hemispheric Difference in Serial Versus Parallel Processing." *Journal of Experimental Psychology*, 97:3 (1973), pp. 349–356.

Crampton, M. "Psychosynthesis." R. J. Corsini, ed. *Handbook of Innovative Psychotherapies*. New York: John Wiley & Sons, Inc., 1981.

238

De Renzi, E., and H. Spinnler. "Visual Recognition in Patients with Unilateral Cerebral Disease." *Journal of Nervous and Mental Disease*, 142 (1966), pp. 515–525.

De Renzi, E., G. Scoffi, and H. Spinnler. "Perceptual and Associative Disorders of Visual Recognition." *Neurology*, 19 (1969), pp. 635–641.

Di Cara, L. V. "Learning in the Autonomic Nervous System." *Scientific American*, 222 (1970), pp. 31–39.

Dimond, S. J. *The Double Brain*. Baltimore, MD: The William & Wilkins Company, 1972.

Dimond, S. J., L. Farrington, and P. Johnson. "Differing Emotional Responses from Right and Left Hemispheres." *Nature*, 261 (1976), pp. 690–692.

Dimond, S. J., and L. Farrington. "Emotional Response to Films Shown to the Right or Left Hemisphere of the Brain Measured by Heart Rate." *Acta Psychologia*, 41 (1977), pp. 255–260.

Eccles, J. C. "The Physiology of Imagination." *Scientific American*, 199 (September 1958), p. 135.

Efron, R. "The Effect of Handedness on the Perception of Simultaneity and Temporal Order." *Brain*, 86 (1963), pp. 285–294.

Ellis, A. *Reason and Emotion in Psychotherapy*. New York: Lyle Stuart, Inc., 1963.

Festinger, L. *A Theory of Cognitive Dissonance*. Stanford, CA: Stanford University Press, 1962.

Filbey, R. A., and M. S. Gazzaniga. "Splitting the Normal Brain with Reaction Time." *Psychonomic Science*, 17 (1969), pp. 335–336.

Flor-Henry, P. "Lateralized Temporal-Limbic Dysfunction and Psychopathology." *Annals of the New York Academy of Science*, 280 (1976), pp. 777–795.

————. "On Certain Aspects of the Localization of the Cerebral Systems Regulating and Determining Emotion." *Biological Psychiatry*, 14:4 (1979), pp. 677–698.

Fowler, J. personal communication, 1980.

Freedman, A. M., I. H. Kaplan, and B. J. Sadock. *Modern Synopsis of Comprehensive Textbook of Psychiatry/II*. Baltimore, MD: The William & Wilkins Company, 1976.

Frostig, M., and P. Maslow. "Neuropsychological Contributions to Education." *Journal of Learning Disabilities*, 12:8 (October 1979), pp. 40–54.

Gainotti, G. "Emotional Behavior and Hemispheric Side of the Lesion." *Cortex*, 8 (1972), pp. 41–55.

Galabruda, A. M., M. LeMay, T. L. Kemper, et al. "Right-Left Asymmetrics in the Brain." *Science*, 199 (1978), pp. 852–856.

Galin, D. "Implications for Psychiatry of Left and Right Cerebral Specialization." *Archives of General Psychiatry*, 31 (1974), pp. 572–583.

Galin, D., and R. Ornstein. "Lateral Specialization of Cognitive Mode: An EEG Study." *Psychophysiology*, 9:4 (July 1972), pp. 412–418.

Gasparrine, M. A., P. Satz, K. M. Hielman, et al. "Hemispheric Asymmetrics of Affective Processing as Determined by MMPI." *Journal of Neurology, Neurosurgery and Psychiatry*, 41 (1978), pp. 470–473.

Gatchel, R. J., D. Maynard, R. Turns, and H. Taunton-Blackwood. "Comparison of Heart Rate Biofeedback, False Biofeedback and Systematic Desensitization in Reducing Speech Anxiety." *Journal of Consulting and Clinical Psychology*, 47:3 (1979), pp. 620–622.

Gazzaniga, M. S. *The Bisected Brain*. Englewood Cliffs, NJ: Prentice-Hall, Inc., 1970.

————. "The Split Brain in Man." *Scientific American*, 217 (1967), pp. 24–29.

Gazzaniga, M. S., and J. E. LeDoux. *The Integrated Mind*. New York: Plenum Publishing Corporation, 1978.

Gerstmann, J. "The Problem of Perception of Disease and Impaired Body Territories with Organic Lesions." *Archives of Neurology and Psychiatry*, 48 (July–December 1942), pp. 890–913.

Geschwind, N. "Specializations of the Human Brain." *Scientific American*, 241:3 (September 1979), pp. 180–199.

Geschwind, N. and W. Levitsky. "Human Brain: Left–Right Asymmetries in Temporal Speech Region." *Science,* 161 (1968), pp. 186–187.

Grace, W. J., and D. T. Graham. "Relationship of Specific Attitudes and Emotions to Certain Bodily Diseases." *Psychosomatic Medicine,* 14 (1952), pp. 243–251.

Graham, D. T., J. A. Stern, and G. Winokur. "Experimental Investigation of the Specificity of Attitude Hypothesis in Psychosomatic Disease." *Psychosomatic Medicine,* 20 (1958), pp. 446–457.

Graham, D. T., J. D. Kabler, and F. K. Graham. "Physiological Response to the Suggestion of Attitudes Specific for Hives and Hypertension." *Psychosomatic Medicine* 24 (1962), pp. 159–169.

Grant, D. A. "The Influence of Attitude on the Conditioned Eyelid Response." *Journal of Experimental Psychology,* 25 (1939), pp. 333–346.

Gur, R. E. "Left Hemisphere Dysfunction and Left Hemisphere Overactivation in Schizophrenia." *Journal of Abnormal Psychology,* 87:2 (1978), pp. 226–238.

Hall, P. S., and C. R. Prior. "The Cognitive Factor in the Extinction of a Conditioned GSR Response." *Psychonomic Science,* 16 (1969), p. 74.

Harman, D. W., and W. J. Ray. "Hemispheric Activity During Affective Verbal Stimuli: An EEG Study." *Neuropsychologia,* 15 (1977), pp. 457–460.

Hebb, D. O. *The Organization of Behavior.* New York: John Wiley & Sons, Inc., 1949.

————. *A Textbook of Psychology.* Philadelphia: W. B. Saunders Company, 1966.

Heilman, K. M., R. Scholes, and R. T. Watson. "Auditory Affect Agnosia." *Journal of Neurology, Neurosurgery and Psychiatry,* 38 (1975), pp. 69–72.

Henschen, S. E. "On the Function of the Right Hemisphere in Relation to the Left Brain in Speech, Music, and Calculation." *Brain,* 49 (1926), pp. 110–123.

Hohmann, G. W. "The Effect of Dysfunctions of the Autonomic Nervous System on Experienced Feelings and Emotions." Paper read at Conference on Emotions and Feelings at School for Social Research, New York, 1962.

Holland, J. G., and B. F. Skinner. *The Analysis of Behavior.* New York: McGraw-Hill Book Company, 1961.

Holmes, T. H. "Life Situations, Emotions, and Disease." *Psychosomatics,* 19:12 (December 1978), pp. 747–754.

Hudgins, C. V. "Conditioning and Voluntary Control of the Pupillary Light Reflex." *Journal of General Psychology,* 8 (1933), pp. 38–48.

Humphrey, M. E., and O. L. Zangwill, "Effects of a Right-Sided Occipitoparietal Brain Injury in a Left-Handed Man." *Brain,* 75 (1952), pp. 312–324.

Jackson, J. H. "On the Nature of the Duality of the Brain." J. Taylor, ed. *Selected Writings of John Hughlings Jackson,* Vol. 2. New York: Basic Books, Inc., Publishers, 1958.

Janis, I. L. *Victims of Groupthink: A Psychological Study of Foreign-Policy Decisions and Fiascos.* Boston: Houghton Mifflin, 1972.

Jones, M. C. "The Elimination of Children's Fears." *Journal of Experimental Psychology,* 1 (1924), pp. 383–390.

————. "A Laboratory Study of Fear: The Case of Peter." *Pedagogical Seminary,* 31 (1924), pp. 308–315.

Katzman, R. *Dementia.* 2nd ed. Philadelphia: Davis, 1978.

Kimma, D. "The Asymmetry of the Human Brain." *Scientific American,* 228 (March 1973), pp. 70–78.

Korzybski, A., *Science and Sanity.* 4th ed. Lakeville, CT: The International Non-Aristotelian Library Publishing Co., 1958.

Lacey, J. I., and R. L. Smith. "Conditioning and Generalization of Unconscious Anxiety." *Science,* 120 (1954), pp. 1045–1052.

Lacey, J. I., R. L. Smith, and A. Green. "Use of Conditioned Autonomic Responses in the Study of Anxiety." *Psychosomatic Medicine,* 18:3 (1955), pp. 208–217.

Lamendella, J. T. "The Limbic System in Human Communication." H. Whitaker and H. A. Whitaker, eds. *Studies of Neurolinguistics,* Vol. 3. New York: Academic Press, Inc., 1977.

Lee, I. J. *Language Habits in Human Affairs.* New York: Harper and Row, Publishers, Inc., 1941.

Levy, J. "Possible Basis for the Evolution of Lateral Specialization of the Human Brain." *Nature,* 224 (1969), pp. 614–615.

Levy, J., C. Trevarthen, and R. W. Sperry. "Perception of Bilateral Chimeric Figures Following Hemispheric Deconnection." *Brain,* 95 (1972), pp. 61–78.

Levy-Agresti, J., and R. W. Sperry. "Differential Perceptual Capacities in Major and Minor Hemispheres." *Proceedings of the National Academy of Science,* 61, (September–December 1968), p. 1151.

Lishman, W. A. "Emotion, Consciousness, and Will After Brain Bisection." *Cortex,* 7 (1971), pp. 181–192.

Luria, A. R. *The Role of Speech in the Regulation of Normal and Abnormal Behavior.* Bethesda, MD: U.S. Department of Health, Education and Welfare, Russian Scientific Translation Program, 1960.

_____. *Human Brain and Psychological Processes.* New York: Harper & Row, Publishers, Inc., 1966.

_____. *Higher Cortical Functions in Man.* New York: Basic Books, Inc., Publishers, 1966a.

_____. *The Mind of a Mnemonist.* New York: Basic Books, Inc., Publishers, 1968.

_____. *The Working Brain.* New York: Basic Books, Inc., Publishers, 1973.

_____. *Cognitive Development: Its Cultural and Social Foundations.* ed. Michael Cole and trans. Martin Lopez-Morillas and Lynn Solotaroff. Cambridge, MA: Harvard University Press, 1976.

Maclean, P. D. "Some Psychiatric Implications of Physiological Studies on Frontotemporal Portion of Limbic System (Visceral Brain)." *Electroencephalography and Clinical Neurophysiology,* 4 (1952), pp. 407–418.

Maultsby, M. C. "Systematic, Written Homework in Psychotherapy." *Psychotherapy: Theory, Research, and Practice,* 8 (1971), pp. 195–198.

_____. "Rational Emotive Imagery." *Rational Living,* 6:1 (1971a), pp. 22–26.

_____. "Patient's Opinion of the Therapeutic Relationship in Rational Behavior Therapy." *Psychological Reports,* 37 (1975), pp. 795–798.

_____. "The Evolution of Rational Behavior Therapy" (paper). Presented at the First National Conference of Rational Emotive and Behavioral Therapists, Chicago, IL. (June 2–5, 1975).

_____. *Help Yourself to Happiness Through Rational Self-Counseling.* New York: Institute for Rational Living, 1976.

_____. *A Million Dollars for Your Hangover.* Lexington, KY: Rational Self-Help Aids, 1978.

_____. "Overcoming Irrational Fears." (Series A) (audio cassette series). Chicago, IL: Instructional Dynamics, Inc., 1978.

_____. "Overcoming Irrational Fears." (Series B) (audio cassette series). Chicago, IL: Instructional Dynamics, Inc., 1978a.

_____. *Freedom From Alcohol and Tranquilizers* (a series of five Rational Bibliotherapeutic booklets). Lexington, KY: Rational Self-Help Aids, 1979.

_____. *Your Guide to Emotional Well Being.* Lexington, KY: Rational Self-Help Aids, 1980.

_____. "Rational Behavior Therapy." Samuel M. Turner and Russell T. Jones, eds., *Behavior Modification in Black Populations: Empirical Findings and Psychosocial Issues.* New York: Plenum Publishing Corporation, 1982.

————. "The Professional's Self-Training Kit for Group RBT." Lexington, KY: Rational Self-Help Aids, 1982.

————. *Your "Create Your Own Happiness" Kit*. Lexington, Ky: Rational Self-Help Aids, 1982.

Maultsby, M. C., and D. J. Graham. "Controlled Study of the Effects on Self-Reported Maladaptive Traits, Anxiety Scores and Psychosomatic Disease Attitudes." *Journal of Psychiatric Research*, 10 (1974), pp. 121–132.

Maultsby, M. C., and A. Hendricks, *You and Your Emotions*. Lexington, KY: Rational Self-Help Aids, 1974a.

Maultsby, M. C., P. J. Winkler, and J. C. Norton. "Semi-automated Psychotherapy with Preventive Features." *Journal of Preventive Medicine* (Fall 1975), pp. 27–37.

Maultsby, M. C., R. T. Costello, and L. C. Carpenter. "Classroom Emotional Education and Optimum Health." *Journal of the International Academy of Preventive Medicine* (December 1976), pp. 24–31.

Mavissakalian, M., and D. H. Barlow. *Phobia: Psychological and Pharamacological Treatments*. New York: The Guilford Press, 1981.

McFie, J. "The Effects of Hemispherectomy on Intellectual Function in Cases of Infantile Hemiplegia." *Journal of Neurology, Neurosurgery and Psychiatry*, 24 (1961), pp. 240–249.

Menzies, R. "Conditioned Vasomotor Responses in Human Subjects." *Journal of Personality and Social Psychology*, 4 (1937), pp. 75–120.

Miller, N. E. "Learning of Visceral and Glandular Responses." *Science*, 163 (1969), pp. 436–445.

Monrad-Krohn, G. H. "Dysprosody, or Altered Melody of Language." *Brain*, 70 (1947), pp. 405–415.

Mowrer, O. H. *Learning Theory and Behavior*. New York: John Wiley & Sons, Inc., 1960.

————. *Learning Theory and the Symbolic Process*. New York: John Wiley & Sons, Inc., 1966.

Nebes, R. D. "Superiority of the Minor Hemisphere in Commissurotomized Man for the Perception of Part-Whole Relations." *Cortex*, 7 (1971), pp. 333–349.

Olds, J. "The Central Nervous System and the Reinforcement of Behavior." *American Psychologist*, 24 (1969), pp. 114–132.

Osgood, C. E., and G. J. Suci. "Factor Analysis of Meaning." *Journal of Experimental Psychology*, 50 (1955), pp. 325–338.

Osler, W. S. *Sir William Osler: Aphorisms from His Bedside Teachings and Writings*. ed. W. B. Bean. New York: Henry Schuman, 1950.

Patton, L. P. *The Effects of Rational Behavior Training on Emotionally Disturbed Adolescents in Alternative School Settings."* Ph.D. Thesis, North Texas State University, 1976.

Paul, G. L. *Insight vs. Desensitization in Psychotherapy*. Stanford, CA: Stanford University Press, 1966.

————. "Insight vs. Desensitization in Psychotherapy Two Years After Termination." *Journal of Consulting Psychology*, 31 (1967), pp. 333–348.

Pribram, K. H. "The Neurophysiology of Remembering." *Scientific American*, 220:1 (January 1969), pp. 73–86.

————. *Languages of the Brain: Holograms*. Englewood Cliffs, NJ: Prentice-Hall, Inc., 1971.

Quinn, G. *The I'ACT Handbook*. Appleton, WI: The International Association for Clear Thinking, 1980.

Razran, G. H. S. "Conditioned Responses." *Archives of Psychology*, 28:191 (1935–36), pp. 110–120.

————. "Some Psychological Factors in the Generalization of Salivary Conditioning to Verbal Stimuli." *American Journal of Psychology,* 62 (1949), pp. 247–256.

————. "Attitudinal Determinants of Conditioning and of Generalization of Conditioning." *Journal of Experimental Psychology,* 39 (1949a), pp. 820–829.

————. "The Observable Unconscious and the Inferable Conscious in Current Soviet Psychophysiology." *Psychological Review,* 68 (1961), pp. 81–147.

Rosenthal, R., and R. A. Lawson. "Longitudinal Study of the Effects of Experimenter Bias on the Operant Learning of Laboratory Rats." *Journal of Psychiatry Research,* 2 (1963), pp. 61–72.

Ross, E. D., and M. Mesulam. "Dominant Language Functions of the Right Hemisphere? Prosody and Emotional Gesturing." *Archives of Neurology,* 36 (1979), pp. 144–148.

Ross, G. "Reducing Irrational Personality Traits, Trait Anxiety and Intra-Interpersonal Needs in High School Students." *Journal of Measurements and Evaluation in Guidance,* 11 (1978), pp. 44–50.

Rotter, J. B. "Generalized Expectancies of Internal versus External Control of Reinforcement." *Psychological Monographs,* 80 (1966), pp. 1–28.

————. *Social Learning and Clinical Psychology.* Englewood Cliffs, NJ: Prentice-Hall, Inc., 1954.

Ruhnow, M. personal communication, 1977.

Russell, P. *The Brain Book.* New York: Hawthorn Books, Inc., 1979.

Sackeim, H. A., and R. C. Gur. "Lateral Asymmetry in Intensity of Emotional Expression." *Neuropsychologia,* 16 (1978), pp. 473–481.

Schwager, H. A. *Effects of Applying Rational Behavior Training and a Group Counseling Situation with Disadvantaged Adults.* Counseling Services Report 22. Glassgo, MN: Mountain-Plain Education, Economic Development Program, Inc., 1975.

Schwager, H. A., and S. M. Cox. "The Use of Behavioral Medicine as an Adjunct Therapy in the Treatment of Systematic Lupus Erythematosis: A Case Study." *Journal of the International Academy of Preventive Medicine,* 5:1 (1978), pp. 97–102.

Schwartz, G. E., R. J. Davidson, and F. Maer. "Right Hemisphere Lateralization for Emotion in Human Brain: Interactions with Cognition." *Science,* 190 (1975), pp. 286–288.

Silverman, A. J., G. Adevai, and E. McGouch. "Some Relationships Between Handedness and Perception." *Journal of Psychosomatic Research,* 10 (1966–1967), pp. 151–158.

Skinner, B. F. *Science and Human Behavior.* New York: The Free Press, 1953.

————. *Verbal Behavior.* Englewood Cliffs, NJ: Prentice-Hall, Inc. 1957.

Smith, A. "Speech and Other Functions After Left Hemispherectomy." *Journal of the Neurology, Neurosurgery and Psychiatry,* 29 (1966), pp. 467–471.

Smythies, J. R. *The Neurological Foundations of Psychiatry: An Outline of the Mechanisms of Emotions, Memory, Learning, and the Organization of Behavior with Particular Regards to the Limbic System.* New York: Academic Press, Inc., 1966.

Sperry, R. W. "Cerebral Dominance in Perception." F. A. Young and D. B. Lindsley, eds. *Early Experiences and Visual Information Processing in Perceptual and Resting Disorders.* Washington, DC: National Academy of Science, 1970.

————. "Hemisphere Deconnection and Unity in Conscious Awareness." *American Psychologist,* 23 (1968), pp. 723–733.

Sperry, R. W., and M. S. Gazzaniga. "Language Following Surgical Disconnections of Hemispheres." in C. H. Millikin and F. L. Darley, eds. *Brain Mechanisms Underlying Speech and Language.* New York: Grune & Stratton, Inc., 1967.

Staats, C. K., and A. W. Staats. "Meaning Established by Classical Conditioning." *Journal of Experimental Psychology,* 54 (1957), pp. 74–80.

Staats, A. W., and C. K. Staats. "Attitudes Established by Classical Conditioning." *Journal of Abnormal and Social Psychology,* 57 (1958), pp. 37–40.

Staats, A. W., C. K. Staats, and W. G. Heard. "Language Conditioning of Meaning Using a Semantic Generalization Paradigm." *Journal of Experimental Psychology.* 57:3 (1959), pp. 187–192.

Strong, O. A., and A. Elwyn. *Human Neuroanatomy.* Baltimore, MD: The Williams and Wilkins Company, 1943.

Swisher, L., and I. J. Hirsch. "Brain Damage and the Ordering of Two Temporally Successive Stimuli." *Neuropsychologia,* 10 (1972), pp. 137–152.

Tucker, D. M., R. S. Roth, B. A. Arneson, et al. "Right Brain Activation During Stress." *Neuropsychologia,* 15 (1977), pp. 697–700.

Volgyesi, F. A. "School for Patients: Hypnosis, Therapy, and Psychoprophylaxis." *British Journal of Medical Hypnosis,* 5 (1954), pp. 10–17.

Wada, J. A., and A. E. Davis. "Fundamental Nature of Human Infants' Brain Asymmetry." *The Canadian Journal of Neurological Sciences,* 4:3 (August 1977), pp. 203–207.

Watson, J. B., and R. Rayner. "Conditioned Emotional Reactions." *Journal of Experimental Psychology,* 3:1 (1920), pp. 1–14.

Watzlawick, P. *The Language of Change.* New York: Basic Books, Inc., Publishers, 1978.

Wechsler-Adam, F. "The Effect of Organic Brain Disease on the Recall of Emotionally Charged Versus Neutral Narrative Texts." *Neurology,* 23 (1973), pp. 130–135.

Weisenburg, T., and K. E. McBride. *Aphasia: A Clinical and Psychological Study.* New York: Commonwealth Fund, 1935.

Weissman, M. M. "Management of Depression in Women." *Weekly Psychiatry Update Series.* Lesson 4, Vol. 3. Princeton, NJ: Biomedia, Inc., 1979.

Werito, L. personal communication, 1981.

Wexler, B. E. "Cerebral Laterality and Psychiatry: A Review of the Literature." *American Journal of Psychiatry,* 137:3 (March 1980), pp. 279–291.

Wexler, B. E., and G. R. Heninger. "Alterations in Cerebral Laterality During Acute Psychotic Illness." *Archives of General Psychiatry,* 36 (March 1979), pp. 278–284.

Wolf, J. L., and E. Brand. *Twenty Years of Rational Therapy.* New York: Institute for Rational Living, 1977.

Wolpe, J., and A. A. Lazarus. *Behavior Therapy Techniques.* New York: Pergamon Press, Inc., 1966.

Wolpe J. *The Practice of Behavior Therapy.* New York: Pergamon Press, Inc., 1973.

Zajonc, R. B. "Feeling and Thinking." *American Psychologist,* 35:2 (1980), pp. 151–175.

Zangwill, O. L. "Agraphia Due to a Left Parietal Glioma in a Left-Handed Man." *Brain,* 77 (1954), pp. 510–520.

Index